The Greatest Need

The Greatest Need

the creative life and troubled times of

Lily Tobias, a Welsh Jew in Palestine

First published by Honno

'Ailsa Craig', Heol y Cawl, Dinas Powys,

Wales, CF64 4AH

1 2 3 4 5 6 7 8 9 10

ISBN 978-1-909983-23-6

Published with the financial support of the Welsh Books Council.

Cover design: Sue Race

Printed by Bell & Bain Ltd, Glasgow

Author's Note

Lily Tobias was always 'Lil' to acquaintances, friends, and family members: it is as Lil that she signed her letters, and as Lil that relatives still refer to her. In her own way she was a formidable woman, and as I have grappled with trying to tell a story about the tensions of her life and the challenges that she faced, my respect for her has only grown. However, at no point in writing about her life did I feel I had earned the right to call her 'Lil', as if I had known her personally. Even 'Lily' still feels presumptuously familiar.

I've come to the end of writing about her life and I worry about whether I've done her justice: I'm conscious of all the details I've had to leave out because of space, or uncertainty or narrative requirements, and I'm painfully aware of the possibilities that I did not have the time or resources to pursue. Above all, I am conscious that, despite knowing something about her, I really hardly know her at all.

As with any factual book there are, of course, omissions in this one – perhaps in this case more than in a scholarly biography, for I have not set out to write a comprehensive text weighed down with footnotes and historical sources, but simply to try to tell a story which, I hope, will give a flavour of Lily's difficult and interesting life. A biography, of course, always touches on the sensitivities of family history, and here I have endeavoured only to refer to more private matters where they have been central to that story, and to an understanding of Lily's experience.

A very large part of this portrait is based on Lily's own writing, and in this way I hope it will serve as an introduction to her work. The outcome of a commission for Honno Press's popular biography series, this volume is published in conjunction with the republication of *My Mother's House*, Lily's 1931 novel (her 1933 novel, *Eunice Fleet*, was republished in the Honno Classics series in 2004).

There is a great deal more to know about Lily Tobias: she 'got about' with extraordinary chutzpah. No doubt there is further material in archives in England, Wales, Israel and South Africa – and in the memories of friends and relatives. I hope that readers will get in touch to share additional information (and of course to correct any misapprehensions or oversights).

A NOTE ON THE TEXT

In quotations from texts and letters I have retained without comment the idiosyncrasies of style or spelling, which sometimes differ from the style and spelling conventions of the book. It is difficult to convey the dynamism of hand-written letters, but I hope that the idiosyncrasies in the reproduction of Lily's will give a flavour of the original.

Contents

Preface

Murder in Haifa

It is a hot Monday afternoon in July 1938, and Philip Vallentine Tobias, a middle-aged British-Jewish businessman in Palestine, is returning home from his business, the 'Palmira' Palestine Plate Glass and Paint Works factory in the Haifa Bay industrial zone. He is giving a lift to three of his employees – Lothair Kach, Hermann Steiner, and the factory foreman, Israel Geller. It's about 4.30 in the afternoon, and as they approach the outskirts of town near the Tel Amal crossing, they hear an explosion ahead of them. Philip brakes sharply, then slowly drives on along the heat-hazed dusty road, cautious and fearful. There have been increasing numbers of attacks on Jews, and in recent days bombings, shootings, and ambushes have become frequent, particularly in Haifa. Two years earlier, a strike in protest against land sales to Jews, and against the level of Jewish immigration to Palestine allowed by the British Mandatory authority, turned into the sustained Arab Revolt, and by the summer of 1938 it has reached a new peak of violence.

As Philip and his passengers reach Haifa's outskirts, a shanty town of tin huts at the edge of the industrial neighbourhood, their fears are realised: a large crowd of young men has gathered around a bus that has just been bombed. Fearing their approach, the Jewish driver of the bus fires into the air to try to frighten them off, and members of the crowd, seeing that two Arab men have been wounded, and believing they've been injured by Jews, become enraged.

It's a chaotic scene that Philip has driven into, and the police, arresting the bus driver in the confusion and trying to disperse the crowd, have also become its target – the young men start throwing stones at them.

Philip stops the car a little way from the crowd, and Lothair and Hermann tear open the doors and make a run for the Tel Amal crossing, in order to escape up the road. There are about a thousand people gathered in the crowd around the bus in Istiklal Street, and some of them, seeing a new target, begin stoning Philip's car. A police constable named Horowitz identifies the passengers as Jewish, and shouts at them in Hebrew not to leave the car, and then turns away to try to disperse the crowd. But it's a mob scene, and other police nearby are doing nothing to intervene, but simply watching from the safety of a cafe. Israel Geller, terrified, tries to escape. He is stoned, injured, and knocked down. A crowd of about thirty men pull Philip from the car and heave stones and rocks at him. Like Israel, he tries to make a run for the Tel Amal crossing, dodging the stones, but he is hit and he falls. The men close in, stoning and knifing him in a frenzy, and one man, leaning over his prone body, stabs him in the neck.

A little later, the police manage to disperse the crowd and rescue both injured men. They lift them into a car, and drive them to Government Hospital. Israel is seriously injured, but he is given first aid and survives. Philip, stoned and stabbed, has died.

Not far away, in the spacious villa they share up on the heights of Mount Carmel overlooking that scene, Philip's wife, Lily, is writing in her study, completing the last chapter of her fourth novel. Unaware in those hours before the start of the evening curfew that she is already a widow, she drafts the novel's conclusion – and its final words are prescient: 'Jews and Arabs were standing together, brothers with heads bowed in a strange truce, the sons of Israel and the sons of Ishmael. The corpse of the murdered policeman lay in the dust at their feet. And between them, hostage or deliverer, was borne the body of the Samaritan.'

It is too late for it to be the postman when the fateful ring sounds at her door. Perhaps she puts down her pen, curious, puzzled, and goes to open the door; perhaps she sees standing there a uniformed British policeman, sweating and awkward in the heat, or an associate of Philip's from the factory, his face betraying his horror. Ever afterwards, an unexpected ring at the door will alarm her, triggering the memory of the 11th of July, 1938, which is about to change her life forever.

Later that day, in shock, she is driven to the mortuary to identify Philip's mutilated body. She will never be free of that trauma, of knowing what butchery he experienced in the minutes before his death, of seeing him transformed. Nor will she ever be free of the certain knowledge that his death could have been prevented, for soon afterwards she learns the details of what happened from the constable, Shimon Horowitz, who witnessed the attack, and arrested the main perpetrator.[1] According to Horowitz, his superior let the man go, and then disclaimed all knowledge of him, in an apparent act of police collusion with the murderer –

an injustice that will haunt and torment Lily for the rest of her life.

In accordance with Jewish tradition, Philip's funeral takes place the next day, but at the unusually early hour of 5.30 a.m., while the night curfew still provides some safety to the mourners in that time of heightened conflict, and before the morning's summer heat becomes again suffocating. Then, seventeen days after his death, Lily packs into trunks her clothes, books, typewriter, and draft manuscript, and boards the S.S. *Sphinx* at the Haifa port to sail back to the UK. There she takes what comfort she can with her family, particularly the two siblings to whom she is closest – her brother Joseph, in London, and her sister Kate, in Cardiff.

Only two years have passed since she and Philip left the UK and finally moved to the country she hoped for and dreamed of with a political and religious zeal from her earliest years. Even as a child growing up in Ystalyfera, an industrial village in Wales, Palestine offered to her a dream of possibilities: 'The authentic voice of Israel pleads for "Peace – Peace – Peace." It is not for us to hush a single note of that compelling cry,' she wrote eighteen years earlier in the *Zionist Review*. 'For, unless we fulfil its message on the soil of Palestine, we shall be false alike to the most vital teaching of our past, and to the greatest present need of racked mankind.'[2]

Now, at the age of fifty-one, her dreams of building a shared Jewish life with Philip in Palestine are at an end. Palestine, once the site of all their joint hopes and ideals, and now site of such trauma, has become a place of horror. When she boards the *Sphinx*, it isn't clear, in the shock of her grief, if she will return. 'Early in July a fresh holocaust of terror broke over Haifa and overwhelmed my life,' she would later write in a note to *The Samaritan*, which was to be finally published at the end of 1939. It would take her more than a year before she would be able to pick up her pen to write that note, and to 'fill in a few bare outlines and revise some of the text'. That intervening year was to be full of terrible grief, and a futile search for justice. Nevertheless, she would recover – with difficulty, and never completely – and return again to Palestine to carry on alone what she and Philip had begun together.

One

An Ystalyfera childhood

Philip's death marked the centre point and fulcrum of Lily's near century-long life. Before that darkened summer day there lay the passionate hope and idealism of the years in Wales leading up to their marriage in Swansea in 1911, and the shared quarter-century of their life together in Cardiff, London and Haifa, during which she had become a writer of note; after it lay a weight of despair and disillusionment, against which she fought with an extraordinary and determined act of will for more than forty-five years.

Lily's family had arrived in Wales in the late nineteenth century by a circuitous route. Her father, Tobias Shepherd, had grown up in Siemiatycze, a largely Jewish town in Russian Poland, and he left in 1877, when the Russian Ottoman war began, to escape the draft. When he came ashore from the ship at Plymouth in 1877, he had big plans for his new life in the UK. Many of the thousands of Jews who, over the next few decades, left Eastern Europe in search of a better life, fleeing persecution and then pogroms, believed, mistakenly, that they had bought tickets to the *goldene medina*, America, where the streets were paved with gold; some had sold all they owned and sewed their worldly wealth in coins into the hems of their gabardines and long dresses. But Tobias – at that time still bearing the surname Rozinky – arrived before that great flight from hardship and pogrom, and he did not end up in England because he was tricked, or because he misunderstood where he was going. He'd seen possibilities in the growing Jewish community in London, and that was his destination. He planned to establish himself as a religious teacher, and, once established, he intended to fetch his wife Chana Beila, and their son, Moshe, from Siemiatycze, where his extended family lived. But though he knew where he was going, he was, nevertheless, tricked. Apart from a little cash in his pocket for the journey, he had invested his portable wealth, the means by which he was to establish himself, in fish oil, which he'd arranged to have shipped to England in barrels. But when he went to the dock to collect his cargo he found that the fish-oil barrels were empty. Like so many migrants, he'd been the victim of a cruel fraud.

Jews arriving in the ports of England often had little more than a scrap of paper, much unfolded and refolded, with the name or address of a relative or the friend of a relative. Arriving without English, lightheaded with hunger, seasick, and itchy with lice, traumatised and bereft, forced to flee first hardship and persecution and then pogroms and pillage, the increasing number of Jewish refugees had swelled to thousands, and then tens of thousands, by the end of the century. The increasing numbers led to political debate and calls in the press about the need to curb immigration before Britain was 'swamped' and 'overrun'. But by the time the new Aliens Act that resulted had been debated and voted into law in 1905, Tobias and his wife, and their now eight children, had become naturalised citizens, and he had changed their family name from the foreign-sounding Rudinsky to the safely neutral English one of Shepherd.

By then Tobias had been back to Poland several times. In 1883 he'd visited Chana Beila, his wife, which resulted in the happy outcome of their second son, born in 1884. Tobias's parents were well-to-do: later, theirs was to be the third house in the town of Siemiatycze to have a telephone installed. Siemiatycze was a thriving, busy, predominantly Jewish town – only a quarter of its approximately 6,000 residents in the late nineteenth century were not Jewish, and Jews were involved in all aspects of the town's economy. London's growing East End was also at that time heavily Jewish, including both a long-established community and new immigrants. Visibly different, with its inhabitants' traditional Polish Jewish dress and Yiddish speech, the Jewish East End was seen as deeply foreign and alien, and increasingly dangerous, both because of incendiary political movements and because of growing health risks from overcrowding and poor sanitation.

Soon after his arrival in London, Tobias left, moving first to Portsmouth, where his half-brother Aaron had set up in business, and later to Swansea, where he set up his own travelling salesman route. Swansea, like Portsmouth and many port cities, had a growing Jewish community. In fact, with roots that could be traced to the mid-eighteenth century, Swansea's was the UK's oldest Jewish community outside London. It was here that Chana Beila and their two sons came to live, and where Lily was born in 1887, at 291 Carmarthen Road.

By the turn of the century, Swansea's population had swelled to more than 100,000, but its Jewish community was a mere fraction of that (at its greatest extent before the First World War, the entire Jewish community of the south Wales industrial area is estimated to have been no more than a few thousand). Compared to the familiarly Jewish town of Siemiatycze that Chana Beila knew so well, Swansea must have seemed an overwhelming and alien metropolis – but the family did not stay there long: soon after Lily's birth, they moved twelve miles up the Swansea valley to the industrial village of Ystalyfera, where Lily's father Tobias had opened up a painting and decorating shop.

Ystalyfera has a vibrant history. Its transformation from farming village to smoky, noisy, bustling industrial town followed a similar pattern to neighbouring villages to the east and south, but unlike the better-known industrial areas in the mining valleys of east Glamorgan, which drew in their burgeoning coalmining workforce from north Wales, England, Ireland and elsewhere, the development in Ystalyfera and the other industrial villages of the Swansea valley was more local. Further from urban centres, and with a growing iron, steel and tin industry, the village attracted workers from the surrounding rural counties, and it developed a unique political and social life that remained predominantly Welsh in language and in culture. Its many political radicals, and its sustained social foment at the turn of the century – in particular its newspaper, *Llais Llafur* (Labour Voice) – gave Ystalyfera an important place in the story of industrial south Wales.

Lily's family moved to Ystalyfera during the period of its renaissance, after an initial rapid industrial growth had shifted pace and caused it to suffer a temporary setback.[3] A century earlier it had been a farming village with one large landowner who leased agricultural land to tenant farms scattered along the river valley and across the densely wooded mountain slopes. The Twrch River, which gave its name to many farms and villages such as Abertwrch and Cwmtwrch, might well have been uncomfortable for its new Jewish residents once they learned its meaning – hog or boar, perhaps retaining an earlier memory of wild boar, or perhaps recalling even earlier folk memory of the prominence of pigs in Celtic culture. Mostly, however, the names reflected the features of the pre-industrial landscape: *allt* and *rhiw*; *craig* and *carreg*; *grug* and *wern*, with the mountain of Alltygrug dominating the village.

All that changed when coalmining began in earnest in the 1790s. The early colliery workings were small private affairs, but the area was rich in coal, and coalmining expanded rapidly, particularly when iron ore was discovered, and leases for foundries were signed. Four foundries were built in 1840, but by the 1850s there were forty, along with sixteen tin mills and tin houses. Smoke from the foundries and tin mills, and the coal tips and slag heaps that mining and smelting produced, soon poisoned the waterways and transformed that wild landscape of alder and bramble, now cut through by new access and transport roads, and a new canal. In 1841 the population had been just above 1,000; by 1861 it was nearly 5,000, and the ironworks at the time were said to be the largest in Europe. But iron began to be overtaken by steel, and the ironworks declined and then closed in 1885, leading to unemployment and depression. The population of Ystalyfera shrank, and it wasn't until the ironworks were reopened as tinworks, followed by the new Pwllbach, Tirbach and Ystalyfera collieries, that the town began to prosper again.

By the time Lily's family arrived in Ystalyfera the town had begun to thrive once more, with a proliferation of specialist shops and businesses, from butchers and grocers to cobblers and drapers and tailors (including Tobias's own T. Shepherd & Co., which sold paint, paper, and glass). Despite cultural differences, and its heavy industry, in population size Ystalyfera was comparable to the scale of Siemiatycze, and for Chana Beila at least perhaps was more manageable than Swansea's bustling urban density. However, unlike Siemiatycze (and unlike Swansea), there were no Jews at all living in Ystalyfera, so it was an odd and rather difficult place for a devout Jewish couple to move to in the late 1880s. By strange coincidence, a Jewish family had lived in the very house that Tobias rented (there was still a *mezuzah* on the doorpost); that family had died or fled in the cholera epidemic some twenty years before.[4]

The isolation from other Jews proved challenging for Lily's mother, but for Lily herself, growing up in Ystalyfera was to prove fortuitous, because of the political vibrancy that developed at the turn of the century. Her younger brother Joseph claimed that the family's move from Swansea was a purely commercial one: Ystalyfera offered opportunities, and their father Tobias was ever an entrepreneur. But there were tensions in the Jewish community of Swansea, tensions between an older, established elite, and the newer immigrant Jews, whose visible and audible 'foreignness' reflected badly on the establishment, or so members of the elite felt. The newcomers were often poor, and spoke limited or no English and Welsh, but they were also made to feel like second-class citizens within the communal organisations, particularly in the synagogue. All these tensions led to the establishment of a new 'immigrants' synagogue, the Beth Hamedrash *shul*, something in which Tobias himself was involved, so it was likely to have been a combination of opportunity and escape that drew the family to the growing commercial possibilities of Ystalyfera. Apart from anything else, there was little competition in Ystalyfera: the company owning one of the industrial works had had a monopoly with its store, but now new shopkeepers and tradesmen were beginning to meet the needs of a growing population.

Chana Beila, Lily's mother, was pious and careful, Yiddish-speaking and uneducated; she had grown up in the thoroughly traditional and predominantly Jewish milieu of Siemiatycze, and for her the twelve-mile distance from a Jewish community was a considerable hardship. All the communal aspects of Jewish life presented a major challenge: a community of fellow Jews is needed for prayer, for festivals, for celebration and grieving, for the provision of kosher food and the marking of important moments of transition in an individual's life. The welcome of a new baby into Jewish life marked by a *bris*; the welcome of a child into adulthood with a *bar mitzvah*; the riotous celebration of marriage – to mark any of these, the family had to traverse the distance to Swansea's Jewish community and synagogue, when there was no public transport.

However, if there were inconveniences to being so far from Jewish life – such as having to travel the twelve miles and back by horse and trap to have your chickens slaughtered according to Jewish practice by the *shochet* – there were also advantages. Swansea's well-established Jewish community stretched back a century and a half, and social tensions vibrated alarmingly between prosperous members and the new 'foreigners'. Without much English or Welsh, Chana Beila never was able to integrate in the community in Ystalyfera, and her distance from the security of a Jewish community no doubt deepened her sense of isolation as an immigrant. That isolation was expressed at least in part in her anxiety about her children's Jewishness, and this caused some tension for Lily, her brothers, and the growing number of their younger siblings, who, unlike their mother, were fluent in Welsh and English, and became very much part of the community in which they lived.

Ystalyfera had its problems. Conditions were primitive: very few houses in the town had running water at the end of the nineteenth century – Joseph himself recalled that 'there was no tap water in the house' when they were children.[5] Ystalyfera's sewerage provision was appalling, with inadequate shared outhouses and open drains in the streets that emptied into the canal. In some very impoverished areas there was no provision at all, and the street itself served as outhouse. Not surprisingly, this led to disease. In 1866 there had been a cholera outbreak that spread rapidly, and many died in the epidemic, and others fled. It provoked public outcry, but even so a sewerage system was not built until 1912, and the town remained notorious for its foul sanitation. The nightsoil accumulated in the gullies and by the sides of the road until it was carted off once a week. Even after 1912 there were problems with water and sewage: public standpipes were still sited by the side of the road, and the authorities complained about property owners who had not connected their homes or businesses to the sewerage system.

The poor sanitation in Ystalyfera was an ongoing subject of concern and discussion for its inhabitants and for the authorities, and it certainly must have impressed itself upon Lily when she was young, for it appeared later in her novel, *My Mother's House*. In this, her first novel, she fictionalised Ystalyfera as 'Blaemawe'. Blaemawe's town crier and nightsoil-man is called Dai, but in all other respects he is a portrait of a prominent Ystalyfera resident called Morgan Davies. This public employee, nicknamed 'Moc yr Eidon' ('eidon' means bullock or ox), was a strange and memorable figure. He became Ystalyfera's only crier in 1866, the year of the cholera outbreak, and continued in that role until his death in 1920. He was prominent and idiosyncratic enough to merit a biographical portrait in the unofficial history of Ystalyfera by Bernant Hughes, alongside other prominent figures of the town.[6] Uneducated, and almost illiterate, Morgan Davies had to rely on a relative to help him 'read' the notices that he was to announce, and he would then memorise these and walk the town's streets, ringing his bell three times every quarter mile, and call out, in Welsh, 'Daliwch sylw bawb ohonoch chi' ('Pay attention all of you'). The only English he knew was the exclamation with which he would close his public announcements – 'God save the Queen' (changing, of course, in 1901 to 'God save the King').

Morgan Davies worked variously as town crier and as gravedigger for Capel Caersalem, one of the town's many chapels, but he was also the sanitation worker for the council, and his happy disregard for the conditions in which he worked – and ate and drank – made its way into Lily's fiction. The reaction of her protagonist, Simon, in the novel *My Mother's House* no doubt expressed her own feelings, too. Here Dai, a 'short stout figure in official cap and coat' walked with 'a heavy, lumbering gait', which might have been the basis for the nickname 'bullock' attributed to the real 'Moc yr Eidon', whom Lily was clearly describing. As town crier, Dai would ring his bell and call 'Cymrwch sylw, bawb ohonoch chwi', but Simon was horrified by the man, 'who, for all his official garb, and spruced appearance, was present to his consciousness as a drunken, evil-smelling reprobate. That was, perhaps, rather a strong picture of the Council's odd-job man, who was overfond of his glass and quarrelsome at home, but genial enough in the course of even the most unpleasant of his occupations. Simon had seen him, horridly, unforgettably engaged, knee-deep in the filth of cesspools.'

Lily must have seen the real Morgan Davies knee-deep in the filth of cesspools. She also described Ystalyfera's notorious sewage problems, and expressed through her protagonist Simon what was probably her own strongly felt and clearly recalled disgust: 'The primitive lack of sanitation in the valley had no terrors for old Dai, who conducted his disgusting cleansing operations in the public view, to the accompaniment of songs, curses, ribaldry and hymns. Simon had been sick the whole day, after seeing the old man drink his beer with relish in a ditch of excreta, his hands fouled on the mug as he tilted it to his lips. The recollection was still powerful and nauseating.'[7]

Evidently by the time the family moved to Ystalyfera, Tobias Shepherd had dispensed with their 'foreign' name, Rudinsky, but though his shop, T. Shepherd and Co., gave no indication of its owner's Jewish identity, it was still known locally as 'Siop y Jew' ('the Jew's shop'), for everyone knew in that small community that he was Jewish. To a modern ear this might sound hostile, but in fact it is likely to have been merely descriptive in the same local way that a shop might be identified by its position ('Siop y Gornel' – the corner shop, for example). Nevertheless, even if not hostile, it suggests how the family, though being part of the community, was identified as still being different in their Jewishness, and it is likely that Tobias had decided to change his name at least in part to alleviate this sense of obvious difference.

The way in which an immigrant family accounts for the origin of its anglicised name is often comical, sometimes because the true cause for the change of name is embarrassing or less than salutary. Interviewed at the age of eighty, Lily's younger brother Joseph recalled a well-known and often repeated story about why their father, Tobias, had changed the family name to Shepherd. 'He had a half-brother who had preceded him, who was related to the Zangwill family,' Joseph remembered, referring to the prominent Anglo-Jewish author, Israel Zangwill. 'And it was Israel Zangwill as a boy who told my uncle, who preceded my father in coming here, that you should change your name from *Pastech*, which is the Yiddish and the continental for "shepherd", into *Shepherd*. So we became Shepherd, which is a translation of Pastech. Who was the *pastech*? The shepherd who looked after the flock. The community – I don't know if the rabbi regarded the flock as his sheep – anyway the Christians do, you see. And the rabbi is the shepherd of his flock.'

In this case, Israel Zangwill was indeed a relative by marriage to Tobias's half-brother Aaron, and this story about the change of name acquired a kind of gloss by association with him. Zangwill was the leading figure in Anglo-Jewish literature, and was a well-known author throughout the UK and internationally.[8] Effectively the association ennobled what to all immigrants marks an uncomfortable point of change: the moment when the family tries to distance itself from the past and make a claim to belong in the new homeland. Though Joseph did correctly recall the Yiddish word for shepherd, *pastech*, Tobias and his brother Aaron probably chose the nicely English-sounding name Shepherd as a humorous – or respectful – salutation to their father, whose given name was Shepsel. But Shepsel is a diminutive of 'sheep', rather than the slightly more respectable 'shepherd'. A variant of the story, which claimed that Tobias changed his name because his children were 'like a bunch of sheep', was, according to another family member, John Minkes, 'purely apocryphal'.[9] It seems much more likely that Tobias changed the name from Rudinsky to Shepherd for shrewd business purposes – and, given the growing hostility to immigrant Jews at the end of the nineteenth century, for reasons of personal safety.

Like the surname, the first names of family members became anglicised too: Moss, for Moshe, and Anna-Baila for Chana Beila. Anna-Baila was by reputation the most beautiful woman in the Swansea valley, and she was 'a very pious, shrewd and gentle mother', according to her son Joseph. Finding the world around her difficult and foreign, she was superstitious and anxiously religiously observant, which was the picture of her recalled by two of her grandsons, Leo and Dannie Abse, sons of Lily's sister Kate. Living isolated from a Jewish community, and trying to maintain an impeccable Jewish home, she found the non-Jewish industrial world around her threatening.

Indeed a great deal going on in the immediate vicinity was to threaten the Jewish observance and identity of her family. The coincidence of Lily's birth and Ystalyfera's rebirth was a fortuitous one, because in its second industrial life the town began to develop into a vibrant cultural community with vigorous and varied literary, political and social events and gatherings, and a great deal of public discussion and debate. This was a period of growing politicisation and national revival: Wales enjoyed a quite remarkable cultural, educational, and political renaissance, not least with the Cymru Fydd movement, and the growing possibility of Home Rule. Some of this engagement with political and literary life, and in particular the growth of the periodical press in Welsh, was a response to – and repudiation of – the notorious Blue Books, a nineteenth-century English inspectors' report on the allegedly atrocious state of Welsh education.

The timing of her birth meant that Lily could enjoy an education until the age of thirteen, which was by then compulsory, but perhaps the development that was most important to her directly was the establishment of the printworks by Ebeneser Rees in 1895. It was the printworks, or more specifically the newspaper printed there, that was instrumental in creating an atmosphere of possibility and potential quite at odds with the protective and careful atmosphere cultivated at home by Lily's mother.

Ebeneser Rees had grown up in nearby Cwmtwrch and, like most boys in the area, he had started work in the mine when he was only seven. Later he'd become active in the trade union movement and been dismissed and gone to America, before returning in 1872 to the Swansea valley. At first, in a manner rather similar to many early Jewish arrivals in the south Wales valleys, he worked as an itinerant salesman, selling watches and jewellery, and subsequently he set up shop as a jeweller in Ystalyfera.[10] The printworks was one of several ventures, and for a few brief months it published a paper entitled *Y Gwladwr*, which wasn't a success, but it laid the groundwork for Rees to try something else. A committed trade unionist, he saw the need both for a local paper and for a paper that represented working people. In 1898, when the South Wales Miners' Federation was established in the wake of severe mining disputes, and the year also when a group of residents formed a branch of the new Independent Labour Party in Ystalyfera, Ebeneser Rees launched *Llais Llafur*, the radical socialist paper.

Llais Llafur (Labour Voice) was, in its early years, a progressive and vibrant socialist paper. Published weekly, and predominantly in Welsh, it was determinedly international in outlook and content, with a quite radical editorial slant.[11] The paper served an important and influential role in south-west Wales, and Lily was closely associated with it: she knew the editor, and her earliest work allegedly appeared in it, when she was twelve years old (although given that most work is unattributed, this is hard to confirm).[12]

Llais Llafur was widely read in the area. It supported the ILP and the labour movement, contained informative and highly political articles and editorials attacking the Liberal stance, and took progressive positions on everything from education reform to literature, but it also published fiction and poetry (including a lovely pastiche of Walt Whitman's 'Leaves of Grass'). The paper thus offered a window on the world that was in sharp contrast to Lily's constrained, pious, and religiously observant home. Those contrasts that she struggled with in Ystalyfera, between religious observance and political engagement, between dutiful daughterhood and radical action, helped lay down a path she would follow all her life, and she would return to her roots in Wales repeatedly – especially at times of crisis. Even when she was at the greatest distance, in South Africa during the Second World War, and through her decades in Palestine and subsequently Israel, she retained a connection with the place, the politics and the culture of her childhood and upbringing.

In all its poverty, hardship and transformation, its complexity and vibrancy, Ystalyfera shaped Lily, and had a lasting impact on her. The village appeared, barely disguised as 'Trwyntwll', in her earliest stories, before reappearing under a thin fictional veneer as 'Blaemawe' in *My Mother's House*, and the dedicated socialism she encountered there as a child and in her early teens recurred as a kind of touchstone throughout her work.

When she was sitting in her study in Haifa in 1937 and 1938, drafting *The Samaritan*, which was the sequel to her first novel, *My Mother's House*, she recalled the terrible effect of the Depression which transformed Swansea and the Swansea valley in the 1930s, something she had seen before she'd left the UK for Palestine, and which she saw, in its worsening conditions, on her return after her husband's death in 1938. By the 1930s her family had been long gone from Ystalyfera. There were other changes in the town too: several Jewish families had taken up residence, and there were visiting salesmen or 'packmen' as well – 'Solly the Jew' and 'Levene y Jew' among them. In the final form *The*

Samaritan took, the fictionalised Ystalyfera is seen through the eyes of the protagonist, Edith, with a poignant nostalgia that Lily herself felt. Like Lily, Edith had grown up in the village of 'Blaemawe', and returned for a visit in the 1930s to see 'the river that wound to the sea; the mountain slopes from which pitheads rose and little black-leaved purple berries sprouted; the high valley road along which young and old ambled, exposed to stares and greetings of slow, odd-speaking folk at cottage and shop-doors. Public-houses and chapels alternated like the strips of pavement with terrace wall and dump or thistly waste. An occasional cinema reared a gaudy, unfamiliar head. There was a slight increase, perhaps, of speed in human and machine, for bus and car now rolled where once only carts and horse-traps jolted, with the rare spectacle of the Hafod coach. Otherwise little seemed changed. The Welsh accents brought a curious sense of nostalgia, such as no other place produced.'[13]

Two

Welsh and Jewish

Lily was a small, passionate and idealistic girl who, as an adult, would recall being fired from an early age by the melodrama and romance of nineteenth-century English literature – particularly the novels of Grace Aguilar and George Eliot. But these were illicit pleasures: her mother was anxious to the point of zealousness about any threat to her children's Jewish outlook and practice, and the literature that her daughters began to discover in school was forbidden. Lily and her younger sister Kate resorted to reading their banned books in the outhouse. Their mother might have calculated that forbidding something to children – and more so to independently-minded teenagers – would only increase its allure. At least in part because of her fears over what unkosher contamination might be found between the covers of books, Anna-Baila inadvertently produced a family of writers: three of her many grandchildren became well-known and successful authors, but the first author in the family was her oldest daughter, Lily.

Anna-Baila ensured that her daughters had a thorough knowledge of domestic Jewish practice, from the separation of meat and milk, to the Shabbat blessing over the candles, and she was zealous with her teenage sons, too: 'My mother would never give breakfast to any child who didn't wear *tefillin* in the morning,' Lily's brother Joseph recalled, remembering with difficulty, long after he had abandoned the practice, the Hebrew name for phylacteries, which, according to religious tradition, all men over the age of thirteen are required to wear for morning prayers. Assiduous about keeping her milk and meat dishes separate, Anna-Baila was no doubt the model for the mother in *My Mother's House*, who worried over the cleanliness of a lustre jug bought to adorn her dresser in imitation of the Welsh households around her – might it be *treif* from contact with pigs? Was it unclean?

Anna-Baila was worried about the dangerous influence of the outside world, but its effect was more strongly felt by her daughters than her sons, no doubt in part because she relied on them for help and support in the home. This hardworking, simple woman gave birth at barely two-year intervals to twelve children, nine of them in primitive living conditions. She had little help or support, isolated as she was from the community around her by language and by inclination, and from her own people by a distance of twelve miles that only later was linked by rail. To her grandson Leo she seemed a superstitious, rather cold and unaffectionate woman. Though this contrasts rather sharply with Joseph's characterisation of her as 'very pious, shrewd and gentle', Joseph's own recollection of her withholding breakfast from her sons if they did not say the morning prayers suggests that she was also quite capable of being harsh.

Though Anna-Baila was deeply concerned about her children's Jewishness, such concerns did not turn Lily against her religion. Her mother's close attention to Jewish practice was balanced and enriched by her father's Talmudic learning, and deepened by his profound concern with Jewish ethics: her background, Leo recalled, 'essentially was permeated with religion'. Lily's father, like her mother, was deeply religious, but though he taught his children the rudiments of Hebrew for the purposes of reading, they understood little of what they read. Lily adored and respected her father, and until his death when she was fifty, only lived apart from him for a few years early in her marriage. Leo remembered his grandfather in his old age as a wise and benevolent patriarch. Tobias had 'a passion for learning and spent all his days reading – reading the Talmud, reading the Commentaries', he recalled. Tobias's influence on Lily was stronger than Anna-Baila's meticulous religious observation, Leo thought: Lily 'could identify with her father, who valued learning, in a long Jewish tradition.' Leo remembered his grandfather as a learned, scholarly and thoughtful man, whose religious observance was more philosophical – and unusually Zionist – than the careful religious observance of his grandmother.[14]

Lily loved her father, but her brothers found him very difficult. Moss and Barnett, the eldest two, left home as soon as they were able, at the age of seventeen or eighteen, because they could not 'stick' their father and argued with him; they moved to Swansea where they established their own businesses. Lily's younger brother Joseph remembered him as overbearing. 'My father was an extremely religious Jew,' he said, 'but he was rather a dictator, and a tyrannical father', who had minimal interest in his children. He was 'a despotic, difficult, uncompromising man, neglectful of his children, harsh in words', though he was never violent, and never hit them. However, Tobias changed as he got older. 'He became more liberal,' Joseph recalled. 'He became sager in every way. Instead of age souring him, it ennobled him.' He had not been a good father when they were young, but in old age he was considerate and kind, and he became a good grandfather. 'From being harsh and tyrannical, he became ... ripened, mature, tolerant, compassionate, liberal.' Nevertheless, one granddaughter – Lily's niece, Naomi – didn't find him mellow in old age: in her memoir, *Alarms and Excursions*, she described Tobias Shepherd as 'a tyrannical white-bearded patriarch'.[15]

By contrast, Dannie Abse described their grandfather in a rather telling way in *There Was a Young Man from Cardiff*, an 'autobiographical fiction':

The Shepherds, especially Grandpa and Grandma, were observant Jews. The Shepherds thought the Abses to be ignorant atheists who did not know the Talmud from the back of a horse; the Abses thought the Shepherds enslaved by piety and superstition. Wilfred, my eldest brother, thought Grandpa Shepherd was a religious nut and I usually agreed with Wilfred who had recently taught me which was my right hand and which was my left. Grandpa Shepherd gave you the feeling that he had known Moses personally.

'You're the third son,' he said, pointing his grey beard at me, 'so here are three pennies for you. God favours the third.'

... I told my mother that Grandpa had said I was lucky to be the third in the family. She said, protesting, 'I have four children, not three. You're the fourth, the baby, the afterthought. There's your sister Huldah Rose. You're the third son, but our first-born is Huldah.'

'I think Grandpa thinks girls don't count,' I said.[16]

Certainly girls did not count in the family in the same way as boys. Compared to the sons, expectations of Lily were minimal: to remain a Jew, to meet and marry a nice Jewish boy and to have, in due course, good Jewish children. In that regard, Kate, her younger sister by eighteen months, had the advantage of good looks. Leo remembered his mother's beauty as an asset that she relied upon. 'That's why she was so tactless,' he recalled; 'she never had to use charm.' Dannie made gentle fun of a certain kind of silliness in his mother, and also alluded to her good looks. In *Ash on a Young Man's Sleeve* his uncle Isidore tells the young Dannie 'you know, lad, she used to be the prettiest girl in South Wales – Jewess or Goy.' Dannie objects that she still is. 'No, no,' the uncle replies. 'Now she's the most beautiful.'[17]

Lily had none of Kate's giddiness or foolishness, and none of her good looks: she was, according to Leo, 'the ugly duckling of the family, short and dumpy, with her three younger sisters very pretty girls'.[18] Although her brothers had aspirations towards learning, from her parents Lily 'had no encouragement at all. As long as the girls could read enough Hebrew to say the prayers and go to *shul*, that was regarded as sufficient', he recalled. His grandparents 'had the same attitude as the general Victorian attitude to women'.[19]

As a girl, no matter how bright – and evidently Lily was very bright – her educational opportunities stopped at the age of thirteen. At school, within the classroom, Lily learned in English, but in the playground and with friends the language was Welsh, while at home her mother's first language – and the only language Anna-Baila was ever comfortable in – was Yiddish. The village school, which had separate classes for boys and girls, and separate playgrounds, was non-denominational, but the vast majority of the residents were Welsh-speaking and chapel-goers. The Church of England was something of an alien body – only the snobs were Anglican, Joseph recalled; they were anglicised, too, and would not speak Welsh – '*Saesnegs*', he said, contemptuously, a distinction that Lily also made in *My Mother's House*, in which the experience of the protagonist, Simon, closely matches that of Joseph. This was not to be the last time Lily wrote about Joseph's experience, either – she and Joseph were close, and remained close throughout their lives, and later his experiences as a conscientious objector during the First World War informed her writing of the pacifist novel *Eunice Fleet*.

Unlike Lily, whose schooling was brief by virtue of her being a girl, Joseph won a scholarship to the County School. He remembered the inequities with some passion. 'What access had the working class to education?' he exclaimed. 'You feel it more in Wales than in England. I believe the English working class don't believe in education. Now in Wales they strove.' In the school he attended, he recalled a total count of some 220 pupils of whom only twelve could have a scholarship each year. 'Now, how many of the colliers' sons could afford fees? In the school I went to, in Ystalyfera, it served a wide community. It covered Ystalyfera, Pontardawe, Gwaun, Cwmtwrch – an area of ten miles, and there were only twelve scholarships given to an intake of

forty each year. So it was lower middle class, tradesmen...
So that was there, in the school, the son, say, of a carpenter,
a collier, of a tinplate worker? I don't think there was one.'

That inequity in access to education was one of the many
obvious injustices that informed his and Lily's early and
natural socialism, a socialism which, late in his life, in 1976,
when he was interviewed, he felt he had lost. 'It was very
easy to be a socialist then,' he said, recalling that early
passionate politicisation, 'because there was so much
injustice.'

With compulsory schooling ending when she was
thirteen, Lily's formal education was brief, but she was a
voracious reader, and her curiosity and interest was not
stopped by her lack of education. The only aspiration that
her parents had for her might well have been merely a good
marriage and the provision of grandchildren, but Lily was
excited about other things. She had been lit up by reading
forbidden works of English fiction, but by the turn of the
century she had also begun to read the social and political
writers who were being widely discussed in lectures and
talks. These were put on by the many literary and cultural
societies that were springing up all over Ystalyfera as part of
the national cultural revival, and the growing politicisation
of the south Wales valleys. In her teens, the town was buzzing
with debate and discussion, and the Welsh periodical press
was booming. The pages of the Ystalyfera paper, *Llais Llafur*,
were full of local and international news and international
culture, and Lily read her first paper at a meeting of Urdd y
Ddraig Goch, a cultural society set up in the town. This
vibrant world could not be kept at bay, though her mother
tried to keep her close to home, and soon the pull of

Swansea and all that the city had to offer began to draw her further away.

The family rarely went to Swansea, however, except for the High Holy Days – Rosh Hashanah (the Jewish New Year) and Yom Kippur (the Day of Atonement). For those festivals they would attend services at the synagogue in Goat Street. Years after their arrival in Ystalyfera, the Shepherds were still the only Jewish family in the town, but Tobias had a Torah scroll of his own, and a handful of other isolated Jews had moved into the surrounding villages – Mr Neft, a dentist who lived just down the valley in Pontardawe (his daughter Rosa would marry John Silkin, who later became Lord Silkin), and others further away. They, combined with Tobias and the older boys who still lived at home, were enough to make up the required ten Jewish men to form a *minyan* for prayers, and they would gather in the Shepherd house to mark Passover and other festivals. After the oldest boys, Moss and Barnett, had moved to Swansea, there were still four boys left in the family home – Isaac, Solomon, Joseph and David – and the four girls: Lily, Kate, Freda and Fay. Two other children, as was typical of that period, and in that environment of poor sanitation and health care, did not survive infancy.

Tobias was entirely caught up with his shopkeeping business, an ironmongery and furnishing shop at Wern, but his fortunes waxed and waned. His first business, T. Shepherd and Co., had sold wallpaper and glass, paint, paraffin oil, and petrol, but it had failed, and in the autumn of 1897, when Lily was ten years old, her father had appeared in bankruptcy court in Neath. The process dragged on for months, and he was eventually declared bankrupt in April the following year. The high public profile of the bankruptcy gave the family unwelcome attention, with notices appearing in the *South Wales Daily Post* and elsewhere. Two years later Tobias was in the *South Wales Daily Post* again because of the escape of a sheepdog of his, which was suspected of being rabid and had been ordered contained. The paper reported the following week that the dog had been found in Brecon, declared a serious case of rabies by a Brecon vet, and put to death with poison. This wasn't to be the last time that the family was named in the local press for negligent behaviour – worse was to come some years later.

Soon enough after his bankruptcy, Tobias bounced back into business. From its first issue in 1898, *Llais Llafur* carried advertisements for what had become T. Shepherd & Sons, proclaiming its stock of wallcoverings and curtains 'for the classes as well as the masses'. Tobias also sold furniture, and he described himself as a furniture dealer on his 1904 naturalisation certificate. The Wern shop in Ystalyfera was in the front part of the house in which the family lived, but, as the business grew, it began to take over the home, so the family moved into a terrace house a little further away. Tobias also employed a few people to go out with horse and trap to sell wallpaper and paint in the surrounding villages. His sons opened shops in Swansea, but the main business of the Shepherds was, in the end, to be glass – first selling glass, and later making glass – a successful enterprise that would have branches in Cardiff and London, and, eventually, in Haifa in Palestine.

Glass, being the family business, made its way into one of Lily's earliest stories, 'Glasshouses'. Here a glass merchant, like Lily's father, supplied itinerant Jewish glaziers and picture framers who went from town to town carrying glass in a pack on their backs. Lily's sympathetic portrayal of the near-indigent itinerant glazier, written before the First World War, recalled the Jewish refugee packmen who tramped the industrial valleys selling everything from brushes and sponges to Catholic painted-glass icons. Packmen like those in her story – no doubt drawn from her early childhood experience of her father's shop – were usually poor refugees who had fled Eastern Europe and Russia at the end of the century. They often became charity cases for the Swansea Jewish elite, who, over-sensitive about their own tenuous social status, sent them out of the town, where they would be less of a social liability and embarrassment. 'Glasshouses' wasn't the only story in which Lily would write about the experience of Jewish refugees: her sympathies were engaged early by the people she saw in her father's shop, and by the accounts of their shameful treatment by others, particularly better-off urban Jews.

Tobias had removed his family from the Jewish community in Swansea, and they were not subjected to the same snobbery, but inevitably as they grew up his sons and daughters gravitated towards the city. Moss, who had been unable to get along with his father, set up a glass business in Swansea, and a little later his wife, Fanny Foner, opened a corsetry shop (a shop which, more than a hundred years on, is still going strong, and still enjoys the original name, 'Madame Foner'). Lily was able to stay with Moss when she visited the city. For a while she came and went, and perhaps this accounts for the mistake that Tobias made in his naturalisation document in 1904, when he listed Lily with the wrong age. She was sixteen at the time, not thirteen as given on the form, but as Kate is not included in the list of his children living at home, perhaps he simply confused the two of them – after all, there were ten children and he may have lost track of who was where. Shortly afterwards, Lily left Ystalyfera permanently, and moved in with Moss in Swansea. There she encountered a different world.

It was a period of heady social change in Wales. These were the years of the Edwardian Golden Age, a time of growing wealth and opportunities in the years before the war. But where there was money and opportunity, and an increasingly vulgar and ostentatious display of wealth, there was also a rapidly growing disparity between the newly industrial rich and the industrial workers. Liberalism was in firm control, but membership in the Independent Labour Party was increasing, and in south Wales, both in the cities and in the industrial valleys of east and west Glamorgan, every stripe of socialist, communist and anarcho-syndicalist affiliation found its expression and organisation, as did a renewed cultural and later political small-nation nationalism. Lily was a socialist by inclination, from her childhood and early adolescence in the coal and tinplating town up the valley: her socialism, like that of her younger brother, was a natural embrace of sympathies with the rights of working people to a decent wage and better living conditions. In Swansea this socialism was soon informed by urban social inequalities, too, and by a new class-consciousness of her own: her father, like so many entrepreneurial immigrant Jews, was a small tradesman, and in Swansea she was made aware of her lower social status for the first time. But it was not just as the daughter of a tradesman: she was also the daughter of an immigrant, and she was made conscious of her social status as much by fellow Jews as by middle-class Welsh people.

In Ystalyfera, her Jewishness had been a cause of separation, but not of social inequality. On the contrary, with the rare exception of those whom she and her brother recalled as anglicised Anglicans, the diverse chapel culture of nonconformist Welsh-speaking west Glamorgan accepted and respected her family's Jewishness. Indeed her father, as a former Yeshiva student and as someone versed in the Torah and the Talmud, was invited regularly to speak in various chapels on aspects of Judaism and Zionism. But in the socially hierarchical urban milieu of Swansea, Lily found that being Jewish was quite another matter. Here, although there was a sizeable and visible Jewish community, there were limits to its members' integration in non-Jewish society. The social hierarchies of birth and money, and, importantly, of degrees of Anglicisation, had their unhappy, limiting counterparts within the Jewish community, which emulated some of the worst inclinations of the society of which it could not quite be a part. Concerned about social appearances, so-called 'provincial' Jewish communities looked to Jewish centres in London for guidance on proper behaviour and social progress, a situation in which any overt Welshness was looked down on.

Growing up in Ystalyfera, where the first language outside her home was Welsh, Lily spoke in the distinctive accent and idiom of the working-class Swansea valley, something that was at odds with the heavily anglicised Swansea Jewish community. Later, in *My Mother's House*, she wrote about the painful awkwardness of the efforts by two Swansea

Jewish girls to rid themselves of their Welshness. These city cousins of Simon, the novel's protagonist, are described as 'Gay, smart, grown-up, superior,' with '"Welshiness" as well as "Jewishness" carefully eliminated from voice and manner.'[20] But earlier in their lives, that 'Welshiness' showed through despite their best efforts – for example when one cousin, Nettie, was embarrassed by the breach of etiquette by a member of 'that Besamedrash set' (an unusually undisguised identification by Lily of the Beth Hamedrash, the 'immigrants' synagogue): '"But there, indeed!" she said in a loud whisper to her sister, forgetting to avoid being "Welshy" in her indignation. "What can you expect of *foreigners*? No idea how to behave, only anxious to pry into everything."'[21]

Unlike the protagonist and his cousins in *My Mother's House*, and unlike many people who had grown up in the valleys and left for Welsh cities and then for England or elsewhere, Lily never tried to denude herself of her Welshness by acquiring an English accent. In Swansea and in Cardiff, and later in London, and on the radio in South Africa in the 1940s, and through all the years in Haifa until the end of her long life, she retained in the way she spoke the sound of the place that she came from.

Lily's portrait of tensions felt by working-class Jews suggests some of the difficulties caused by the family's location in Ystalyfera. Joseph was critical of his father's move there from Swansea because of the alienation from the Jewish community that this caused them: 'Commercially it was good, but from the alienation point of view of it was bad,' he told his interviewer in 1976. 'You'd think … only a man who had really in emotion ceased to be a Jew, or was a defector from Jewry, who had alienated himself from the community … would go there voluntarily,' he mused, looking back.

Lily's father might have been a difficult man, but he was no defector from Jewry, for he was strictly observant and devout. Nevertheless, his early and strong espousal of Zionism was decidedly unfashionable in the late nineteenth century and was perhaps provocative to the Swansea Jewish establishment. That too might have been a factor in his distancing himself from the Jewish community in the city. By the turn of the century, various strands of political and cultural Zionism had been organised, and although still not yet a major part of British-Jewish life, it had become central to Jewish discussion throughout the UK and on the continent. Nevertheless it was still a decidedly challenging political movement for British Jews. Officially readmitted to Britain only in the eighteenth century, after the expulsion in the thirteenth century, Jews in the UK still sought to prove their credentials as loyal British citizens, fighting against the slurs of anti-immigrant campaigners, against the allegations of international Jewish conspiracies, and against the charge of 'dual loyalties' (slurs and accusations that continue in only slightly different form into the present). Though there were followers and devotees of Zionism among prominent members of the Anglo-Jewish establishment (who often supported the idea of a Jewish homeland for Jews less fortunate than themselves), it continued to be a troubling political movement.

Lily was fundamentally shaped by her father's unfashionable Zionism. The form of Zionism that she embraced and began to write about was bound up with a vision of a world free from militarism, and, just as importantly, with the equal rights of women. Most importantly, Lily felt from an early age that Zionism was inextricably part of Jewishness. The title of her first novel, *My Mother's House*, is taken from the Song of Solomon, and the novel's epigraph provides the context for it: 'I held him, and would not let him go, until I had brought him into my mother's house.' The mother it evokes (and the home she creates) is simultaneously the Jewish mother, Judaism itself, and Palestine, or Zion. 'Bleib nor a Yid, Shimke, et sein alles gut', a prominent member of the family pleads with the novel's protagonist, Simon: 'only remain a Jew and all will be well.'[22] This injunction to remain a Jew, which Lily learned from earliest childhood, and which she believed was only truly possible in a Jewish homeland, was so deeply internalised by her that it informed all her writing, and shaped her whole life.

Lily had grown up in a world of sharp contrasts in Ystalyfera – sharp social contrasts, where there were extremes of wealth and poverty, and sharp contrasts between her public and domestic life. Unlike her younger brother, she did not find a conflict between Judaism and the social and political movements of the time; like him, she embraced the radical socialism of the mining community in Ystalyfera, and early on became a member of the Independent Labour Party, which had established a branch there in 1898. None of this was ever in conflict with her life-long religious devotion, which sustained her. She found in Judaism, both in its practice, its texts and traditions, a high order of spirituality and ethics that informed not only her sense of self as a Jew, and her understanding and espousal of Zionism, but also her embrace of Welsh nationalist aspirations, her pacifism, and her involvement in the movement for women's rights. Common to all these political commitments, which she first encountered in Ystalyfera, was a vision and a hope for social justice, equality and the right to self-determination, both individual and national.

Leo later identified W. H. Stevenson, a journalist with Ystalyfera's paper *Llais Llafur* (later editor of the *South Wales Daily Post* and subsequently of the *Daily Herald*) as having a considerable political influence on Lily. '*Llais Llafur* was a quite important journal in a way in the life of the Welsh Labour Movement,' he observed. 'The group around [Stevenson] were of course socialists, pacifists, and she would have come into contact with that. And the nationalism that she would have picked up was, of course, of a type that could marry in to her Jewish nationalism.' Leo struggled to reconcile what politically he saw as being quite at odds – her socialism and pacifist nationalism – but he understood it in terms of her anti-imperialism, an anti-imperialism that was 'part and parcel of the Labour Movement'. The pacifist nationalist element was, he thought, 'a bit of a mush if you look at it politically – it was all mixed up; it wasn't clearly defined. But it arose in no small degree by being anti-imperialist.' Consequently, he thought, Lily 'would romantically identify with the nascent Welsh nationalism … which was also anti-imperialist.'[23]

In herself, however, Lily did not find it difficult to reconcile those disparate elements. Around her in Ystalyfera, and later in Swansea and then in Cardiff, she undoubtedly encountered contrasts and tensions in the Labour movement, the national movement, and the Zionist movement, but for her they nevertheless worked together to create not contradictions but a coherent whole, which she explored in her writing.

Even if Leo couldn't share his aunt's later political views, he recognised how little encouragement and how much constraint she had to struggle to overcome as a young woman, and praised her for 'stepping, as it were, out of the constrictions which she had, to identify with that.' It was not only the heady promise of a socialist future and the exciting possibilities of a Jewish homeland that drove her, however, but also a stubborn determination that she showed throughout her life, whether it was defying the authorities during the First World War, insinuating herself onto public radio in South Africa, or struggling, always, through difficult times, with courage and strength of will.

Lily was also a romantic, steeped in the melodrama of English Victorian literature, and a budding writer, and in Ystalyfera and then in Swansea she found all the material she would need for her first short stories. When she moved to live with her brother Moss in Swansea, she was free at last of her mother's anxious strictures, and she began to explore. She soon came to know the employees, stories and workings of her sister-in-law's corsetry shop, where she too worked for a while, and, as with her brothers' experiences and her childhood in Ystalyfera, she would later use this rather racy setting in her second novel, *Eunice Fleet*, though fictionally transplanted to London in the early 1930s. One of Fanny Foner's sisters, Angie, was sent to Paris, where she was to learn about the fashion side of the growing business; in Paris she met Prince Kropotkin, the anarchist leader, and that adventure was to form the basis of Lily's slightly scandalous account of illicit sex and corsetry decades later.

Swansea opened up other worlds, too. Lily started to attend Zionist meetings and congresses, to take part in literary society conferences in south Wales and in London and elsewhere, and to get involved in the growing women's movement. She also began to enjoy Swansea's expanding cultural life, including theatre productions, such as Israel Zangwill's new play, *Merely Mary Ann*. After a successful run at the Duke of York in London in 1904, his play had gone on tour in the 'provinces' in 1905, starting with Cardiff's Theatre Royal in April, and moving to Swansea's Grand Theatre in May. It was after a night out seeing the play at the Grand that Lily wrote her first piece of journalism for a major paper. Hesitant, but daring, she sent it to the *South Wales Daily Post*. Not only was it accepted, but the editor, W. H. Stevenson, whom she had known from Ystalyfera, visited her for tea. His purpose, to her surprise and shock, was to ask her to join his staff at the *Post*, and she did not hesitate in accepting.

Despite her limited education, the absence of support by her parents, a strict and constrained home life and an extended family more interested in getting on in business than with a life of the mind, she had nevertheless absorbed her father's Talmudic learning, and been stimulated by everything she had read, secretly, in the toilet, in those suspect, possibly unkosher novels of the previous century. Ystalyfera's progressive political, social and literary scene had opened up a huge sense of possibility for her, and that first unsolicited review of Israel Zangwill's play marked the beginning of her long career as a writer.

Three

The making of a Zionist

Lily's work as a junior jobbing journalist did not give her the opportunity to write on the topics about which she cared most, nor under her own name. However, conditions around her, and abroad, meant she was soon taking a public position in other ways – on the precarious position of Jews, and the necessity, as she saw it, of a Jewish homeland.

Zionism, the movement to establish a Jewish homeland in Palestine, based on a sense of historic origin in the land, meant many things to Lily – it was a religious and cultural attachment to the place of Jewish origin, and a natural facet of her Judaism, but she also believed in the political right to self-determination, and the necessity of a full national Jewish life. In that respect, her beliefs were influenced by the cultural and political nationalism of the world in which she'd grown up – the Cymru Fydd movement, and the hope, if not for Welsh independence, then at least for Home Rule.

Not all of her beliefs drew from positive national aspirations, however: her conviction also had roots in a deep and pervading sense of insecurity – a sense that Jews could not be safe from persecution without their own homeland. She knew too well the history of violence against Jews, whether in ancient, medieval or modern times, and her convictions were strengthened by the ever-present, ever-recurring evidence of Jewish vulnerability, from mild hostility, to violent attack and murder, and, later, genocide.

That sense of insecurity was something she'd been born into: although apparently safe from active persecution in the UK, her family nevertheless remembered terrible events and experiences in Russia and Eastern Europe, and the sense of safety in the UK was always tenuous. Between 1903 and 1905, that security was shaken again by renewed pogroms in Russia, and by an increasingly hostile atmosphere to Jewish immigration in the UK. Persecution of Jews in Eastern Europe had contributed to mass Jewish emigration at the end of the nineteenth century, and now that same immigration raised social and political anxieties for British people, which led to the Aliens Act of 1905, intended to restrict and control immigration. The characterisation of immigrants, predominantly Jews, in the debates and the media leading up to passage of the Act was hostile and threatening, but it was the Kishinev massacre in 1903 that focused Lily's fears.

Lily was not yet sixteen and still living at home in Ystalyfera when stories began filtering through about Kishinev in the spring of 1903. Jewish readers of *The Times* and the *Jewish Chronicle* were shocked by it, but not surprised. It wasn't the worst Russian pogrom – that was to come two years later – but it was particularly violent and nasty. The prominent Anglo-Jewish writer Israel Zangwill characterised elements of the pogrom as particularly barbaric, including the disembowelling of men, and atrocities against women in the style of Jack the Ripper.[24]

Official figures put the deaths at forty-nine, and more than five hundred Jews were injured during the long days of violence. Some seven hundred homes were destroyed, and six hundred businesses were looted. In this pogrom, as in pogroms that preceded it and the pogroms that were yet to come, there was complicity by the police and the military: police were directly involved and soldiers did nothing to quell the violence.

Young and impressionable, and directly connected through her parents and uncle with similarly vulnerable family members who would later suffer terrible oppression in Russian Poland, Lily understood the events in stark terms. Coupled with the many other expressions of hostility to Jews in the period, including the infamous Dreyfus Affair, the massacre grotesquely illustrated what became for her a lifelong conviction about perpetual Jewish insecurity. Published reports about the pogrom in Kishinev were accompanied by calls for protest and a proliferation of appeals for the relief of its victims. Lily and other members of her family were quick to donate. A short while later, Lily also responded to an appeal to support by subscription the publication of a pamphlet revealing what had really happened in Kishinev.

The Kishinev massacre occurred at a particularly awkward time for British Jews. News came just a few short weeks before the year-long Royal Commission on Immigration was to complete its investigations and make recommendations that would lead to the Aliens Bill of 1904 and the Aliens Act of 1905. The Commission had been set up largely as a consequence of the very large-scale Jewish immigration from Russia in the preceding twenty years, and it raised two very different sets of anxieties for Jewish residents of the UK.

Members of the Jewish establishment, made up of families that had long been resident in the UK, and descended from Spanish and Dutch and mid-European Jewish immigrants, were anxious to keep the status quo. They wanted nothing to interrupt the steady progress they were making, climbing rung by rung up the social and political ladder. They wished to present themselves, and to be seen, as Englishmen and Englishwomen (even when they lived in Wales or Scotland): English people whose Jewishness was a matter of belief and community, not one of nationality and ethnicity – merely 'Englishmen of the Jewish persuasion', as the common and uneasy term would have it. Wealthy and comfortable, they were nevertheless socially anxious and apologetic, wishing for social admission and putting from them as much association as they could with anything 'foreign'. They already had enough to worry about with the notorious East End of London full of foreign Jews – immigrants, refugees from Imperial Russia, who were impoverished, indigent, traumatised, who spoke little English, or a kind of Yiddish-English pidgin, and who dressed traditionally and clung to 'foreign' and 'old-fashioned' habits; in all ways it was felt that they presented an embarrassing and inconvenient spectacle of 'otherness' that could hamper social progression for 'English' Jews. Israel Zangwill brilliantly played on those tensions in his 1892 portrait of East End Jewry, *Children of the Ghetto: A Study of a Peculiar People*, as did Amy Levy in her novel of middle-class Jewish anxieties, *Reuben Sachs*, while in *Daniel Deronda* George Eliot's protagonist sees with some distaste and unease the various 'types' of Jew to be met in the city.

Established British Jews were anxious about anything that might undermine their status as Englishmen of the Jewish persuasion, but there were different and more pressing concerns for Russian Jews, who, since the 1880s, had been taking up residence in great numbers in cities throughout the UK, augmenting the Jewish areas that the established Jews had been leaving as they acquired wealth and stability. The violence of the pogroms had been extreme – Jews had been murdered, burned out of their homes, and raped, and years later such memories among those who had left as refugees and fled for the UK and America were brought again to the fore by the events of Kishinev. By the 1920s, more than 2 million Jews had left Russia in the great wave of emigration that began in the 1880s. Some who arrived in England, Scotland or Wales believed they had reached America. Most of them were transmigrants, and they continued their journeys from the UK's busy imperial ports on the west coast, but some 150,000 people stopped and stayed.

The great influx of new Jewish arrivals in the last two decades of the nineteenth century and the early years of the twentieth century, particularly in London, where the majority settled, led to intense anxiety in Britain about cultural change, and heated discussion about the need to curb immigration. The burgeoning Jewish population of the UK, increasing from some 50,000 to 200,000 in a twenty-year period, particularly with many newcomers living in overcrowded conditions with poor sanitation, was seen as severely threatening to the British public. Some of that threat was the same that any large-scale immigration causes – a perceived threat to employment and housing. But other elements were particular to Jewish immigration. Jews were seen as carrying disease both physiological and metaphorical

– they were understood to be poor, racially inferior and contaminating, and were also characterised as carrying among them the plague of political sedition. The terms of the debate in the press and in parliament, and in the Commission of Enquiry, revealed an intense anxiety and fear-mongering about contamination, flooding and pestilence. The Bishop of Stepney, for example, stated to the Commission of Enquiry in 1902 that 'the East End of London was being swamped by aliens who were coming in like an army of locusts eating up the native population or turning them out. Their churches were being continually left like islands in the midst of an alien sea.'[25]

With the Commission still sitting, the Jewish establishment had some difficulty in responding to the news from Kishinev, and achieved a precarious balance between calls of protest and support, on the one hand, and a careful characterisation of the problem as a distant one. But it was immediate and pressing for those like Lily who were close to the experience of immigrants and refugees.

As a child Lily had heard the stories of East European persecution from her own parents – her father had left in the 1870s, before the outbreak of violence against Jews that occurred in 1881, but he had witnessed atrocities as a child, and had gone back and forth to Poland several times, remaining in close contact with his family still living in Siemiatycze, while Lily's mother had not left for the UK until the mid-1880s. In 1914, Lily's father recalled his childhood experiences in a conversation reported in *Llais Llafur*. "'I well remember," he said, "the Revolution in Russian Poland occurring over 50 years ago. I was living with my father and mother in a village on the river Buge.

One night a troop of Cossacks came to the village, burnt all the buildings and drove the people into a big field on the outskirts. I was then six years old, and clearly recollect being taken by my father and mother, holding each hand, over the bridge spanning the river. Here the people had made some resistance to the soldiers and the bridge was crowded with dead and dying men and women who had been shot down. We had simply to walk over them in our haste to escape. I can recollect all the incidents as though they occurred only yesterday."'[26]

The atrocities of Kishinev, coming when Lily was a teenager, was just the latest and most immediate of a long line of abuses, and it cemented her Zionist convictions. It wasn't just Kishinev, however. The turn of the century was a precarious time for Jews worldwide. The Dreyfus case, which swelled and ebbed and swelled again for some nine years between 1895 and 1904, heightened Jewish anxieties, particularly those of established Jews throughout Western Europe, for here a French Jewish officer – an emblem of Jewish social arrival – was framed and jailed for life as a spy (he was later retried and convicted, pardoned and eventually exonerated). The trial itself, and the famous accusation of a cover-up and institutional antisemitism in Emile Zola's letter 'J'Accuse', as well as the subsequent retrial and pardon, highlighted the problem of Jewish insecurity. Famously, it led the Austrian Jew Theodor Herzl, who observed the trial as a reporter, to propose that Jews could only be safe in their own state. His book *Der Judenstaat, The Jewish State*, published in 1896, was the foundational text of the new political Zionist movement for which he became the figurehead.

For Lily, that movement, which she would work for all her life as a practical organiser and as a passionate writer, had its beginnings closer to home. There had been an important meeting in Cardiff very early in the political organisation of the Zionist movement: in 1895, Herzl had travelled to Cardiff with Israel Zangwill to meet Colonel Albert Goldsmid, who headed the Welsh Regiment stationed in the city. Goldsmid famously introduced himself to Herzl as the embodiment of Daniel Deronda, that Jewish character in George Eliot's novel of the same name, who discovers his hidden Jewish identity and becomes a Zionist. Goldsmid, with his newly discovered identity, became a prominent supporter of the Zionist cause.

Although Lily was only eight years old at the time of that meeting, it was widely known about in Wales: Goldsmid was an important figure in the Welsh Jewish community.[27] This important early meeting of Zionist leaders laid some of the groundwork for the nascent political movement, which had its first international Congress in Basel in 1897. If Lily was too young for it to make an impression on her at the time, it was certainly impressed upon her later.

In many other ways, it is no surprise that Lily should have become a lifelong Zionist, one for whom Zionism initially offered an ideal of international peace and harmony, but who later reluctantly came to view armed nationalism as a necessity. It wasn't only her relatives' memories of having been persecuted, nor the terrible atrocities of Kishinev that affected her, nor her father's Zionist beliefs. In Ystalyfera and Swansea she had also encountered victims of those atrocities, and later wrote about them with poignant sympathy.

Following the findings of the Royal Commission on Alien Immigration, a new Immigration Bill restricting immigration, aimed primarily though not explicitly at curbing the immigration of 'Jewish undesireables', was presented to parliament in 1904. It did not pass that year, but an amended bill passed in 1905, and a few months after it received Royal Assent, there was a new outbreak of hostilities against Jews in Russia, which resulted in another surge of emigrants.

Though the worst restrictions of the 1905 Aliens Act were toned down, the discussion in the press, in demonstrations and in parliament, had been damaging and distressing, and it had raised the temperature of hostility to Jews. It was discussions by politicians in particular that worried Jews. Harry Lawson, an East End MP, asserted in May 1905: 'The truth is that we get the floating scum', while another East End MP, Major William Evans-Gordon, a major contributor to the shape of the 1904 Bill, asserted that there was not 'a responsible resident in the East End of London who does not see this process of transformation and wholesale substitution of foreign for English population going on daily'.[28] In April 1904, the *South Wales Jewish Review* noted a discussion of the issue by Evans-Gordon in the pictorial supplement to the *London Illustrated News*, and in particular Evans-Gordon's reference to 'Alien Immigrants' in Dowlais, and 'quite a large colony' in Cardiff. 'It is a pity,' the writer in the *South Wales Jewish Review* observes, 'that it is not made clear to which "large colony" this alludes. It might refer to the coloured seamen, Greeks, or any of the nationalities which one naturally expects to find in an important seaport. Are these not also alien "colonies" in the ordinary sense?'[29]

The 'alien immigrant' colony – which is to say a Jewish group of workers – at Dowlais, near Merthyr, had brought disturbances much closer to home for Lily. Jewish workers newly arrived from Russia in 1903 encountered difficulties at the Dowlais Ironworks. There were widespread reports of a conflict between Jewish and non-Jewish workers at the Ironworks, and the situation was brought to the attention of the Jewish Board of Guardians in London. The Board of Guardians arranged for some of the single men and married men without families to emigrate, mostly to Canada, but the conflict continued.[30] In early 1904 these were characterised as being antisemitic incidents, but the *South Wales Jewish Review* quickly reported in its February issue that this had been misrepresented: an Irish worker, 'in an unsober condition', had assaulted Jewish fellow workers.[31] Feelings were running high, no doubt fuelled in part by the viciously antisemitic rhetoric of a Father John Creagh in Limerick, in Ireland, who, in January 1904, called for the boycott of Limerick's small Jewish community, a boycott that continued for two years.

One aspect of immigration considered by the Commission was the proposal to make certain areas off limits for new arrivals, particularly in those places, like the East End of London, where overcrowding and its accompanying problems had resulted from earlier immigration. While some refugees, following the pattern of immigration around the world, made their way to join distant family members who were already established in the new country, others arrived without family connections and without resources, either financial or social. Indigent and often traumatised, many were sent on from centres in London and Manchester to 'the provinces' by the charity arms of the more established Jewish communities, who were anxious about how their status might be affected by these new, poor, foreign-looking and foreign-sounding arrivals. This was true also in the decidedly provincially minded Cardiff and Swansea communities, where the status of the Jewish establishment was still felt to be tenuous, and where relations with the dominant society were also anxiously protected. As Lily sympathetically described in her earliest stories, refugees who became charity cases, cared for by the Jewish relief committees of various sorts, were often sent on from the cities into the valleys as pedlars and packmen.

Less sympathetically, Lily's nephew Leo would later speculate that some of the worst of new arrivals were sent to Cardiff and Swansea. 'The bulk of the Jews in Cardiff weren't very nice,' he recalled. 'Bernice Rubens has written some books cruelly about the Jews in Cardiff, but justifiably. What she was depicting wasn't very nice because they weren't very nice. They were ghetto Jews who had come over, and I strongly suspect, but I can't prove it, that some of the Jews that came to south Wales were the ones which the establishment Jews in London didn't want to keep in their lives ... And I think Wales had more than its quota of some of the refuse from the ghettos. They weren't criminals, but they were anti-social, and that group ... prayed morning, noon and night, and played cards almost morning noon and night. Obsessional traits, both of them.'[32]

This wasn't Lily's response to Jewish refugees in south Wales at the turn of the century. The people she encountered then, as a very young woman, and the stories of their experience of persecution, along with the wider hostility expressed against Jews between 1899 and 1905 both abroad and, on occasion, closer to home, all showed up later in her writing. Those experiences and encounters also deeply coloured her politics beyond the particular needs of Jews, just as an understanding of wider social injustice coloured her Zionism.

That Zionism was adamantly pacifist, and that pacifism fed into her sympathy for conscientious objectors during the First World War, a sympathy that took practical expression. Nevertheless, although her concerns about war, her support for political and social equality, the needs and rights of working-class people, the aspirations of minority nationalities and cultures, and the rights of women all led in many directions – to the suffrage movement, the No-Conscription Fellowship, the Independent Labour Party and the Cymru Fydd movement for Welsh emancipation – she felt most strongly the call of the Zionist movement, and it was with the cause of Jewish nationalism that her first allegiance always lay.

The right to self-determination for Jews mirrored and reinforced Lily's understanding of Welsh national aspirations. She explored this 'link of common aspirations' in one of her earliest stories, written before 1914, in which echoes of Kishinev and the immigration debates surrounding the Aliens Act can also be heard. An English boy, Bert Hanson, insults the only Jewish girl in the village of Trwyntwll, clearly Ystalyfera, calling her 'a dirty little foreigner'. When the girl, Leah, protests that she was born there, he replies: "'I don't care … Your father comes from Russia and he says 'dat' instead of 'that.' My dad says you ought to go back to Russia, to your own country. We don't want dirty foreigners in England.'" But a Welsh boy, Idris, comes to Leah's defence: "'Look here, Bert Hanson, you mind your own business or I'll be telling *you* to go back to *your* own country. This is Wales, not England, and it's you are the foreigner here.'" To Idris, at the beginning, this constitutes 'a blow struck for the honour of Wales', but as a friendship develops between him and Leah they empathise with one another's parallel dreams of national independence. There are distinctions, however: Leah observes that 'while the Welsh had been deprived only of their independence, the Jews had lost land, home, and liberty'. Idris objects that the Jews are treated well in Wales, and though Leah agrees, it is with reservations:

'Ye-es,' she admitted. 'In England and Wales we are not trampled on, we have the same rights as other citizens. But that is not like being free in one's own—'

'No! No!' cried Idris enthusiastically. 'A people can only be free in its own country, with its own head and its own laws and its own soldiers. Hurrah for the freedom of the nations!'

In contrast, another Jewish boy, a more recent arrival in the valley town, has no time for nationalism:

'Why fritter away our energies in creating another political entity?' he asked with a shrug.

'We are frittering them very rapidly as it is,' answered Leah warmly. 'If nothing happens we shall fritter ourselves to extinction. And there's another side: you know that only last week we heard of a fresh pogrom in Russia—'

'Oh, Russia.' He waved his hand in dismissal. 'Russia is

barbaric. In really civilised countries like this, where we are free and respected, and have equal citizen rights—'

'But only a national life can restore self-respect to a people,' interrupted Idris, 'and bring out the best that is in them. The noblest ideal is to serve one's people.'

'The noblest ideal is to serve humanity,' retorted Israel. 'Nationality is narrow. Art is universal.'

'I have read somewhere,' said Idris, 'that fire burns brighter when you narrow the draught.'[33]

If experience only seemed to reinforce for Lily the idea, formed early on, that Jews could not be safe anywhere but in their own country, sadly, later in her life, she would find that Jewish independence had come at a cost, and that even achieving national statehood had not brought that longed-for security. But at the turn of the century her Zionist vision was clear – and her near-devout dedication to Theodor Herzl, so-called father of political Zionism, was beginning to emerge.

At the beginning of the twentieth century, Zionism in Britain was still very much in its infancy, and full of tensions, contradictions and infighting. While many British Jews supported Zionist ideas, in its early days this was as a solution to the problem of East European Jews who were suffering oppression. Many felt quite opposed to the idea of whole-scale Jewish emigration from the diaspora; support of the Zionist movement was support for other Jews, and did not apply to them. Though according to tradition, Jews recite the words 'Next year in Jerusalem' each year at Passover, and though there had been a sustained and unbroken cultural form of Zionism based on a spiritual relationship with Palestine, and a strong sense of connection to origins, for most this did not necessarily translate into a desire to settle there. A more practical Zionism, which proposed and supported Jewish settlement of Palestine, emerged in the nineteenth century in various forms, both among Jewish continental thinkers, and among western non-Jewish writers, such as George Eliot. However, so-called political Zionism, the movement to establish a Jewish nation-state through political negotiation with European governments, rather than through settlement, was a product of the later nineteenth century and the ideas of Theodor Herzl. Herzl, the figurehead and promulgator of this political Zionism, had been stimulated to action not only by witnessing the antisemitism of the Dreyfus trial, but also by the national independence movements of the late nineteenth century in continental Europe.

Lily responded passionately to his call for the establishment of a Jewish national homeland and the creation of a Jewish state, and her attachment was, from its first expression, profoundly aligned with the political movement. For some, this national home had inevitably to be in Palestine as the historical birthplace of Judaism and the Jewish people, although Palestine was then under Ottoman rule. Others suggested alternative locations for settlement, however, including Uganda and, like the Welsh colonial project in Patagonia, Argentina. The Uganda proposal (actually concerning Kenya) was made in the wake of the Kishinev massacre – Joseph Chamberlain, the British Colonial Secretary, made the offer of an area of land to representatives of the Zionist Organisation as an immediate solution to a pressing British problem as much as to the distressing predicament of Russia's Jews.[34] He, like many politicians, anticipated an ever-growing Jewish immigrant population in response to Russian persecution, and he proposed that these persecuted Jews should be helped to live as Jews elsewhere, rather than threaten British resources and, indeed, 'Britishness'.[35]

Lily objected vehemently to the Uganda idea. She was from the beginning adamant that the Jewish national home had to be in Palestine, and in 1904, when she was sixteen, she wrote a passionate letter to the editor of the *Jewish Chronicle* arguing against the Uganda proposal, and for Palestine.

The East Africa or Uganda idea, proposed as an immediate short-term solution to the situation of Jews in Russia in particular, was strongly supported by some prominent Zionists, including Israel Zangwill. Another fervent supporter was an Irishwoman named Kathleen Manning. It was she who, the previous year, had appealed for subscriptions to support the publication of a leaflet detailing the Kishinev atrocities – an appeal to which Lily had responded. Kathleen Manning was engaged in extensive fundraising, and in the organisation of relief for Russian Jews affected by the pogrom. Her first publication in the *Jewish Chronicle*, the previous year in June 1903, had concerned Kishinev, but subsequently she began to write in the *Chronicle* about Palestine, against missionaries' conversionist activities, and in support of the Zionist cause. She wrote and lectured frequently on Jewish and Zionist subjects, including a letter to the *Chronicle* expressing her horror, as an Irishwoman, at the boycott in 1904 against the Jews of Limerick. But it was her representation of the East Africa proposal, published in the *Jewish Chronicle* on August 12 1904, shortly after Theodor Herzl's death, that provoked the sharp response from Lily.

Kathleen Manning's tone was categorical and absolute: 'While it is touching in the extreme to note the deep feeling of sorrow occasioned by the death of Dr. Herzl,' she wrote, 'we must not forget that the best tribute we can offer his beloved memory is by following in his footsteps, and by carrying on the work he began. As Mr Zangwill said, "I cannot bring myself to write 'late' Dr. Herzl for his influence has not departed and never will depart from among us."' Kathleen was more than a little accusatory: 'Dr. Herzl is still with us if we feel moved to continue his life work – the work he wore himself out in doing – but he has, indeed, left us if his people only sit and wail helplessly over his loss,' she wrote. He had a goal before him, 'and he fell by the way in trying to reach it. Let us prove we were really his followers by acting, not talking. For instance, a definite plan lies before all Zionists.' It was this 'definite plan', and Kathleen's call for financial support towards its realisation, that would provoke Lily. 'East Africa is still open for settlement by the Jewish people, but the requisite funds are needed to send out a Commission of Enquiry in the autumn,' Kathleen wrote. 'Dr. Herzl was very keen on the acceptance of this colony, for we know he saw in it a stepping-stone to Zion.' There should be, she went on, 'no holding back now, no sitting on the fence' – everyone should 'prove their loyalty by coming forward and practically aiding those who are unselfishly working for the Zionist cause by enabling them to carry out his plans for the good of his people.' Put your money where your mouth is, she urged: 'every Jew ought to be a Zionist if he has the temerity to call himself a Herzlist. A Herzlist must be a Zionist, and every Zionist must help to complete the work the leader began for his persecuted brethren.'[36]

Lily objected categorically – but politely – to the premise of Kathleen's call; her letter appeared in the *Chronicle* the following week:

Sir, — I have ever looked forward with great interest to Mrs. Kathleen Manning's communications, and I have almost always coincided with her opinions, but I beg to dissent from some of the views set forth in her letter of last week.

I agree with the writer that it is the duty of every Jew to follow in the footsteps of our lamented leader, and to carry on to the utmost of individual ability that work which he so nobly began and died in his strenuous endeavours to fulfil. But a harshly discordant note is struck in [her] assertion that it is equally obligatory on those Zionists who wish to identify themselves with the work of Dr. Herzl to strive for the proposed Jewish Colonisation of East Africa. Never by any of his actions or words did Dr. Herzl signify his concurrence with the East African scheme; he simply laid it before the mass of Zionists to accept or reject as they themselves desired, while his own attitude remained perfectly and imperially neutral. Within his own pure heart the vision of Zion alone sat enthroned, and not for a single instant did he swerve from the idea he had proclaimed of reaching the original goal – Palestine!

By all means let us strive earnestly and courageously to tread in the steps of our late beloved leader, and march along the path which he clearly marked out for us; but let us not be blinded by the treacherous light which has arisen across the bright pure rays of his teaching into wavering from the straight road and falling into boggy bypaths.

The murky sideways *may* eventually lead to the desired destination, but such vague possibilities should not induce us to abandon the direct way which Dr. Herzl himself walked in. Our aim, like his, should be the Palestinian goal – and the Palestinian goal alone!

Yours obediently,

Lily Shepherd

Ystalyfera, near Swansea[37]

This was Lily's first foray into the pages of the *Chronicle*, and the beginning of an association with Kathleen Manning that would prove lasting. Kathleen was later much better known for her campaigning work against slavery, and for her marriage to Lord John Simon. But at the time that she was a vociferous and active Zionist, in the early years of the twentieth century, she was working as governess to John Simon's son; her letters and articles were written from addresses in France and London and elsewhere. Two years on, in 1906, John Simon became Liberal MP for Walthamstow, and in 1910 he was knighted. In 1917, years after the death of his first wife in 1902, he married Kathleen, who became Lady John Simon.

John Simon served as Home Secretary, Foreign Secretary and Chancellor of the Exchequer, but the notable moment in his career for Lily was to be his resignation as Home Secretary in 1916, as an objection to the introduction of conscription, something against which Lily would campaign vigorously.[38]

In those early years of the twentieth century, when Lily was in her teens, the connection with Kathleen Manning was a strong one: Kathleen became a prominent organiser, frequently mentioned in relation to the London Zionist League, and she lectured throughout the UK on her views on Jewish nationalism.

Some fifteen years later, when C. W. Daniel came to publish Lily's first book, *The Nationalists and Other Goluth Studies*, in 1921, Lily would remember and honour the connection with Kathleen Manning that had been created through their shared Zionist work. The book's dedication reads: 'to Kathleen Manning (Lady John Simon), in honour of an old bond.'

Four

A political engagement

In 1905, with renewed anti-Jewish violence in Russia, Kathleen Manning once again went into action, trying to muster relief for those affected, and Lily donated to her 'Russo-Jewish Committee appeal on behalf of Victims of Massacres and other outrages'.[39] Lily had herself now become publicly active on behalf of oppressed East European Jews. The persecution affected her own family directly, for in the autumn of 1905, during the festival celebrating the Jewish New Year, Russian Tsarist police attacked a group of Jews in Siemiatycze, where Lily's extended family still lived. The response there was remarkable: Jewish residents organised themselves into resistance units the next day. They managed to disarm the police and they took control of the town for a period of three weeks.[40] It wasn't just in Siemiatycze, however: self-defence was being organised throughout the affected areas, and a Russian Jews' Self-Defence Association was established in the UK to fundraise for these groups, and to offer them practical support. Lily helped set up the Swansea branch of the Association, and the *Jewish Chronicle* reported briefly on the branch's activity on September 22, 1905: 'A public meeting, under the auspices of the Russian Jews' Self-

Defence Association was held at the Albert Hall last Sunday. Mr S. Green, president, was in the Chair and addresses were delivered by the Revs S. Fyne and W. Tudur Jones, Ph.D., and Mr Mat Giles. Miss Lily Shepherd (Secretary) read several messages of sympathy.'[41] On the same day a much longer report of the meeting appeared in the *Cambrian*. This article included detailed accounts of the speeches that were given. 'The objects of the association are to "provide the victims of persecution in Russia with the means of self-defence,"' the reporter explained. The meeting was well attended, with a 'good gathering present comprising apparently all nationalities and creeds', including councillors. The accounts of the speeches evoke the kind of oration and rhetoric that was used at the meeting to drum up support in the shape of donations – not to relieve afflicted Jews, but to support their efforts to defend themselves:

Mr. S. Green (who presided) explained that the association was a charitable organisation, established in many towns in the United Kingdom, to enable Russian Jews to defend their rights against opponents who made use of misrepresentation and calumny. Since the association had been formed good news had been received from Russia in that Jews were to receive a little better measure of legislative representation. He was glad, from a humanitarian point of view, that peace had been concluded, but he had hoped that the Russians would have received another few thrashings in order to bring the Czar to his senses. (Laughter and cheers.) The Russian Jews did not want their freedom by bribery; they wanted their freedom the same as the other Czar's subjects, among whom none were more loyal than the Jews. It was useless, however, to expect the police to protect them, and therefore an association of courageous young Jews had been formed to defend the Jews in communities and their property in times of Anti-Semitic riots, 'by any means and by all means.' The movement did not partake of a revolutionary or socialistic character, but was purely one of self-defence. (Hear, hear.) The speaker instanced a recent case in which the association had prevented another probable Kishineff. Money collected for the association was sent to Switzerland and thence to Russia. In concluding a vigorous speech Mr. Green alluded to the unusual loyalty of the Jews to the rulers in the countries they resided in. All they wanted was freedom. (Applause.)

In fact in Siemiatycze at least it was revolutionary groups that organised self-defence, but no doubt this political element was downplayed, just as the Jewish loyalty was emphasised, in order to maximise support from beyond the Jewish community and across political affiliations.

The Reverend William Tudur Jones used the opportunity to relate Welsh and Jewish rights, and – ever a believer in the liberal progression of Welsh nonconformist Christianity – to denigrate the Russian Orthodox Church (Tudur Jones, author of several works of philosophy, was originally from Pontrhydfendigaid in Ceredigion and was minister of the Unitarian church in Swansea from 1899 to 1906; in 1900 his *The rise and progress of religious free thought in Swansea* had been published). 'Let them be Jews in the truest, fullest sense of the word; let Welshmen be real Welshmen; and let both act and work together for the welfare of the world,' the summary report of his speech reads. 'It was only by escaping from the influence of the Russian Orthodox Church of superstition and corruption that hope for Russia by means of her young men lay. If a religion taught them nothing of sympathy with peoples' troubles, it was not worth the getting. There must be more humanity, chivalry, and honour in their religion, and then the downtrodden people would begin to see the dawn of a brighter, happier, and nobler day (Applause).'

Simon Fyne, the rabbi of the Swansea synagogue, 'addressed his hearers as "Jews and Gentiles"', the reporter wrote. Fyne asserted:

> they were all there as brothers of the great British Empire. The meeting showed that there was real sympathy with a downtrodden nation. The Jews in Russia had tried the policy of submission to oppression and injustice. They were now going in for retaliation – not a policy of revenge. That was not their idea for a moment. Russia, however, did not care one jot what became of her children so long as her Czar and Grand Dukes were maintained. Protest meetings and petitions were useless. Petitions never reached the Czar, Jews had had enough of the 'turn the other cheek' policy. They were going in for self-defence now, and it would be eye for eye, tooth for tooth, hand for hand. (Applause.) If they as Gentiles believed that the Russian treatment of Jews was wrong, let them speak out to that effect loudly and unequivocally. (Applause.)[42]

A third speaker, Mr Mat Giles, pointed out that 'the Anti-Semitic movement was not unknown' in the UK, and referred to the Aliens Bill. The speaker 'worked in some

Socialistic allusions to "the right to live," and "the brotherhood of man," and "capital and labour," and said he was there on behalf of his comrades in expression of the "solidarity of sympathy".'

Lily was seventeen at the time of this meeting, when she served with her brother Barnett as secretary of the Russian Jews' Self-Defence Association, sitting with him and the speakers on the platform, and reading messages of sympathy to a substantial crowd. The public role she took then could not have been very easy, for only the previous year both her older brothers and her parents had once again been in the newspapers, and in court, in two embarrassing and difficult proceedings – Barnett for non-payment of a bill, and Moss for fraud and bankruptcy. Tobias and Anna-Baila were dragged into proceedings, too, and both appeared as witnesses.

The previous year, in 1904, Barnett, then living in Swansea and working as an itinerant jeweller, had bought a Remington typewriter, for which, apparently, he did not pay. When the suppliers took him to court, his defence seemed, in the confused and bizarre proceedings, to rely on the typewriter having been supplied to an 'infant' – but Barnett's apparent claim to being underage (younger than twenty-one) proved no defence. His parents were required to give evidence of his age, and both Tobias and Anna-Baila recalled that he'd been born twenty years previously in Warsaw, though Anna-Baila could not recall the year of his birth. There was clearly something of a communication problem in court, and evidently for immigrants, precise dates and documents might cause some difficulty. One account of the court case described Tobias recalling his son's birthday as falling on 1 March twenty years earlier, making it 1884, but a document allegedly supplied to the Ystalyfera school that he'd attended gave his birthday as 12 January 1883 – a document that Tobias said he had no knowledge of.[43] Whether or not the defendant was underage proved immaterial: the judge ruled that Barnett was guilty, and he was required to pay for his Remington typewriter.

Though this must have been an embarrassment for the family, and perhaps was in part what led Joseph to remember the rift between his father and his older brothers, worse was to come, for a mere five months later, Moss appeared in bankruptcy court and was subsequently charged with fraud. The reporting of the case was prominent in the Welsh press, as was his arrest, which he tried to evade. In a headline that declared 'Bankrupt Swansea Jew's Arrest', the *Cambrian* indicated just how vulnerable immigrant Jews remained.[44]

The convoluted case against Moss revolved around a suspicion that he had attempted in several instances to evade creditors by amending his books, concealing assets by setting up a non-existent company in the name of others, and hiding goods; he was also investigated for making significant purchases for which he did not pay at a time when he allegedly already knew he was insolvent. In all ways the business dealings looked, in court, to be suspect: cash transactions instead of payment by cheque; missing bank accounts and payments; pages torn from account books, and vague and evasive responses to questions about directors, owners, shareholders, business expectations and even an engagement to a Jewish woman, perhaps non-existent, perhaps real. This engagement was made in court to look very suspect: the marriage had allegedly promised sufficient monetary interest to save Moss from bankruptcy. Equally, all these business dealings could, perhaps, have been a consequence of informal cash transactions, word-of-mouth agreements, and family business networks, as much as simple incompetence.

In the court proceedings, Moss claimed that the items in the list of goods he was alleged to have withheld from his creditors belonged, in fact, to his mother – including furniture, bedding, blinds, rugs, candlesticks, pictures and two volumes of the *Jewish Encyclopaedia.* The list indicates how, despite Tobias's earlier bankruptcy, and now Moss's bankruptcy, the family was becoming quite well-to-do by 1904.

In the end, although the evidence against Moss was strong, only one charge against him was sustained. At the Quarter Sessions in Swansea, it emerged that his bankruptcy was a consequence of a fire at his Ystalyfera business for which no insurance had been payable, as the insurance company itself had gone bankrupt; he had also imported glass from Holland but it suffered bad breakages in transport, and again he had been unable to claim compensation. The only charge for which he was found guilty was that of passing off as his mother's certain goods that were his own, and unpaid for – for that he received a four-month custodial sentence.

Moss did not marry the Polish-Jewish woman of means named in the court-case; instead he married Fanny Foner, of south Wales, and went on to become a successful glass merchant in Swansea. His sons would later emigrate to Palestine, but his daughter remained in Wales and carried on what had been a corsetry business, and became, in time, a lingerie shop.

All in all, that year, 1904, was rather an important one for Lily and for her family: Lily left home, got her first journalism job, published her first articles, and became publicly active in political affairs; her two older brothers appeared in court, and her father became a naturalised British citizen, nearly thirty years on from his arrival. This meant that he was no longer subject to possible deportation – a risk that immigrants faced if they came to the attention of the authorities, particularly if they were deemed criminal or destitute – and it gave his whole family a greater degree of security. With this new status he was able to return once again to Poland for a period, and that year he stayed abroad for some months.

Despite his new citizenship, and the sense of safety this conferred on all members of the family, the public shame of the court cases must have made it an anxious time for them. Later on, Lily based many of her short story plots and elements of the plots in her four novels on the experiences and stories of her extended family, and on personal experience, but she kept these particularly difficult affairs well out of sight.

In addition to being active in Jewish affairs in Swansea and Cardiff, Lily became involved with the Jewish literary and debating society movement, and this was how she met her husband Philip Tobias, when she was in her early twenties.

The years of prosperity before the war, the so-called Edwardian Golden Age, were a great period for societies, whether literary, cultural or political, including mutual help or Friendly Societies. Members enjoyed public display of their association with parades, processions, and pageants.[45] Jewish literary and debating societies were springing up all over south Wales, both in the cities and in the smaller mining towns. Lily took part in the Swansea Jewish Literary Society, which held regular public talks and social events, including social dances. These kinds of social gatherings, as much as communal festivals and synagogue-related events, provided matchmaking opportunities for young Jews – a particularly important function for people living in communities where the chances of meeting a Jewish partner were limited. For Lily, coming from a traditional family, and herself religiously observant, marriage outside Judaism would have been impossible – so although her political and literary activities were of interest in and of themselves, they were also the means by which she and other young people widened the pool of their Jewish acquaintances and contacts. It would have been in both capacities that she attended a conference of the Union of Jewish Literary and Debating Societies in London, which was where she met Philip.

As the grandson of the founder of the *Jewish Chronicle*, Philip was an eligible young man, and a desirable catch for any Jewish girl, but even more so for a Jewish family with social aspirations. He was born in Portsmouth, but his parents had emigrated to South Africa, which was where he spent his childhood and adolescence. Like Lily, he was a committed socialist and Zionist, and although Lily was by all accounts shy, this never kept her from speaking in public or taking strong positions. They must have found they had a great deal in common when they met for the first time. No doubt their first encounter at the conference was a public one; certainly they enjoyed the challenge of public debate both before and after their marriage, and on occasion spoke in support of opposing motions during subsequent formal debates.

Soon after they met, Philip moved to Swansea and took up work as a paper and paint merchant; at the time Lily had a clerical job in the family glass merchant business, in addition to her occasional newspaper work (after their marriage, Philip would became involved in the Shepherd family's glassworks business, which was renamed Shepherd, Tobias and Co.).

Their family backgrounds might have differed, but this was not an impediment to their marriage. After all, although Philip was related to a prominent Anglo-Jewish family, his father, like Lily's, was a merchant, a tradesman – and although Lily's parents had immigrated from the continent, by the time she and Philip became engaged, in 1910, her parents had been resident in Wales for some thirty years. By then the family's financial and legal difficulties, which had created a temporary notoriety in the south Wales press, were safely in the past.

Philip asked Lily to marry him in the early spring of 1910, and their engagement was formally announced on 25 March. In fact, the announcement in the *Jewish Chronicle* was a dual one: Lily, eldest daughter of Mr and Mrs T. Shepherd, of Ystalyfera, was betrothed to Philip Vallentine Tobias, son of Mr and Mrs P. Tobias of Durban, Natal, while Kate, second daughter of Mr and Mrs T. Shepherd of Ystalyfera, was engaged to Rudolf Abse, son of Mr and Mrs L. Abse of Bridgend.

Dannie's grandmother and grandfather Shepherd might

have thought, as he claimed, that the Abses were 'ignorant atheists who did not know the Talmud from the back of a horse', but by contrast the association with the Vallentine Tobias name, through Philip, and hence association with the *Jewish Chronicle*, must have been a source of some pride to Lily's parents.[46]

Lily became engaged to Philip at a fierce time in the struggle for the right of women to vote, and her involvement in the women's movement took public expression. Two months after her engagement to Philip was announced, the Swansea branch of the Women's Freedom League staged a pageant in Swansea, in which Lily took part. It was written by Cicely Hamilton, who performed in the main role as 'Woman'. A *South Wales Daily Post* journalist enjoyed the spectacle, and reported, rather snidely:

The sceptic may not have been exactly converted to the side of the Suffragette by the 'Pageant of Famous Women,' as produced under the auspices of the local branch of the Women's Freedom League, but, nevertheless, the audience that crowded the Swansea Albert Hall on Thursday evening were highly delighted with the entertainment. Mere man can and does admire the important part that woman has played in the world's history. Miss Cicely Hamilton, the gifted authoress of the production, who played by far the most important part in it, was in herself a living witness to the fact that women as well as men possess brains. The libretto is brimful of literary talent, and the writer displayed rare histrionic tastes. The wisdom of giving votes to women is perhaps another matter, and this was the feeling of many who saw the pageant.

The tableau included a dramatic enactment of the argument between 'Woman' and 'Prejudice' before an enthroned figure of Justice, and a tableau and pageant of Learned Women, Saintly Women, Heroines, Artistes, and Rulers. Among the latter, Deborah was played by Lily – the Biblical Deborah having been one of several powerful Jewish women leaders.

Lily was supported by Philip in her political activities, and in particular her involvement in the campaign for the right of women to vote, for although both were observant Jews, their Judaism took a modern socialist form. In this as in other respects, the two of them enjoyed a politically progressive relationship as equals: later on, after they married, Philip's support enabled Lily to concentrate on her political work and writing.

Lily's involvement with the suffragette movement also took expression in her Zionist activities: she was a founder member of the Cardiff and Swansea Daughters of Zion Association, the women's section of the Zionist organisation, and in 1910 was elected President; the following year, in January 1911, she was re-elected. She and Philip were together active in Jewish events and in the Zionist cause, both before and after their marriage later that year. But Philip also supported the work of women's groups: both of them were involved in the organisation of a Hanukkah ball, under 'the auspices of the Daughters of Zion Association' – Lily, as President, along with the Honorary Secretary, was responsible for the practical arrangements, while Philip served as one of the MCs.

Like Kathleen Manning some years earlier, Lily also began to lecture, giving a talk on 'Miriam' in 1911 that was well received. It is evident that until then the local associations had

had to rely on outside speakers, for the *Jewish Chronicle* reported that the proposal of thanks to the lecturer 'laid great stress on the fact that at last a local Jewish lady had come forward as a public speaker and expressed the hope that the precedent set by Miss Shepherd would help in bringing other members of her sex on the public platform'. The report, as always given in 'the provinces' section of the *Chronicle*, also mentioned that 'an enjoyable programme, arranged by Mr P. V. Tobias was then gone through'.[47] Philip was Secretary of the local Zionist Society, and Lily's father had also become a public speaker, giving presentations on Jewish tradition and on Zionism in chapels in Ystalyfera, and speaking on 'The Need for Zionism and the Cause of Delay in its Consummation' to the Beth Hamedrash, the newer of the two synagogues in Swansea.

That year, Lily and Philip's political engagement took a symbolic turn, too. Throughout the UK, women's organisations, considering how to protest against women being denied the vote, found a new target in the ten-year census, which was to be conducted in April 1911. Many decided to boycott it as a protest against being denied the vote. Women – and some men – resorted to an inventive range of strategies to avoid being counted, staying out over night, or hiding in cupboards and caves. A group of women from Cardiff spent the night of the 2nd to 3rd of April in the surrounding hills, and Lily organised a similar event in Swansea, taking her sister Kate and a group of other young woman to some secret place where the census-takers would not be able to count them. Though this protest may have gone unnoticed, it became part of the family's folklore.[48] Equally unnoticed was the manner in which their fiancés supported their protest – for neither Lily, Kate, Philip nor Rudolph appear on the census record for 1911.

Lily's socialism meant that she was also involved in campaigning for Independent Labour Party candidates, and for a period she served as secretary of the Swansea branch of the party. She and her sister Kate attended ILP meetings and events throughout Wales, but at the same time Lily remained closely involved with Zionist events. As well as serving as President of the Daughters of Zion, in which capacity she attended meetings and conferences and the Zionist Congresses, she also began to engage in public debates. On one occasion, on 22 November 1912, under the auspices of the Zionist Society, the Daughters of Zion Association and the Order of Ancient Maccabeans, she and Philip participated on opposite sides of a debate on the question 'Is Zionism less progressive in England than in other countries?' Lily spoke for the proposition, and Philip against it.

Lily and Philip were engaged for nearly a year and a half before they married at the synagogue in Goat Street in Swansea. Herbert Sandheim was minister by then, having replaced the rabbi Simon Fyne. Philip's occupation was 'Paper and Paint merchant', and he lived at the time in a house called Havalah, in Hazel Mere Road, Sketty; Lily was employed as a Managing Clerk, and lived at 7 Grove Place in Swansea. Although her nephew Leo later remembered her as 'the ugly duckling of the family, short and dumpy', a photograph of the couple taken at the time of their marriage shows something else entirely: Lily is a slim, elegant and attractive young woman, with large expressive eyes, an endearingly sweet, rather melancholy smile and a mass of wavy dark hair.[49] Lily was twenty-four years old, Philip twenty-five, when their marriage, 'according to the rites and ceremonies of the Jews', took place on the 7th of August, 1911.

A wedding was a joyful occasion in the Jewish community, and Lily's extended family was by 1911 well established. Despite her father's involvement with the Beth Hamedrash, the 'immigrant' or 'foreigners' synagogue, it was not there but at the establishment Swansea synagogue that the ceremony took place. Many would have gathered to witness their marriage at the Goat Street synagogue that August day. The gathering included elite members of the Swansea establishment, who enjoyed special privileges, and family and friends from nearby Cardiff, as well as people from the growing Jewish communities in the industrial towns in the Swansea valley and beyond, and Lily and Philip's political friends and associates. It would have been a noisy and festive occasion, for a Jewish wedding was not only a celebration of a couple's happiness but also an event that celebrated the promise, in due course, of the community's perpetuation.

At the time, the synagogue membership was split down the middle in a conflict over the rabbi, Sandheim, who was under pressure to resign. There would have been much gossip and restless whispering about this and other social matters by the congregation that hot day as the couple married under the *chupah*, the marriage canopy.

Nothing on that joyful day nor in the days immediately after could have alerted Lily and Philip to what was about to happen – an event, or series of events, that forever after marked the consciousness of the Jewish community of Wales.

The building where Lily and Philip got married no longer stands – like large areas of Swansea it was destroyed during heavy bombing of the city during the Second World War. At the time, however, it was a symbol and focus of the flourishing Jewish community, and a centre to which the outlying communities still gravitated, though by 1911 even Ystalyfera had a large enough Jewish community to set up its own synagogue. But that flourishing community was about to suffer a profound shock, for just twelve days after Lily and Philip's wedding the so-called anti-Jewish riots broke out in Tredegar.

The 1911 rioting, which began in Tredegar and then spread to other towns in the south Wales valleys, is the most contested matter in Welsh Jewish history. A hundred years on, historians still disagree about what happened. What no one disputes, however, is that the riots, in which looting was initially aimed at Jewish shopkeepers, has to be considered in the wider context of the extended strike, riot and political unrest of that time. There were sustained strikes, regular outbreaks of rioting and looting and, in some notorious examples, organised violence against strikers by the authorities – notoriously in the Tonypandy riots in 1910, and in Llanelli in August 1911, when strikers and protesters were assaulted and killed. The Tredegar riot began at the culmination of a year-long miners' strike, and directly after events in Llanelli. Almost immediately there was contradictory reporting of the riot, which both played up and played down the fact that Jewish shopkeepers were apparently the target of the rioters.

Lily's strong sympathy was with the striking workers, and the events drove her to write the polemical short story, 'The Nationalists', shortly afterwards. At the same time, what had happened in Tredegar and elsewhere also reinforced her belief that, ultimately, the only way that Jews could ever be truly safe was in an independent national homeland. In 'The Nationalists' she presented the striking workers' predicament side by side with an exploration of Welsh and Jewish national aspirations. The protagonist, Leah, had hesitantly agreed with her friend Idris that Jews were not trampled on in Britain, and had the same rights as other citizens, but shortly afterwards, the 'rigorous tyranny of the English manager of the new mines' brought labour tensions to a crisis in Trwyntwll, Lily's fictional Ystalyfera. 'It was this man's harshness and uncompromising contempt which finally forced the strike – a desolating procedure that dragged on for months, bringing disturbance into the newly cohered life of the valley, and starving peaceable citizens into desperate brutes.'[50] Leah feels the effects painfully, and helps relieve the families who are worst off with secretly donated food. "'It's too cruel – this strike,"' she says to Idris. "'I don't think the men can – or ought to – stand it much longer."' Idris, a political orator, has been arguing against the men returning to work, and the two don't agree. Idris, in a passion, bursts out a confession of love, to which Leah responds with dismay, wrenching her hand from his and staring at him in disbelief. As she is Jewish and he isn't, such things are impossible between them, she explains, and when he objects that religion need not be a bar, she rejects him utterly:

'Religion!' she exclaimed passionately. 'It is more than religion. How can you think I would be false to all the ideals of my people? We are a separate race – intermarriage is death to us. And – and I thought you a true Welshman.'

'Do you mean I should choose a Welsh girl?' he asked quickly. 'I don't know one who appreciates Welsh traditions as you do. And such intermarriage as ours would strengthen, not kill, our joint ideals … '

'I can't listen to you,' she said in distress. 'I tell you it's impossible.'

Idris rushes away to walk in wild and passionate distress on the common, and when he returns at twilight, he passes the house of Trwyntwll's other Jewish family, 'where the sound of a violin and subdued chatter issued from behind drawn blinds', followed by the voice of a child singing *HaTikva*, 'The Hope' (the song that would, years later, become the Israeli national anthem).

A group of sullen men stood leaning against the wall without, their faces haggard, their clothes scant and ragged.

'Them damn Jews,' came a muttering voice on Idris's ear. 'Enjoyin' thesselves, whatever. Made plenty of money out of us, they 'av.'

'Ay,' said another. 'Wish I had the coin I've paid this feller for lessons to my lil gell. She an't got no bread now, let 'lone lessons.'

'Ay, they've sucked the blood out us,' continued the first voice. 'Feller at the "Cow" last night tol' us it's all bad luck where the Jews are. So it's been since this lot 'av come here.'

In the pain of his rejection by Leah, Idris neglects to consider the 'influence that sane words from him might have wielded on these ignorant, hunger-maddened men', and later in the day, the effect of his exhortations to the miners to maintain the strike proves 'electric, notably on some idlers who had lately drifted into town, and who had scarcely been associated with the aggrieved men. "Cam on boys," went up a sudden shout from among the mutterings. "Let's show some of these bloodsuckers."' In trying to prevent the looting of two Jewish shops that ensues, Idris is stabbed.

He gasps out the word 'scapegoats', and tries to motion towards Leah. "'She said – the Jews – and I, too— " His head fell heavily back on the couch.' As Lily often did, here she left the ending ambiguous – it is not clear whether Idris dies or not.

Lily's picture of starving workers stirred up by outsiders and provoked into taking action against those they saw as profiting from their difficulties – the shopkeepers – echoes how her father saw the events. He was harshly critical of the Jewish victims of the looting in Tredegar, some of whom had bought properties, raised rents, and forced tenants to buy exclusively from their shops. With the new railway strike, just preceding the outbreak of looting, they allegedly raised the prices of their goods – a Michael Cohen was particularly noted for profiting from the workers' hardship.[51] Leo remembered learning about it from Lily's father, who, according to Leo, thought much as Lord Rothschild had at the time, that they were 'a bad lot' who probably deserved what they got. 'My grandfather, nearer the area, formed the same view,' Leo recalled. 'At his knee, I heard the full story of the Jews whose shops were smashed. He regarded them as loan sharks, and instilled in me such a repugnance of money-lending that when, many years later, I became a solicitor, although in accordance with my professional duty, I defended murderers and rapists, I would never make on behalf of a client any application for a money-lender's licence.'[52]

Like Lily, in her depiction of events in that early story 'The Nationalists' and later in *My Mother's House*, Leo did not see the riots in Tredegar and elsewhere as significantly anti-Jewish, and attributed them to the tense social conditions at the time. Remembering what Lily's father had told him, he was dismissive of 'the well-worn tale of the 1911 Tredegar riot', describing how, 'after a bout of Saturday night drinking, some louts smashed 18 Jewish shops; no Jew was injured, although the intervening police put 15 of the mob in hospital. Given the tension in existence in labour relations that year, and given the disreputable character of most of the Jews in Tredegar, notorious as tough pawnbrokers, money lenders or minor Rachmans, the occurrence is not surprising.'[53]

Some historians have interpreted the riots as being indicative of an insidious underlying antisemitism in Wales, but Lily discerned no such undercurrent. 'About the Welsh folk as a whole I can only say that I have always found myself perfectly at home with them, and have been able to sympathise with them in their aspirations,' she told a *Western Mail* reporter years later, in 1927. 'As you know, a fellow feeling makes us wondrous kind.'[54]

By then she and Philip were living in London, in Hampstead Garden Suburb, which had been designed and built as part of the wider garden suburb movement – but back in 1911, when she married Philip, Lily had not yet moved far from the place where she had grown up. Soon after their marriage, however, she and Philip moved into their newly built home at 3 Lôn Isa in Rhiwbina, the Cardiff

Workers' Co-operative Garden Village. Here, in the early years of their marriage, they attempted to live out some of their socialist beliefs: Rhiwbina was a tenants' cooperative, originally intended for working class and lower middle class tenant-investors, though as with many of the garden suburb developments, soon enough those were the very people who would be unable to afford to live there.

Rhiwbina was established by Sir Daniel Lleufer-Thomas, Professor Stanley Jevons and W. J. Gruffudd – but another key figure, Edgar L. Chappell, was an Ystalyfera man whom Lily would have known from her early ILP activities in her hometown. Chappell had worked in urban planning in the Swansea valley, and had written about the planning problems in Ystalyfera. He later became secretary of the Welsh Housing Association, and published widely on planning and on politics; his name turns up regularly in the pages of *Llais Llafur* in relation to his vigorous campaigning for the ILP as a dedicated socialist.

The first prospectus inviting new members to buy into the Rhiwbina scheme was published in 1912; the planned community offered well-appointed properties, with baths, hot water, electric light, and gas-stove heating in the living rooms. Entertainingly – from the perspective of the twenty-first century – the prospectus was written in 'reformed' spelling, which, progressively, was meant to ease learning to read, although reading the following description is quite challenging: 'The Sosiety haz purchast 10 aicers ov the Pentwyn Estate, Whitchurch, which liez immeedeaitly North ov the Cardiff Railway between the Rhubina Road and the nyu Whitchurch Station.'

Building of the first thirty-four homes began in October

of that year – including numbers 2 to 20 on Lôn Isa, where Lily and Philip were to live. It was W. J. Gruffudd who was responsible for the Welsh place-names. The official opening ceremony for the first completed houses took place in July 1913 and the first phase of development was completely finished in June 1914, when the war intervened and the planned expansion was put on hold.

Rhiwbina attracted a truly remarkable array of intellectuals, literary figures and cultural shapers. Leo recalled visiting Lily and Philip in Rhiwbina when he was a boy – this, he remembered, 'was where the nest of local intellectuals then lived; the dominant figure there was Sir J D Morgan, a wealthy shoe factor, given his knighthood by Ramsay MacDonald whom he had sheltered in MacDonald's pacifist days in World War I. As a lad, not yet in my teens, I would frequently visit my aunt; the ambience of the gatherings in her home was a combination of pacifism, ILP socialism and the William Morris ethos – J D Morgan gave money to establish meeting-halls in Cardiff for the ILP and lived in a ménage a trois.' Lily enjoyed a close friendship with the second Lady Morgan, who was a 'redoubtable figure'; Leo described her as 'the doyenne of the whole Rhiwbina set' and someone who 'made a significant contribution to the Labour movement in Cardiff'. He remembered with affection and acknowledged the influence on him of 'the idealism and vitality that had reigned' in the 'little bijou house in Rhiwbina'.[55]

The Morgans were funders from the outset, but Rhiwbina was home to another set of people whom Leo would not have met or recognised: a group of Welsh-speaking intellectuals, nationalists rather than ILP socialists, who created a different ambience. Later, the folklorist Iorwerth Peate, who was responsible for establishing the Museum of Welsh Life at Sain Ffagan, would make his home in Rhiwbina; in his memoir *Rhwng Dau Fyd* (Between Two Worlds) he describes Rhiwbina as a vibrant intellectual enclave during the inter-war years, populated and visited by a phenomenal array of prominent figures from both the English and Welsh-speaking worlds of the 1920s.[56] This included W. J. Gruffydd, R. T. Jenkins, Tom Bassett, publisher of *Y Llenor* (and conscientious objector during the war), Sir Cyril Fox and Kate Roberts, among many others. Kate Roberts, the most influential Welsh-language novelist of the twentieth century, had also previously lived in Ystalyfera between 1915 and 1917, and Lily would undoubtedly have met her there when she returned for visits to her family. Similarly, although Kate Roberts moved to Rhiwbina shortly after Lily and Philip left, it is very unlikely that their paths did not cross, for Lily retained her connections both with friends and family in Cardiff all her life. Nevertheless, it's mere speculation about the coincidence of time and place to put them together: as writers they diverged greatly, not least in language, for Lily's Welsh, though fluent, was not literary or formal, and she wrote for publication only in English.

Although Lily retained close links with Swansea and with Ystalyfera and *Llais Llafur*, after her move with Philip to Cardiff it was the experiment of organised community in Rhiwbina on which she focused. Rhiwbina was the first of three garden suburbs in which she and Philip got involved – from Cardiff they would move to Hampstead Garden Suburb in London (that planned community too was originally intended to be affordable to lower-income residents), and subsequently they also invested in the planned community of Karkur-Pardes Hanna in Palestine, under the auspices of the First London Achuza Company. However, when they moved to Palestine to live, it was in Haifa that they would settle.

In the intellectually stimulating atmosphere in Rhiwbina, Lily would write the many sketches and stories that would later be collected in 1921 in her first book *The Nationalists and Other Goluth Studies*; it was in Rhiwbina, too, that she wrote a good deal of her first novel, *My Mother's House*. Encouraged and supported by Philip, 'a delightful and gentle man who worshipped her' and gave her the financial and emotional wherewithal to write and to 'engage in political activity', Lily was able to begin to focus on fiction. But not long after their arrival in Rhiwbina, war intervened, and that part of her life was put on hold. For both as a socialist and as a Jew Lily was profoundly opposed to militarism and conscription, and with the outbreak of the First World War her energies and interests were diverted into the pacifist movement.

Five

War, and resistance to war

War made Lily into an effective, tireless, courageous political organiser – or rather, opposition to war did. Lily's first and dearest cause, Zionism, and the pressing cause of women's suffrage which split apart over how to respond to the war, were both displaced by the immediate and horrifying reality of the conflict.

Women were to feel a bitter gladness that it was, in the end, war that resulted in their gaining the right to vote, and for many Jews, and all Zionists, there was a similar grimly joyful outcome: the conquest of Palestine by the British and Commonwealth forces, which raised hopes about the possibilities of Jewish settlement. There was also a heady delight and disbelief, after years of campaigning, when, in 1917, Lord Balfour wrote his infamous brief letter that came to be known as the Balfour Declaration – the declaration that was in fact to signal the beginning of a new conflict, over Palestine, one that has lasted a century.

Initially for Lily, however, the war meant something very different: it was an imperialist war, fought for imperialist reasons. As socialists and pacifists she and her family opposed it utterly, and when conscription was introduced in 1916 her brothers were among approximately 16,500 conscientious objectors who refused to undertake military service.

'Conscientious objectors?' a nephew in Israel remarked, remembering Lily's brothers. 'I doubt they had a conscientious bone in their bodies. Shirkers, more like.' He was wrong, however, for three of Lily's brothers went to prison for their beliefs as conscientious objectors, and experienced 'a hell, a living hell', as Joseph described it, looking back on his five months in Wormwood Scrubs.

Joseph had been a source of pride to his family the previous year, when the papers reported him winning prizes, distinctions in his school exams, and highly competitive scholarships to support university study at Cardiff. *Llais Llafur* congratulated him warmly on his success, pointing out that his gaining a Glamorgan Exhibition for four years of study at the university was his 'crowning achievement' after a long series of successes. As a student at the Ystalyfera County School, the note in *Llais Llafur* observed, he 'has always been recognised as an exceptionally brilliant student, and for his years (we believe him not yet 18), this latest success is one that he has good reason to be proud of. His future career will be followed with much interest by many local educationalists' – as, indeed, it was.[57] But in 1916 the refusal by Joseph and his brothers Isaac and Solomon to do military service for reasons of conscience brought a different kind of attention to the family.

In May 1916, Joseph and Isaac wrote appealing for help from a detention hut where they were being temporarily held in Kinmel Park jail in north Wales:

No 11 Hut
Camp 19
Kinmel Park
Near Rhyl

Thursday, May 11th, 1916

My brother Isaac and I are being kept in the above hut owing to our conscientious objection to all forms – combatant and non-combatant – of military service. We are the sons of extremely orthodox Jewish parents. Our upbringing has always tended to uncompromising hostility to military service, and we intend, Sir, to be faithful to the Jewish atmosphere which we have always breathed.

My brother and I were both arrested at Pontypridd about 8.30 A.M. last Tuesday week (May 2nd). My brother was on the way to our business, I to my daily lectures at University College, Cathay's Park, Cardiff. We were put into different cells tried by a "civil" court, refused any remand and fined £2 and ordered to await escort. The armed escort soon appeared and took us to the Castle Arcade Recruiting Office, Cardiff. Here, in addition to the jeers and abuse that always assail the conscientious objector, we had sneers and threats of a very anti-semitic flavour. Despite all attempts at intimidation (threats to be shot, tortured, etc.) we refused to sign anything or to be medically examined. We were incarcerated in the guard room, Dumfries Place Barracks, Cardiff, from Tuesday the 2nd to Wednesday the 10th. Yesterday (the 10th) we were taken by armed escort from Cardiff to this place. At Cardiff we had no complaints to make about our treatment or our food. We expected to suffer hardship and we must not complain when suffering it. At Cardiff our friends and relatives kept us well supplied with food, a hot kosher dinner being sent in every day. Here we don't know what to do about dinner; we shall probably have to go without any, unless arrangements can be made with the commanding officer whereby we might have some food instead of dinner.

We feel, Sir, that your intervention with regard to this matter would be of much influence. The name of the Commanding Officer is Colonel Wynn Edwards.

We are the sons of Mr. and Mrs. Tobias Shepherd, Cambria View, Tyfica Road, Pontypridd (lately of Ystalyfera, Swansea Valley).

Yours very sincerely
Joseph Shepherd (19)
Isaac Shepherd (24)[58]

Joseph and Isaac were arrested and detained in May 1916, just a few short weeks after conscription came into force, but the introduction of obligatory rather than voluntary military service had been long anticipated, and pacifists who opposed the war, whether for religious or political reasons, had organised themselves well in advance.

Before the introduction of conscription, the efforts of war resisters had focused on arguing the case against enlisting, and resisting the army's recruitment drives. Popular opinion was against them: young men who did not wear khaki in public were targeted as cowards, and women often presented them in the street with white feathers, the symbol of cowardice. Patriotic feeling was feverish, and was augmented with stories of terrible atrocities by the Germans, and highly coloured jingoistic rhetoric that demonised those who spoke against the war. The introduction of conscription in January 1916, as part of the Military Service Act that came into force on 3 March 1916, was a rather desperate move on the part of the British Government two years into the war. The daily and weekly loss of life, recorded in the papers, divided between officers and enlisted men, was in such high figures that it can be hard to credit the reports when reading them long after the fact.

By 1916, voluntary enlistment was not providing sufficient numbers of men to maintain the war effectively, which was being fought on so many fronts. Even so, the introduction of conscription was strongly resisted. Lord John Simon, then Home Secretary (and, a year later, husband of Lily's Zionist associate, Kathleen Manning), resigned his cabinet post in protest. John Simon was not a pacifist. His objection to conscription was based on a belief in the individual's right to decide by conscience, but his objection to the Military Service Act's provisions was also based on an analysis of the figures: he believed that once necessary and legal exemptions had been made, the number of new combatants recruited by compulsion rather than by voluntary enlistment would be negligible. The Prime Minister regretted Sir John Simon's resignation, but disagreed with his assessment of the figures. In introducing the Bill on 5 January 1916, he summarised the provisions for exemption: 'the first is, roughly speaking, that a man is engaged in work which, in the national interest, it is important he should continue to perform. The second is, he has persons dependent upon him, who, if he were called for active military service, would not be able to maintain themselves in comfort or in decency at home. The third is, ill-health or infirmity, physical or mental. The fourth is, conscientious objection to the undertaking of combatant service.'[59]

At his conclusion, he again summarised, with a slightly different emphasis, the provisions for exemption. The detail he gave of exemption on the grounds of conscience and the make-up of military tribunals became the focus of intense scrutiny on the part of those opposed to conscription:

It applies only to unmarried and comparatively young men. It provides for the exclusion from its operation of every man who is engaged in other work which, in the broadest sense of the word, it is in the national interests he should continue to conduct. It exempts those who, though unmarried, are the sole support of the persons dependent upon them. It allows for every form of disability arising from health or infirmity. It respects the scruples of those who on conscientious grounds, object to undertaking combatant service. It prevents a man who, upon any of these grounds, claims to be exempt from being called up until his case has been finally disposed of. It sets up in every locality, as close as may be to a man's doors, a local tribunal, and it gives him in all cases one right, and in some cases two rights, of appeal.

Importantly, the provision for conscientious objection allowed only for objection 'to undertaking combatant service'; on the grounds of conscience there could not be objection to supporting the war effort in a non-combatant role.

Lily and her brother Joseph, in particular, held strong pacifist convictions as socialists; they opposed the war on the grounds that it was fought for imperialist interests against the interests of workers, and opposed obligatory military service on the basis of conscience (although a political basis for a position of conscience was challenged by the military tribunals set up to assess requests for exemption from service). This was the clear position of the Independent Labour Party, which, by 1916, was a strong and rapidly growing political force affiliated with the Labour Party.

From the outbreak of the war in 1914, members of the ILP had believed that conscription would be introduced, and a prominent activist, Lilla Brockway, proposed that young men who intended to resist military service should organise themselves accordingly. She and her husband, Fenner Brockway, an ILP activist and the editor of its weekly paper, *The Labour Leader*, set up the No-Conscription Fellowship, which initially had its headquarters in their home. Fenner Brockway served as its secretary, and Lily and her brothers became active members.

The membership grew rapidly, and with the introduction of conscription its importance became central to those who refused military service on the grounds of conscience. The *Labour Leader* was an important outlet for the No-Conscription Fellowship, which helped support war resisters, reporting on tribunals and courts martial, and sharing vital information on the fate of those conscientious objectors who were sentenced to prison – and, in some cases, to death.

While there was a right to appeal on the grounds of health and conscience, the latter was vigorously and often viciously resisted and challenged in the tribunals to consider appeals and requests for exemption, which were set up all over the country. The *Labour Leader* became a target under the Defence of the Realm Act, or DORA as it became known, a wartime Act that gave the government and police extensive powers to suppress material it considered seditious or treacherous, and to arrest and detain, often without trial or evidence, those it deemed a threat to the war effort.

A significant number of the approximately 16,500 men who stood before military tribunals as conscientious objectors between March 1916 and the end of the war in 1918 were Welsh, among them Lily's brothers.[60] Their experience galvanised Lily. While her pacifist beliefs had been informed by Jewish tradition, and by a family history of forcible conscription by the Tsarist army (something her own father had fled from, and something her brothers obliquely refer to in their letter written from prison), it was her brothers' experience of arrest, trial and imprisonment that turned her beliefs into action.

Leo learned about her activities years later from prominent leaders of the ILP, including Fenner Brockway (by then Lord Fenner Brockway), who remained a committed pacifist throughout his long life. Brockway himself spent months in Wormwood Scrubs Prison for his position on the war (although as a newspaper editor, he was entitled to exemption on the grounds of work of national importance). He remembered Lily well, though he did not mention her by name in his several accounts of that period. He reminisced to Leo about Lily 'as the young, battling, aggressive socialist pacifist', and he praised her 'daring challenges to authorities during the war days'.[61] She had become, according to Leo, 'an active and belligerent pacifist ... showing great resourcefulness and courage in defying the authorities and assisting draft dodgers, and those in prison'.[62]

Brockway doesn't name many women in his four volumes of autobiography, except prominent ones, or the wives of prominent men, but his chapter 'Organising War Resisters' in the first volume, *Inside the Left*, gives a clear picture of the risks they took. The ILP paper, the *Labour Leader*, was on occasion seized and suppressed as seditious, but its producers continued to distribute it secretly – particularly to those in prison awaiting court martial. Lily, often risking arrest, became feverishly involved in helping to distribute the *Leader* and other information of the No-Conscription Fellowship, but she also gathered information and reported on imprisoned COs, and on the progress of the tribunals. In 1916, a No-Conscription Fellowship meeting held at the Friends House in Cardiff featured Fenner Brockway among the speakers, and Lily reported there on the tribunals she had attended, including, undoubtedly, those of her brothers then being held in Kinmel Park. Earlier, her brother Solomon had had his own application for exemption rejected at a tribunal held in Pontardawe. Two weeks after her presentation to the No-Conscription Fellowship meeting, he was arrested for 'desertion', accused of being a shirker, fined £2 and handed over to the military.[63] The news item about his arrest in *Llais Llafur* neutrally noted his position as a conscientious objector, one whose appeal for exemption on the grounds of conscience had been dismissed, but most news coverage of COs was by no means neutral: COs were widely characterised as cowards and shirkers.

Lily portrayed the feverish and risky activity of No-Conscription Fellowship members in some of the most compelling scenes in her second novel, *Eunice Fleet*, published seventeen years later. In the novel she named a few of the most prominent figures of the No-Conscription Fellowship and the Labour Party, including Ramsay MacDonald and Helena Swanwick. Others, such as Fenner Brockway, whom she knew personally, she recalled by a play on names in her fictional characters. The most convincing of these is the small, vibrant, darting figure of Laura Fennick, whose last name combines elements of Fenner Brockway's given and family name, and perhaps refers also to Helena Swanwick. But in part Lily portrayed herself through Laura Fennick, too: like Laura, Lily was small and vibrant and had huge energy – a combination that most people remarked upon when remembering her.

Eunice Fleet, published in 1933, opens in the early 1930s, and deals both with the story of the eponymous protagonist, an anti-heroine, in the 1930s, and her misdeeds years earlier in 1916 – in particular her misunderstanding and mistreatment of her pacifist husband, Vincent. Writing the novel more than fifteen years after her brothers were arrested, Lily recalled in detail the complicated arguments about the right to absolute exemption from military service on the grounds of conscience, primarily expressed through the person of the socialist hero, Vincent. The first military tribunal before which Vincent appears grants him exemption from combatant service, but this is not the total exemption that Vincent seeks. The distinction is an important one to him. Doing work of national importance was one basis on which to gain exemption, and as a teacher he is, indeed, exempt, but he doesn't claim exemption on those grounds. The tribunal informs him that since he is qualified in first aid and ambulance work, he can join the Royal Army Medical Corps. But Vincent seeks total exemption on the grounds of conscience, not merely exemption from combatant service: 'All forms of military service are equally abhorrent to me,' he states. 'In the R.A.M.C. I should be as much a soldier as in the fighting ranks.' A member of the Tribunal objects that he would not be required to fight. 'Surely you cannot object to saving life?' he asks. 'I cannot help to save men in order to send them back to the trenches,' Vincent responds. 'I cannot help others to do what I will not do myself. It is impossible for me to assist in the organisation of war.'

This distinction – Vincent's refusal to accept anything but total exemption on the grounds of conscience – is incomprehensible to his rather giddy and thoughtless wife Eunice, who cites the example of conscientious objectors who accept non-combatant service. 'Conscience,' he tries to explain, 'is an individual affair, and each must judge for himself.' Eunice expects his position to be moderated by the news that she is expecting their baby, and is shocked to find that, though he is delighted, his position remains unchanged: 'According to conviction,' he explains, 'not according to circumstances.'

Vincent is imprisoned, and mistreated. Sullen, resentful, Eunice refuses to visit him, and secretly and dangerously she aborts her pregnancy. Imprisoned in unhealthy conditions, and tortured, Vincent becomes ill, but Eunice does not find out what happens to him until later. Vincent asks a sympathetic soldier at the prison camp where he is being held to smuggle out letters to Eunice, but the soldier only remembers belatedly the bundle he's been carrying around, and, unsure who is wife and who is girlfriend, sends the letters on to the busy campaigner Laura Fennick, who has frequently visited Vincent in prison. The soldier's covering message reveals that Vincent has been sent to the Front in France. Laura, familiar with the workings of the military, knows what this means – that Vincent, like many other conscientious objectors, will have been subjected to a widespread and appalling practice. COs were taken to the Front and ordered to pick up a rifle or given some other military command and then, when the CO refused, he would be threatened with execution, which was the penalty for disobeying a military order, and for cowardice. Some COs were reprieved at the last moment, after having been placed before a firing squad. The practice was widely known, and was intended to demoralise and break COs.

Unfortunately, Laura learns too late about Vincent's predicament. At the Front he is indeed tortured in this way, and then reprieved and sent back to prison in Wales. Here, suffering, isolated, and psychologically and physically broken, he loses hope and the will to live. He dies in prison of pneumonia before Laura can get to him, and Laura holds Eunice responsible for his loss of hope. When Eunice receives Vincent's collection of scraps of writing she is overcome with grief, guilt, and regret, and suffers a nervous breakdown.

Lily described with unapologetic clarity and detail the brutality and inhumanity with which COs were treated. Through the tribunal scenes – both those in which Vincent is questioned, and those in which all kinds of conscientious objectors make their case – she portrayed the complexity and variety of the pacifist and anti-war movement positions.

Like her activist character Laura, Lily kept records of the tribunals, noted prison camp conditions, and informed organisers about the predicament of individual COs. In a letter in 1917 to the No-Conscription Fellowship which was forwarded to Catherine Marshall, then Acting Honorary Secretary, Lily appealed for action on behalf of several Welsh COs. The case of one, she explained in her letter, was detailed 'in the little black book' that she had left with her correspondent at one point.[64] Like Lily, the fictional Laura kept such records, although despite many likenesses, she is not a self-portrait, as is clear from the section of the book set in the 1930s. Here, when Eunice meets Laura again, she finds she has become a Communist, and has just returned from Russia full of enthusiasm for the Soviet system, on which she lectures. Back during the war, Laura had been arrested under the Defence of the Realm Act for distributing seditious literature, and although Lily herself did not get arrested, it was a risk that she ran repeatedly. Lily was unflinching in portraying how some socialists, like Laura, with deepening political conviction moved further left after the war, while others lost their pacifist and socialist convictions, compromised politically, and got elected to parliament, where they betrayed the memory of those who had suffered and who, like the fictional Vincent, had died for their political beliefs.

During his first trial, Vincent explains how such a political belief is also a matter of conscience:

My political and moral views are alike. I think the war is the result of a wrong political conception, which means to me a wrong outlook, morally and spiritually. I am concerned with the welfare of the masses in every country. I regard war in general as a stupid and inefficient method of settling international disputes – I regard it also as organised murder. And I cannot in any circumstances be a party to murder, or pledge myself to commit it.[65]

In the wartime section of the novel some of the most intriguing passages depict the notorious Battle for Cory Hall, which took place on the 11th of November 1916 in Cardiff.

Lily was at the centre of demonstrations and political meetings in the city by then, living in Rhiwbina and vigorously active in the peace movement and the ILP. Like her evocation of the Tribunals, her vivid evocation of events at Cory Hall, seen through the eyes of the uncomprehending Eunice, is evidently strongly informed by her memory of what happened.

The peace meeting at Cory Hall was to feature an address by Ramsay MacDonald, Helena Swanwick and others, and was organised by South Wales Miners Federation leader, James Winstone. Winstone had been the official ILP parliamentary candidate for Merthyr after the death of Keir Hardie had triggered a by-election, but he'd lost the election to his opponent, C. B. Stanton. Stanton, a patriot (which is to say a supporter of the war), had tried to get the event at Cory Hall banned, and when it went ahead he and his supporters organised a counter demonstration and stormed the hall where the speeches were taking place. Lily describes it as a stand-off between pacifists and patriots, and she brings the scenes sharply to life, from the description of the crowds in flight from the conflict, bursting out of the hall and breaking up, to the portrait of the drunken Stanton himself (whom Laura caustically characterises as 'our Bloated Parliamentary Patriot'): hoisted onto the shoulders of his supporters 'was the leader of the patriots. Eunice saw his huge red puffy face, his rolling venous neck and tremendous paunch. Waving his hands, and letting them drop in strangely feeble flaps, he emitted hoarse indistinct sounds. His supporters yelled back and hoisted him still higher, so that his feet in thick, unlaced boots could be seen slipping feebly, like his hands.'[66]

Lily's view of events at Cory Hall as a pacifist versus patriot confrontation was shared by the *Labour Leader*, which reported on the event the following week under the headline 'Mob Rule in Cardiff'. Politically the events were more complex, however: the confrontation was provoked by the inflammatory patriot Stanton, who had competed with Winstone to be ILP candidate in the by-election. Winstone, a somewhat ambivalent anti-conscriptionist, had won the official candidacy, and so in the election Stanton had stood against him as an unofficial ILP candidate, and defeated him. Lily's characterisation of Stanton as 'The Bloated Patriot' mirrors the reaction of many to his extreme anti-pacifist rhetoric, but the detail of his appearance, from his drunken dribbling to his unlaced shoes, is her own.

Unlike Fenner Brockway, who was physically attacked after a similar event in Manchester, Ramsay MacDonald escaped from Cory Hall without harm. The patriotic *Western Mail* saw in this escape an opportunity to depict MacDonald as a coward for slinking away.[67] In *Eunice Fleet*, Lily fictionally enlarges the escape: Laura, dishevelled and harried, running into Eunice in the street, shocks her by the bald familiarity of her revelation that she is 'looking for MacDonald and Mrs. Swanwick'. And then they spy MacDonald getting into a cab, and Eunice is transfixed: 'meeting the eyes of the man who stepped from the arch, she was aware of greatness. There before her, in a brief space which sufficed for vivid impression, was the man who centred in himself the vituperation of British loyalists. The most hated and reviled man in his country: the hero of a small outcast group. She did not know the extent of that faint span of honour. She knew, however, that Vincent worshipped him, as a strong young mind worships a master.'

Evidently Lily did, too: her depiction of MacDonald in *Eunice Fleet* in the early 1930s reflects the huge respect she had for the man whom she no doubt had encountered and admired in 1916 – an admiration and respect that would change shortly after the novel was published, because of his move away from an anti-militarist position.

In the depiction of events at Cory Hall, Lily didn't stop with MacDonald, however. Eunice, taking refuge in a cafe, is struck by the impression of a woman she sees 'quietly drinking tea, looking so calm, so peaceful, so remote from stress and turmoil, that Eunice felt as if a soothing hand had been laid on her own harassed soul'.[68] Then Laura appears, with her characteristic urgency, and bounds across to talk to her – the peaceful seated woman is none other than Helena Swanwick.

In *Eunice Fleet*, written many years after the events, Lily depicted the full range of positions taken by conscientious objectors, although it is Vincent's absolute objection to all forms of military service, combatant and non-combatant alike, that provides the dramatic structure of the novel, and opens up the way to heroic martyrdom. In contrast, Lily only lightly touches on religious objection to military service, both Jewish and Christian. Published in 1933, *Eunice Fleet* appeared in the context of another looming war, and Lily downplayed the religious element to the anti-conscription movement (and disguised the Welsh locale), perhaps in an attempt to make the novel more universally appealing. But back in 1916, just as in the novel Vincent makes no distinction between his political and moral position, Lily's own brothers made no distinction between the political and religious basis for objecting to war and to military service – and Lily too focused on the Jewish aspects of her own and her brothers' pacifism. In January 1916 she engaged passionately in the pages of the *Jewish Chronicle* on this question. This was in the immediate aftermath of the law on conscription being passed, and Lily knew instantly what this would mean for her brothers once it came into effect later in the year.

Lily's letter to the *Jewish Chronicle* was utterly at odds with the editorial position of the paper, which was thoroughly pro-war – for example, in the January 21st issue, the editor appended a note to letters from correspondents on the subject, stating: 'We sympathise entirely with the excellent sentiments expressed by our correspondents though we do not share them as a matter of "practical politics". An evil force, like that of Germany, in the international relations of the world cannot be overcome by sentiment nor by putting into force an ideal, to which, it is clear, mankind has not yet attained.' In the following issue, the regular contributor 'Mentor' argued against Jewish pacifism in his regular column entitled 'In the Communal Armchair'. Under the header 'Jewish Conscientious Objectors: Peace Ideals', he proposed that the religious basis of conscientious objection was Christian, along the lines of the Sermon on the Mount, but that a Jew objected as a citizen, not as a Jew – and further, that a Jew objected to participation as a citizen within a given war, but this objection had no basis in Judaism. 'The Jewish ideal of peace', he argued, was universal: 'How on earth can this prophetic vision be pleaded to justify any Jew refusing to do his duty as a citizen, because that duty involves his fighting the enemies of the country of which he is a citizen?'[69] The ever-present anxiety on the part of nervous British Jews that they would or could be accused of split loyalties was being brought to bear as a kind of pressure against pacifists who were also Jews – against pacifists who might be seen to bring the whole Jewish community into some kind of disrepute by association. It was not very much later that the hysterically patriotic John Bull would be fulminating against the influence of German Jews, which led, among other kinds of censorship, to the suppression of the 1918 film, *The Lifestory of David Lloyd George*, allegedly because of the Jewish identity of its backers.

In this anxious context, to oppose war as a Jew took on a triple risk – to stand accused as a shirker, a coward and an ingrate to the country that harboured you; to fulfil, in short, the age-old allegations of cowardice and split loyalties. Lily's perspective was therefore an unpopular one when she responded to the position taken by 'Mentor' in the *Jewish Chronicle*. Her long, detailed letter expressed sentiments that closely echo the sentiments she would ascribe to the fictional Vincent years later in *Eunice Fleet*:

February 4, 1916
3 Lon Isa
Rhubina, Glam

Sir, —Will you allow me to express not only sympathy with your correspondents who have stated the views of Jewish conscientious objection to war, but my conviction that such views must necessarily become embodied in "practical politics" if there is to be real civil and international peace. That Jews should, in common with fellow-citizens of other faiths, hold war in abhorrence as an irreligious as well as stupid method of settling national disputes, ought not to cause surprise; but it is peculiarly gratifying to find them represented in the *Jewish Chronicle*, which has hitherto voiced only the opposite standpoint.

It strikes me as significant that both Jews and Christians should find common ground in condemning as impracticable the peace ideals of Judaism and Christianity. But I must warn the Jews who take up this attitude that there is danger in the association, and at least one sinister aspect of this partnership in repudiation has already made itself manifest. I was lately occupied in pointing out to a patriotic Christian friend of the conventional "church" order the discrepancy between his conception of Christianity and that held – not only by the author of the Sermon on the Mount – but by some members of the Society of Friends, the Fellowship of Reconciliation, and certain other bodies of what I may perhaps call neo-Christians; and his defence for playing hypocrite was that argument which you, Sir, apparently consider sufficient reason for ignoring the highest Jewish teaching on the subject of the slaughter of one's fellows: "only an ideal to which, it is clear, mankind has not yet attained." Presumably, those who hold an ideal should at least make an *attempt* towards its attainment. Actually to [violate] it is the shortest cut to its abolition.

But the grim feature which unpleasantly illuminated the championship of "the practical" is that the "Christian" I have alluded to in common with many others in public and life, does not hesitate to point to Judaism as the breeding-ground of German militarism – the Old Testament, he asserts, has inspired the war-mongers! And I have quite enough to do to refute this impudent calumny without [finding] the Jewish press apparently ready to endorse it by representing Judaism as the spirit of war.

In conclusion, may I say that while it is plain to some minds that sentiment cannot overcome force, it is equally plain to others that force cannot overcome sentiment. It must also be insisted on that the pacifist does not propose to abolish war by sentiment only. It is necessary to call in reason and construct machinery, revise policies, and create understanding of such a nature as to reduce international friction to a minimum, and in the event of its occurring to proceed to a settlement on lines other than those entailing the barbarity and wastage of war.

She signed herself 'Miss Lily Tobias'. Perhaps this was a mistaken interpolation on the part of the newspaper, or perhaps it was a deliberate self-identification on her part to present herself as an independent thinker, rather than as a wife, notwithstanding the fact that Philip shared her views and supported her in principle and in practice, despite the risks she took.

Lily was twenty-eight at the time, her brothers Joseph and Isaac nineteen and twenty-four. Joseph, Isaac, and their brother Solomon all served prison terms. Isaac was released in mid-September, after having been arrested in May and serving four months; Solomon also served four months in a civil prison and was released in January 1917, when he accepted 'alternative service' and was sent to work at the Llyn-y-Fan water works in Powys. The camp, which housed some eighty COs, lay nine miles from the nearest train station at Llangadog.

Joseph, however, was one of nine men from south Wales who were sent to Wormwood Scrubs after having been sentenced to two years of hard labour for 'disobeying in such a manner as to show wilful defiance of authority a lawful command given personally by his superior officer in the execution of his office'.[70] In the end, Joseph spent five months at Wormwood Scrubs, rather than two years, but he remembered it as a living hell.

The *Merthyr Pioneer* reported regularly on the situation of COs, and in July 1916 published a letter from an anxious correspondent who wondered if the publication had been suppressed when it failed to arrive. 'I must confess that I felt very despondent as a result,' he wrote. 'One likes so much to hear how our brave comrades – Morgan Jones, Isaac, Sol and Joseph Shepherd, Gwilym Smith, and the others – are getting on. The "Pioneer" is the only paper that tells us these things—hence our disappointment at its non-appearance.'[71]

Joseph and Isaac kept that socialism out of the letter they'd written from Kinmel Park appealing for help, and focused instead on the Jewish ethics that informed their objection to war, as it informed that of their sister. In that letter, however, they were not seeking relief from their situation, but simply trying to secure the provision of kosher food during their incarceration. Food was always a concern for imprisoned COs – and not just the provision of kosher food for those who needed it. Lily described the conditions at the Llanddeusant Camp, near Llangadog, as 'quite one of the worst … I knew long ago that the food … is scandalously inadequate for men expected to do very hard work, often in severe conditions. In fact,' she went on, 'I understand that the cook (a woman) and the sub. agent did "very well" out of the business, which speaks for itself.'[72] That camp, where the cook and agent were engaged in skimming off profit at the expense of the internees, was the workcamp to which Lily's brother Solomon had been sent: she knew those conditions suffered by the COs from direct experience.

How wrong their nephew was, decades after the fact, about the principles held by his uncles and aunt: his three uncles were very far from being 'shirkers'. On the contrary, they were principled men who stood by their beliefs despite being subjected to appalling treatment.

Six

Making a name as a writer: The Nationalists *and* Daniel Deronda

In the immediate aftermath of the war, it was Zionism that became once again the dominant concern for Lily as a writer, for one of the extraordinary outcomes of the war, apart from women gaining some semblance of the vote, was the conquest of Palestine and the issuing of the Balfour Declaration.

After the war, Lily's writing career began to take off, and she started to secure publication for articles and short stories in some of the many leftwing and Zionist journals that enjoyed a resurgence after the paper and manpower restrictions of the war years.

Lily's writing about Zionism and her active political engagement was in every way coloured by the pacifist vision that had been formed, tested and strengthened by her courageous support of men resisting conscription, but she also brought an unusual Welsh perspective to questions of Jewish national self-determination, which was noted in particular by editors.

In 1921, C. W. Daniel published her first book, *The Nationalists and Other Goluth Studies*, which collected in one place many of the stories that had been published in the the *Zionist Review* and the *Socialist Review* in 1919 and 1920. However, it was Lily's dramatisation of George Eliot's novel *Daniel Deronda* six years later, with its run at the 'Q' Theatre in 1927, that brought her for the first time to attention beyond Jewish and Zionist circles, and as far afield as Palestine.

The Balfour Declaration, which stated, infamously, that 'His Majesty's Government view with favour the establishment in Palestine of a national home for the Jewish people, and will use their best endeavours to facilitate the achievement of this object' had been issued in 1917, and in its aftermath, Lily wrote frequently about organisational questions of Jewish life in Palestine, and envisioned a utopian national Jewish future there. The Jewish state would be 'a light unto the nations', as many Zionist leaders hopefully characterised it then and since. Lily believed the Jewish homeland could and indeed had to be egalitarian and pacifist: 'The imminence of a revived Jewish Palestine has excited the imagination of the world, and inspired forecasts of the future state marked by varying degrees of kindliness,' she wrote in 1919, introducing her vision of the role of Jewish women in the Zionist movement. 'To create a centre of healing and rejuvenation for the Jewish people,' she continued, 'will be to promote the harmony of mankind, to establish the superiority of the processes of peace over the acts of war, and to hasten the reign of that international amity and concord which alone can save the world.'

The *Jewish Chronicle* approved her vision and sentiments. 'Miss Lily Tobias contributes a bright and neat article on "Jewish Women and Palestine" to the January–March, 1919, number of the *Socialist Review*,' it noted on July 25th of that year. 'Incidentally she points out that "it is only after a long struggle, marked by the extremity of bitterness and passion, that a measure of political emancipation has been gained by British women. But from the first inception of the Zionist organisation – the democratic reflex of true Jewish ideals, as well as the progressive organisation which seeks to realise them – women received the fullest suffrage."'[73]

In that article, 'Jewish Women and Palestine', Lily described some of the practical economic measures taken by the Daughters of Zion, the women's section of the Zionist movement, including Hadassa, the American Women's Zionist organisation: among other activities, they set up training centres, health centres, and cooperative endeavours to support the financial independence and wellbeing of Jewish women in Palestine. Lily, at the time living and participating in the Cardiff Workers Co-operative Garden Village, celebrated the development of cooperative ventures in Palestine too, describing the organisational foundation of the early kibbutz and moshav movement in glowing terms. Throughout the article, however, she made the case, both overtly and subtly, and in historical, Biblical and ethical terms, for equality between men and women – and the foundation of that equality in Judaism. At the end of the article, she included a tableau of Jewish women, organised much like the tableau of 'Women' in the public pageant in which she had participated in Swansea nine years earlier, when she had played Deborah.

'Judaism held a remarkably high conception of womanhood,' she wrote in her 'bright and neat article' in the *Socialist Review*. 'Despite some disabilities, the law to a large extent recognised and protected the private rights of women, asserted their individual claims to legislation, and permitted them to discharge public duties. The moral attitude towards women was exceptionally high, and frequently transcended the limitations of the law, which it moulded and subjected to its demands.' The tradition of subjection, 'which relegates the women of Israel to the position of bond-slaves and parasites, held in the most rigid political, religious, and economic subjection to their men' was not Jewish, she proposed; 'the absurdity of this tradition, created and fostered by Christians who wished to exalt the redeeming powers of the religion which sprang from Judaism, should be clear to the most superficial student of the laws and customs of Palestine.'

Although she was promoting a rosy view of the Zionist movement to non-Jewish readers of the *Socialist Review*, Lily was also fighting for her own tenuous position as a Jewish woman. She and other women had to struggle for a voice, and for the right of women like her to play a prominent role in the shaping of a future Jewish state. She might state that it was 'entirely consistent with the hoariest traditions of Israel that modern Jewish women should expect and receive the rights of emancipated citizens', but the practical expression of those 'traditions' was another thing entirely. She had never been able to take any such recognition of equal rights for granted, but instead from her childhood onwards had needed to struggle to be taken seriously, both inside Jewish society, and beyond. Although she claimed that in Jewish tradition a woman 'is free to act as she thinks best, and by the exercise of her talents gains the love and admiration, not only of her family, but of the "elders of the land," the public functionaries', the exercise of Lily's own talents was insufficient to secure her recognition in the history of the movement. It took a long time to acknowledge the contribution of women in that period and afterwards – Paul Goodman, who, two years later, would write a warmly appreciative review of Lily's first book, neglected to mention her work in his 1929 history of the British Zionist movement, despite being well aware of her contribution both as a writer and an active member. Although he went on to acknowledge the work of women Zionists in his updated edition in 1949, almost all those he cited were the wives of prominent Zionist men.[74]

It did not escape Lily's attention, writing in the *Zionist Review* in the interwar period, that most of the political discussion in its pages was written by men, while the contributions by women tended to be stories, romantic poetry, travel descriptions, and personal and domestic anecdote. Her own contributions, mostly short stories – albeit highly polemical ones – were relegated at times to the 'youth' section. In the story 'Daughters of Zion', for example, which the *Zionist Review* published in 1920, she called on the Zionist movement to embrace equally the contribution of women at the same time as she called on Jewish women to embrace the movement.[75]

With that story, which was a fictional companion piece to the article 'Jewish Women and Palestine', Lily drew on various aspects of her own experience. As she had the previous year in the *Socialist Review* article, in the *Zionist Review* story she presented the Zionist movement as a feminist one. The polemical story was an appeal to Jewish women who had previously put their energies into the women's movement to now take their place in – and make a contribution to – the Zionist movement. Naomi, the story's protagonist, has come to a public meeting where a woman she had known for her suffrage work is to give a speech on Zionism. Naomi, like the speaker (and like Lily herself), 'had been an ardent Suffragette – not, it is true, of the extreme militant order, but sufficiently active to incur the disapproval of most of her family and friends, not to speak of remoter links in the communal chain'. And like Lily, Naomi 'had marched in processions, strewn leaflets broadcast, publicly asked inconvenient questions (though always at question time)', and, reinforcing the Shepherd family anecdote and the suggestive historical evidence, had, like Lily, 'spent a night in hiding to boycott the census, and generally asserted the claim of British women to citizen rights'.

Naomi is not in other respects an autobiographical figure, for this is a story about a suffragette's encounter with Zionism after the war, whereas Lily's Zionism from the outset informed her feminism. Naomi arrives at the public meeting 'in a cynical frame of mind … … It was her habit to avoid this dingy haunt of her local fellow-Jews, who spent some precious hours every alternate Sunday in being harangued by bores from London, and then, by even more wearisome mouthpieces, indulging in doubtfully Anglicised sentiments of approbation or dissent.' Naomi, at something of a loose end, is sceptical. For her, as for others, the war had brought an end to the 'glorious exploits' of campaigning for the vote, and she 'had not found the same thrill in the subsequent activities of women, novel and audacious as many of them were'. Like many others active in the women's movement, 'even when the great consummation of the franchise was actually achieved, it found her in a chastened mood of rejoicing ... and somehow it detracted from her ideal that the boon, which was no boon but a simple human right, had been "granted" as a reward for helping men spill blood.' Now Naomi, waiting for the speech to begin, wonders, 'what was there worthy of serious reflection in this mad hubbub of Jews to set up another centre of reaction? She could not understand the part of an admired Suffrage leader in such a movement.'

'Daughters of Zion' is a polemical story, and Naomi experiences a moment of conversion, which is achieved not so much through an appeal to her concerns for Jewish security – although the speaker 'drew a picture of the social and economic position of Jews all over the world which brimmed with menace' – as through the picture she draws of 'a brilliant future – a national rejuvenation that would not only restore and heal, but light the torch of progress for the world at large'. Naomi is unsure. 'Did the Suffrage leader really believe so much? She was a woman of advanced ideas, who had shown courage and resource in Gentile fields. Was there room for her, too, in this projected Jewish future?'

Lily made the political personal for Naomi: what tips the balance for her is the exchange between members of the audience. Mrs Cohen, an ungainly woman who 'spoke badly in broken English', gets up to thank the speaker, and recalls 'de women of olden times, vat helped de men to build de nation, Sarah and Miriam and D'vora and Chuldah'. Old Mr Shalinsky objects that 'Voomans shall stay in de house and look aff de kinder', to which an elderly widow offers the counter-objection, 'Hoy! ... And if I wasn't goin' out vid my basket every day trampin', how could my kinder have food to eat? None of your charity societies for me, tank you.' The speaker responds to Mrs Cohen's contribution and launches into a new speech about 'sex equality in Palestine to-day', and Naomi's blood 'kindles': she is transported into a fantastical vision, in which she sees a pageant of Jewish women of the past and of the present, and a future New Jerusalem where Jewish men and woman are free and equal, in which 'squalor was gone, ignorance had vanished, brute passion fled before the pure choice of equals. Peace and freedom reigned in Zion, and the Gentile world drew guidance from its lore.'[76]

Lily always drew together these various strands of her political beliefs and engagements – feminism, socialism, pacifism and Zionism – which to her comprised an integral whole. Coloured by her exposure in Ystalyfera to working-class struggle and suffering, by her experience of the Swansea and Cardiff suffrage movement before the war, and by the predicament of wartime conscientious objectors, her humanist political vision would drive her fiction from then on, and would lead to the publication of four novels in the space of seven years during the 1930s. But in 1920 she was writing overtly polemical fiction – and, often, polemic.

'Daughters of Zion' had been rather typical of the acceptable subject matter of women's contributions to the *Zionist Review*, but Lily's article 'Zionism and Militarism: Some Other Considerations', which was published later that year, stood out in that period as an exception.[77] Here she discussed the necessarily pacifist nature of Zionism, rather than arguing for recognition of women's contributions to it and to the future Jewish national home.

She was responding to two earlier articles, one on 'Zionism and Prejudice' and the other 'Zionism and Modern

Problems: Further Considerations', by Arthur D. Lewis in the May and June issues of the magazine. Lewis's views of the necessities of the present and the interpretation of the Jewish Biblical tradition were decidedly militaristic, and Lily's of course deeply anti-war. In her article 'Zionism and Militarism' Lily was roused to a polemical fervour: 'Our leaders have proclaimed the national resolve to make in Palestine a contribution worthy of our past to the lofty labour of humanity – to build afresh a society of individual and social justice, and a centre of reconciliation and fellowship,' she wrote. 'The Jewish genius restored to Jewish soil will there renew the great traditions of the Hebrew prophets', but, she warned, these words 'can mean nothing unless they mean the application of the highest ethical standards to the affairs of everyday life, the actual exercise of reason and goodwill, the consistent practice of the only methods that can lead to universal peace.' Eloquently she rejected Arthur Lewis's assertions about the prophets' advocacy of war: 'Jeremiah and Isaiah not only lived and suffered with the people they admonished, but based their repudiation of war on the experience of their time. They realized that only by the actual beating of swords into ploughshares could the happiness of the world be secured, and they seem to have known that it is not enough to denounce war in any age, that to eliminate the evil thing all its habits and equipments must be discarded at a given moment.' Surely, she wrote, those prophets therefore 'knew that the right way to lessen or abolish war is not, as our critic says, to enlist the spirit of war on the side of peace (that is said to have been done so effectually at Versailles that twenty little wars have managed to ensue, not to mention the wholesale starvation and torment of infants and their mothers), but rather to enlist on the side of peace no other than the spirit of peace.'

As she had some four years earlier in the letters pages of the *Jewish Chronicle*, Lily objected to the claim that Jewish Biblical history was militaristic. In defence of Jewish conscientious objectors she had argued then that Jewish tradition had at its core a deep humanitarian pacifism, something that her imprisoned brothers had also espoused. Now she argued once again that militarism was absolutely antithetical to Jewish tradition, and was an aberration adopted from the non-Jewish world in which diaspora Jews lived:

> We anticipate in a Jewish Palestine a genuinely enlightened public. But can we so easily shake off the accretions of the Exile? Have we taken to heart the lessons still spread before us? It seems to me we have yet to learn a new version of many common terms, such as courage, honour, heroism – or rather, we Jews have to unlearn the perversions of the un-Jewish world in which we are steeped, and sit again at the feet of our ancients, to catch the accents of their highest wisdom.

Arthur Lewis had also proposed a restricted role for women in Jewish Palestine that irritated Lily just as much as his militaristic claims, and she remarked, acerbically: 'Our rambling critic would like to set the limit for the occupations of Jewish women in their homeland. If we are to have that state of individual and social justice which our leaders have proclaimed, then women will recognize no limit to their activities beyond the limit of desire and capacity.' Once again she wove together women's emancipation and pacifism: 'no amount of freedom, nor of its most comfortable curtailment', she continued, 'will render women happy or worthy members of a community which countenances military institutions. In this respect, more than in all else, may the Jewish women in Palestine prove the true inheritors of the ideals of our pacifist prophets … There can be no ghastlier mockery than organized murder waged to "protect women and children": as if women and children were not inevitably the greatest victims of war, the heaviest tolls being exacted when they are being most zealously "protected".'

Lily had opened her article celebrating the 'triumph of Jewish idealism', and she closed with a passionate plea for a Zionism rooted in Jewish pacifism, and one committed to international peace:

> The authentic voice of Israel pleads for 'Peace – Peace – Peace.' It is not for us to hush a single note of that compelling cry. For, unless we fulfil its message on the soil of Palestine, we shall be false alike to the most vital teaching of our past, and to the greatest present need of racked mankind.

Lily poured more hope and scorn into that article than any other, but she wrote energetically and prolifically all that year and the next, producing more than ten publications in an eighteen-month period. She contributed regularly to the *Zionist Review* in particular, and when, the following year, C. W. Daniel published *The Nationalists*, which brought together many of her stories, the book was prominently advertised in the magazine with a promotional leaflet and order form, the only such insert in the five years of the journal between 1917 and 1923.

The Nationalists and Other Goluth Studies included two pre-war stories, 'The Nationalists' and 'Glasshouses', both of which dealt centrally with Welsh and Jewish concerns, as well as a story, 'The Outcasts', which had been first published in the *Socialist Review*. Dedicated to Kathleen Manning, who was by then Lady John Simon, the book also enjoyed the strong endorsement of Leon Simon, a prominent Zionist and the editor of the *Zionist Review* who had accepted several of the stories the previous year. 'I should be happy if I could add any positive service to the negative one of not having refused to print what was so obviously worth printing,' he wrote, in rather convoluted praise in his introduction.

> To me, as one who had been occupied for years in the exposition of Zionism, these sketches came as something new in kind. Zionist literature is rich enough both in reasoned argument and in emotional appeal. But here is neither argument nor pleading, but just a presentation of the way in which the Zionist spirit gets hold of Jews of various kinds, lifts them in some degree out of themselves, gives them a new sense of pride and dignity and responsibility, and makes them feel that to be a Jew is worth the cost.

By Zionist 'literature', Leon Simon meant, of course, the printed word – journalism, argument, polemic, history, and political comment and analysis: in a word, 'propaganda' in its old rather neutral sense of the propagation of a political idea. What he failed to do was to identify the uniqueness of

Lily's contribution as fiction. There were few enough Jewish writers at the time concerning themselves in fiction or poetry with Zionist ideas, and precious few Jewish women writers, despite the tradition established by such Anglo-Jewish novelists and poets as Grace Aguilar and Amy Levy. Lily's fictional depictions of aspects of the Zionist movement, and the effect of Zionism on individuals who encountered, resisted or embraced it, was in that period, unique in the UK.

The book, a slim volume of eight stories, was positively reviewed in *The Zionist Review* by Paul Goodman, another prominent figure in the Zionist movement. He chose to focus on a different aspect of its novelty, however – that of its Welsh locale and concerns. 'Mrs Tobias has introduced us to a new *milieu*,' he wrote, 'for Welsh Nationalism, unknown to most of us, has had its effect on her, blending harmoniously with the Jewish Nationalism with which Mrs Tobias is so deeply imbued. Those of us who only England know are struck by the self-assertion of Welsh Nationalism in its own home.'[78]

Nevertheless, although the locale was almost without exception Wales, only three of the eight stories concerned Welsh nationalism, examining its similarities to and differences from Jewish nationalism: 'The Nationalists', 'Glasshouses', and 'Stray Sheep'. Another overtly Welsh story, 'The Outcasts', concerned Lily's other abiding political interests – socialism and pacifism – but all the stories dealt in some way with concerns over Jewish assimilation and deracination. All appealed simultaneously to the sympathies of the non-Jewish reader to understand the Jewish experience, and, as Leon Simon observed in the introduction, to the Jewish reader, too, to give them 'a new sense of pride and dignity and responsibility'.

The Nationalists and Other Goluth Studies was published when Lily was thirty-four, and over the next ten years she worked hard at her writing, focusing now on developing her fiction, and grappling with the demands of the novel form. It had, after all, been in the forbidden pleasures of the novel that she had first found some escape from her mother's anxiety about the world beyond her home. As both a reader and a writer, Lily was not very much interested in the contemporary world of fiction, but was much more engaged by the drama and romance of nineteenth-century literature, including Scott's *Ivanhoe*, *The Vale of Cedars* by Anglo-Jewish writer Grace Aguilar and, of course, *Daniel Deronda* (though she had also been a close reader of the Brontes: she had gone back to lecture on their work at Ystalyfera's Ddraig Goch society in 1914). It was these novels that she drew on now as she sought to explore through fiction the political movements in which she had taken part and to which she was so committed. However, although she worked hard on her novel in her 'little bijou house' in Rhiwbina with its William Morris atmosphere, and then, through the 1920s, in the comfortable home she and Philip established in London, progress on her novel was frequently disrupted – by the move to London; by many other writing demands (she produced, in 1924, a long article on the work of Grace Aguilar for the *Jewish Chronicle*, and the dramatisation of *Daniel Deronda* in 1927); by frequent travel with Philip as he developed the glass business; and then, tragically, by bereavement.

The Shepherd-Tobias enterprise was developing rapidly. The family business, which had had its roots in Tobias Shepherd's shop in Ystalyfera, had taken off with the glass factory established by Moss in Swansea, and had expanded with a branch in Cardiff. Now Philip and other members of the family, including Lily's brother David, having established a successful branch in London, were looking at new possible outlets – specifically in Palestine, where there were many opportunities for development in business and in industry, particularly after the British Mandate for Palestine was formalised in 1922.

Lily travelled widely in the 1920s, accompanying Philip across Europe, when he and her brothers went in search of contacts and resources to support the opening of their glass manufacturing centre in Haifa. Wherever they went in Europe, at Philip's insistence they visited synagogues and Jewish graveyards, taking a tour of the Jewish cultural mosaic of Europe that would, before long, be destroyed.[79] And it was then, also, that Lily realised her dream of spending time in Palestine – the site of great hope, and the site of grief years before the tragic murder of Philip. In 1926 her mother and father themselves made a visit to Palestine, and her mother, the beautiful and gentle Anna-Baila, fell ill and died after drinking contaminated water from a street seller in Jaffa.[80]

The family marked her grave with an elaborate tomb with chains around a tall central plinth, which carried two inscriptions, one in English and one in Hebrew. The English side reads, simply 'Anna-Baila Shepherd from Cardiff' (Lily's parents had left Ystalyfera when Joseph took up his place at university – by 1916 they were living in Pontypridd, and subsequently they moved to Cardiff). The Hebrew inscription is an oddity, however: it reads 'Chana-Beila Shepherd, from Cardiff, England'. England is transliterated into Hebrew, rather than 'Anglia', the Hebrew word for England – but the greater oddity is that it is not Wales. Perhaps this was a mistake on the part of the stone-cutter to substitute England for Britain, or perhaps it was the family's presumption that Hebrew-speakers would not know where Wales was.

Though her mother's death was a terrible loss for Lily, and although it disrupted her writing, those were nevertheless productive years, and her first-hand experience of Palestine and its realities galvanised her. Every page of her first novel, which would be published in 1931, was informed by the urgent interest of Palestine on the one hand, and by her vibrantly remembered childhood and young adulthood in Ystalyfera and Swansea on the other. But the book was also shaped by her experience of adapting George Eliot's novel *Daniel Deronda* for the stage in 1927.

Strangely, despite the acclaim that several of her novels received, it would be for this dramatisation of *Daniel Deronda* that Lily would be remembered in the UK years after she left. Decades later, when in 1975 the cultural journal the *Jewish Quarterly* published excerpts of her playscript, in advance of the centenary of the novel itself, Lily recalled its genesis:

The first dramatisation ... was suggested to me by the late Lydia Lewisohn when we met in London in the 1920's. Though herself neither a writer nor an actress but being of a theatrical family, she was obsessed by the potentialities for the stage of some of the famous Victorian novels. I was busy at the time writing a commissioned novel and her proposition did not interest me. Not until she mentioned 'Daniel Deronda'. I re-read the book in fascination and agreed to undertake the Herculean task of dramatising that famous novel.[81]

Well before the play opened at the experimental 'Q'Theatre on 14 February 1927, the producer, Jack de Leon, drew attention to the imminent production, aiming it in particular at a Jewish audience – and, indeed, it was primarily a Jewish audience who attended the opening night.[82] 'At the 'Q' Theatre on February 14th will be presented a dramatised version of George Eliot's "Daniel Deronda",' he wrote in a letter to the *Jewish Chronicle*. 'The adapters have sought as far as possible to make the stage version a "translation" of the novel into the form of a play, rather than a play merely *based* on the famous work. The production will come fittingly as it is half a century ago that George Eliot's great Jewish work was first published.'[83]

Despite the rush with which it was produced – the 'Q' Theatre being notoriously chaotic – and the challenges of the adaptation that Lily struggled with, the play was a reasonable success. Unlike the controversial play *Taffy* by her compatriot Caradoc Evans, which had first been staged at the 'Q' two years earlier, it did not subsequently get taken up by a West End theatre. Nevertheless, *The Morning Post* reviewed it favourably, describing it as 'a well-built and moving play', and assuring readers that Jews and non-Jews alike would appreciate its 'sincere portrayal of the complexity and difficulty of human relationships'.[84] A reviewer in the *Jewish Chronicle* was less sure:

To compress 'Daniel Deronda', the book of which occupies some 800 pages, into limits possible for dramatic representation, is no small achievement. In the version by Lydia Lewisohn and Lily Tobias, which was presented at the 'Q' on Monday, this feat has been accomplished successfully, although the result is, perhaps necessarily, a little disjointed and full of recapitulations by the characters of incidents that are supposed to have taken place 'off.' Even with the compression and the cutting that have been done, the play is still much too long, and in common with other members of the audience, I was reluctantly obliged, through the lateness of the hour, to miss the last act.

The reviewer noted Eliot's understanding of the 'inwardness of the Jewish problem', and remarked that 'the statement for the case for Jewish Nationalism by Mordecai in the first act has rarely if ever been bettered'. He conceded: 'This part of the play certainly held Monday's audience.' Although somewhat ambivalent, he concluded that 'the adapters, in attempting the impossible, have failed gloriously; except that the blue pencil might have been used a little more ruthlessly, it is difficult to see how the dramatisation could have been improved upon.'[85]

Lily was well aware of the difficulties with the dramatisation, and felt she needed to explain these and the challenges the adaptation faced. Shortly after the play opened, she spoke publicly about the background at a meeting of the Hampstead Jewish Literary and Debating Society. 'In the course of her remarks,' the *Jewish Chronicle* reported, Lily said that 'the dramatisation had been a difficult enterprise, and had been beset with many obstacles in its hurried production. In the circumstances, if it had succeeded in bringing George Eliot's message to more vivid life, the adapters, at least, would be amply satisfied.'[86]

Two years later, on Sunday April 14th, 1929, the play was produced again, this time under the auspices of the Federation of Women Zionists. The production was by the Jewish Drama League, and was staged at the Palace Theatre in Shaftsbury Avenue; on this occasion it starred Sybil Thorndike and Esme Piercey. This time the review in the *Chronicle* was less positive:

> Such an excellent cause could not fail to draw a large audience, and the house was completely sold out before the performance. The production of the play was elaborate, and the inclusion in the cast of actors and actresses such like Sybil Thorndike and Esme Percy [sic], Joan Pereira and Victor Lewisohn, to mention but a few, ensured an interesting if somewhat protracted performance. Unfortunately, the stage adaptation of George Eliot's famous novel detracts from the literary and political significance of that work and lacks dramatic cohesion as well. The central Jewish theme itself is capable of a dramatic setting unencumbered with the snatches from society life, somewhat grotesquely portrayed, that do so much to dissipate the interest in the present arrangement.[87]

The Palace Theatre offered rather different opportunities, however, no matter the purpose of the staging: unlike the 'Q' Theatre production two years earlier, it led to discussion about a West End run for the play. Lily recalled decades later how Leon M. Lion, 'then presenting Galsworthy plays at his West End Theatre … proposed to put on the play for a six weeks' run'. He told Lily at their meeting that he had in place a cast, and asked for only minor alteration to the playscript. However, the planned production did not come off. The timing was bad: she was completing her first novel, already interrupted by the two years of work she had put into the adaptation of *Daniel Deronda* for the 'Q' Theatre, and she was preparing to move with Philip to Palestine – for those efforts to secure the resources for a branch of the family business in Haifa had paid off, and the plans to establish a factory there were taking shape. That business venture brought together the practical and the political for Lily and Philip: it was a concrete expression of their commitment to help develop a Jewish national home in Palestine, and the means by which they might take their place in it. The political opportunities that the prospective move to Palestine was then offering to Lily took precedence over the possibilities on offer to her in London.

Fifty years later, recalling the production of *Daniel Deronda*, Lily still felt the need to explain the challenges that any adaptor faced: 'My main problem was to contrive the two major themes – the Jewish story and that of the English Society girl – into a dramatic unity. When after two years' work this seemed achieved, the play was produced.' The play, she added, received 'a very favourable press'.[88]

She had recalled those difficulties earlier, too – in 1951, when she mentioned her work on the play in an article about a proposed memorial to George Eliot: 'the book teems with a variety of "plots" and separate spheres of interest, so that any attempt to dramatise it for the stage is fraught with immense difficulties. Nevertheless, at the instance [sic] of a Jewish woman connected with the theatre, I made such an attempt in the decade preceding the last war, and the play was produced twice in London with a certain amount of success. In the West End performance, given in aid of Palestine funds, Sybil Thorndike portrayed the Princess, Deronda's long-unknown mother, in the "big scene" of the play.[89]

The production garnered attention in Wales, too, under the headline 'Well-Known Novel Dramatised – Playwright's Life in South Wales'. The *Western Mail* journalist interviewed Lily in London, but was less interested in the play than in her Welsh connections: he wrote about her Ystalyfera origins and her years in Cardiff prior to her move to London, but nothing at all about the production.[90]

In 1969 a new version of *Daniel Deronda*, adapted by James Maxwell, was staged in Manchester and Lily's production was recalled again. A critic, reviewing the play for the *Jewish Chronicle*, and observing that it 'ran for nearly four hours', remembered that 'an earlier version, adapted by Lily Tobias and Lydia Lewisohn, and put on in London 40 years ago, went on so long that the then critic of the *Jewish Chronicle*' had to miss the last act. 'Lily Tobias, a versatile writer,' he went on to explain, 'was the aunt of Dannie Abse, the poet, and, of course, Leo Abse, MP.'[91]

The following week, the *Chronicle* published a letter of complaint by a reader named Minnie Temkin. What did this critic mean by 'was', she wanted to know. 'To correct the contrary impression conveyed by your contributor, I am happy to inform you that Mrs Tobias who is a relative of mine, is alive and well. She has long been active in literary and cultural circles in Israel, where she has now resided for many years.'[92]

By the time of this letter, in 1969, Lily was nearly eighty years old, and her literary reputation in England and Wales had faded from memory. However, just a few years after her adaption of *Daniel Deronda* had been staged in London, her first and second novels would establish her as a writer of note.

Seven

Lily the novelist

Looking back years later, Lily remembered the plans to move to Palestine as one of the reasons for not pursuing the West End offer for her play of *Daniel Deronda*, but in fact the move to Palestine stalled. Perhaps this was due to the setback of the 1929 riots and their aftermath, when the British colonial authority imposed restrictions on land sales to Jews, so as to limit the increasing problem of landlessness in the Arab population, which was seen as one of the causes of the riots. No doubt developments in Haifa also moved more slowly than she and Philip had anticipated. The factory did not in the end begin to take form until 1934, when the two of them returned for a visit, and they did not move to Haifa permanently until two years later – but in 1929 Lily was more engaged with finishing her first novel than revising the play of *Daniel Deronda* yet again; in fact, in the seven years between the last performance and her emigration to Palestine in 1936, she finished and published not only her first novel, but two others as well. Despite her having bypassed the possibility of the run in 1929, her standing in the London scene, established with that play, enabled her literary work to take off.

Lily was an ambitious writer. All four of her novels published in the 1930s dealt with the big questions of the political movements in which she'd been involved, but in addition to discussing pacifist ideals, or the history of cruelty to Jews, Jewish national aspirations or the Welsh past and its present predicament, Lily also told compelling stories about flawed and complex protagonists struggling with internal conflicts.

As a girl and a young woman, she had been caught up in the sweeping Scottish romance of *Ivanhoe*, and the tragic drama of Grace Aguilar's *Vale of Cedars*, and now as an adult she tried to bring to her own novels something of the heroism and idealism, the motifs of thwarted love and doomed romance, and above all the gripping and moving drama of martyrdom she'd found there. However, it was reworking *Daniel Deronda* for the stage that helped shape her first novel, *My Mother's House*.

In *My Mother's House* Lily created a vivid portrait of a Jewish boy in revolt against his Jewish and Welsh background. In his pursuit of belonging, as an Englishman, her protagonist Simon rejects everything his parents want for him, and seeks to divest himself of all Jewish and Welsh characteristics. Nevertheless, as Lily herself felt, Simon cannot ever feel whole until he embraces his Jewish identity in some way, though the prescription '*Bleib nor a Yid*' – only remain a Jew – is anathema to him in the excitingly modern, assimilating world of possibility that opens up for him when he moves to London.

My Mother's House was published on April 10th, 1931, shortly before Lily's forty-fourth birthday. It was a substantial book of some 500 pages, with a complex series of settings and themes, and a large cast of characters and intertwining stories. The overarching plot was neatly and succinctly summarised by a reviewer in the *Western Mail*:

Simon Black's home at Blaemawe, a Welsh mining village, is all that a poor Jewish boy's home should be, but the influence of his parents is dominated by that of his school and surroundings. He meets Edith, grand-daughter of Lady Hafod, and her English speech, manners, and appearance appeal to him so forcibly that he makes up his mind, while still a boy, to "become an Englishman." He grows up to love Edith. When he discovers that Edith is herself a Jewess there is a struggle between love and loyalty to his new creed. He leaves for London, becomes an English Civil Servant, and marries Jani, a little Welsh girl from Blaemawe. In this close contact Welsh and Jewish wills and ways are soon at war. Then comes disaster. Peace comes to Simon – in Palestine.[93]

Lily wove in many other subplots too, as well as detailed explorations of Jewish identity in London, Jewish attitudes to Zionism, and various conflicting parallel attitudes to Wales and Welshness. Reviewers in Jewish publications tended to note the former, and overlook the significance of the Welsh material, while reviewers in the Welsh press noticed the latter, but tended not to be so interested in the tapestry of Jewish life that Lily presented. Jewish reviewers did not go so far as those non-Jewish critics of George Eliot's *Daniel Deronda* who found the whole Jewish element of the novel inconvenient and thought it better left out – but they certainly didn't recognise the unusualness of Lily's Welsh material, nor what she was trying to do with it.

Simon, the protagonist of *My Mother's House*, grows up, like Lily, in Ystalyfera at the end of the nineteenth century, and his life ends in 1916 in Palestine, where he is fighting as a British soldier in the First World War. Just as she fictionalised Ystalyfera as Blaemawe (and, in 'The Nationalists', as Trwyntwll – a rather ungrammatical rendition of 'nose-hole'), Lily fictionalised almost all the Welsh place-names in this and subsequent novels. Blaemawe is as clearly Ystalyfera as 'Dawport' is Swansea and 'Tavcastle' is Cardiff (renamed 'Taviton' in her second novel, *Eunice Fleet*). Lily's playfulness with the place-names betrays her knowledge of the cities' Welsh names and nicknames, to which some of these fictionalised versions referred, if obliquely. In the name 'Dawport', for example, she incorporated 'Dawe' as a version of the Tawe, the river that appears in Abertawe, the Welsh name of Swansea. With 'Tavcastle' in *My Mother's House* and 'Taviton' in *Eunice Fleet* Lily played on the nickname 'Taffy' and 'Taffytown' – but the castle in Tavcastle is also a reference to Caerdydd, the Welsh name of Cardiff ('caer' meaning castle).

In *My Mother's House* Lily explored intricate layers of class and cultural affiliation and identity in the hinterland of Swansea – a world she recalled with affection, and sharp understanding of its social tensions – but, uniquely, she told the story of a Jewish working-class boy navigating his various Jewish, Welsh and British identities. Accurately, the novel's blurb describes it as a 'story of a young Jew in revolt against Judaism and of the manner in which, after seeing the folly of this attempted renunciation of his race, he eventually finds his soul's satisfaction. Scenes of Anglo-Jewish life, in which all the characters are vital and sharply depicted, move from Wales to Palestine, where the story has its close.' There are indeed scenes of Anglo-Jewish life (in London) but the most important locales are Ystalyfera and Swansea – unusually in British literature, these are scenes of Welsh Jewish life.

Lily shows in painful detail the tensions between English and Welsh people, between immigrant Jews and establishment Jews, and between those living up the industrial valley and those living in town. Though the book is not autobiographical, she used her own experience to good effect, evoking in her characters' experiences the kinds of things she and her brothers and sisters felt as children, acutely aware of their parents' awkward grasp of English, their embarrassing use of Yiddish, and their clumsy working-class manner and clothes next to the middle-class 'sophistication' of the 'townies'. Lily presented discomfort over language and accent at the very beginning of her novel: its opening scene shows Simon encountering upper-class Englishness for the first time. Lady Hafod's apparent sophistication and grace with English sparks in him the deepest desire to emulate it, but though it's a moment of transformation for Simon that will send him off on a doomed quest for belonging and acceptance as an 'Englishman', Lily treated it with humour. 'It was not the voice alone, melodious though it was in pitch and volume; but the accent – the accent was sheer revelation. For the first time in his life Simon heard English perfectly spoken by an Englishwoman.' In a kind of agony, Simon compares the sounds of the Welsh-English of his teacher, the Yiddish-English of his mother, and this – to him – musical and light-filled English-English. 'That Welsh women should speak English badly was, to him, a matter of indifference: that his mother should speak it badly, and in the presence of an English lady, was anguish and mortification in the extreme.' The encounter makes him determined to rid himself of everything Welsh and everything Jewish, both of them aspects of his identity that feel to him not just a social encumbrance but something corrupt and debased, and after hearing Lady Hafod (and, later, a school inspector, whose 'uncymricised Saxon was indubitably agreeable'), he takes to practising his English accent in secret.

Lily depicted Simon's struggle with great sympathy, though his path away from Jewishness was so different from her close identification with Judaism. In her portrayal of a young man in conflict with his own ethnic and cultural inheritance, she mapped out the whole territory of Jewish identity in the UK in the early years of the twentieth century, from devoutly observant families to young secular socialists; from newly anglicised rabbinical students to those going through the motions of minimal Jewish observance – and those in revolt against the constraints of being Jewish, and against suspicion, hostility and rejection, something that all her characters experience in one way or another. But Lily's Jewishness was also shaped by her Welsh upbringing, as her Zionism was informed by the Welsh national movement, and in the novel she presented shades of Welshness, too: the consequences for assimilated and anglicised Welsh people of repudiating the Welsh language, and the value of Welsh culture, are always a counterpart to the Jewish characters' struggles with assimilation.

My Mother's House is the story of a young man's path from childhood into maturity, a *bildungsroman*, but it is also a portrayal of the age-old struggle of second-generation immigrants and the tensions they experience. These are tensions that Lily experienced, like so many sons and daughters of immigrants, as they wrestle to accommodate the old ways to the new, in a society that values one language and one set of values, and either implicitly or explicitly denigrates all others. Lily wasn't merely using a dramatic strategy when she chose to open her novel with a scene showing the impact of 'English as spoken by an Englishwoman'. As a child she had shifted back and forth between four languages, and the experience was formative: Yiddish, her *mamiaith* or mothertongue; Welsh socially and with friends; Hebrew with her father to study Torah, and English, the language of school, of literature, and of getting on in the world, of escape. As for many Welsh people of her generation it was English, the language of Empire, of education and social advancement, that seemed to offer the widest horizons. Welsh Jews had a double disadvantage: many felt that Welsh and Yiddish were both impediments and social burdens that limited access, whereas English offered an escape from constraints of class and background, and gave them a chance to 'get on'.

Through Simon and his foil Edith, Lily explored all that she struggled with in herself, and all that she saw her brothers struggle with, particularly her younger brother Joseph. The question of how to be a Jew in a modern and increasingly secular society lies at the heart of the book, and lay at the centre of Lily's being, too – how to reinvent Jewishness in its new and relatively safe social environment in the UK; how to find a balance between Jewish observance and full participation in British life, and how to reconcile wanting to belong and to blend in on the one hand, and feeling, on the other, the strong pull of tradition, even though it came with constraint, particularly for women.

Above all, Lily struggled with the question of how to behave, publicly, as a Jew, when she was repeatedly reminded that acceptance and toleration of Jews, as with other minorities, was tenuous and contingent on their not making trouble, that it was conditional on their being 'good Jews' – Jews who behaved well. For Lily was not a 'good Jew'. She pushed at the boundaries that her traditional and observant mother wanted her to observe, and, liberated by marrying Philip, who shared her values and beliefs, she behaved according to those political beliefs. Going entirely against the mainstream, she had lobbied for women's rights, had supported COs, and had protested against war. These last two in particular were not the actions of a 'good Jew': to members of the accommodating Jewish establishment in Swansea and Cardiff, who wanted no trouble or undue attention, and who enjoyed tolerant and friendly relations with the 'host' community, this kind of behaviour was provocative and challenging. 'Good Jews' served their country with patriotic fervour – more patriotic fervour than their non-Jewish compatriots if need be, to prove their loyalty. Lily's activities, like those of Jewish COs and their supporters, were threatening to their status, and so too was Lily's public espousal of Zionism, which ran the risk of invoking the libel that Jews always had dual loyalties.

Lily explored this pressure to act like a good Jew in 'The Onus', one of the stories in *The Nationalists and Other Goluth Studies*. Here, a Jewish woman who feels that she represents her people, and has an 'imperative duty to make that impression favourable', tries to pass on to her son 'that it was incumbent on him to display super virtues for his nation's sake'. It isn't until he has a brush with a business competitor, who attributes base dealings to him as a 'smart' Jew, that he comes to the conclusion 'that a Jew is responsible by his deeds for the welfare and good name of all his fellow-Jews'.[94]

No one expressed more elegantly or painfully the hyper-sensitivity to others' awareness of Jewish difference, and the cost of the desire to belong and be wanted, the desire to be thoroughly and completely an 'Englishman of the Jewish persuasion' (since he could not dispense entirely with his Jewish family past) than Lily's character Simon Black. This working-class boy from Blaemawe, who, according to his parents' hopes, would become a rabbi for some Anglo-Jewish congregation, himself secretly harboured the great, impossible dream of a job in the English Civil Service.

Eventually Simon is forced to confront his prejudices and discomforts by his love for the elegant and inaccessible Edith, who is a kind of female Daniel Deronda. In George Eliot's novel, Daniel Deronda discovers he is a Jew, and he sets off in pursuit of all that that might mean to him. This leaves him inaccessible to Gwendolen Harleth, who has been hopelessly in flight from herself and from anything serious, and who must struggle and suffer and change, but who is never able to capture Daniel, the object of her love. In *My Mother's House* Lily's character Edith also discovers her Jewish identity, which her grandmother has tried to keep from her, while the parallel to Gwendolen is Simon, who, ignorant of Edith's Jewish identity, sees her as the repository of all those English qualities that he longs for. He is thrown back on his own rejection of his Jewish heritage by the discovery that Edith is in fact Jewish. Now Edith is inaccessible not because she is gentile, but because she is Jewish: Simon has rejected his Jewishness, and she cannot accept his love until he embraces it again – which, eventually, he does, redeemed through her (as Gwendolen is through Daniel). Unlike the two characters in George Eliot's novel, however, Simon and Edith are united – but it is a love doomed by war. Simon, a soldier in Palestine, is shot by a sniper, and the novel ends with his death: 'A bullet struck sharp and low. Simon's head dropped back ... Nightmare was over. The dream – had it ended, or begun anew?'

As though in fiction Lily had been foretelling from the start her own future loss, all her fictional romances ended in doom and death. Either war, or political betrayal, or sacrifice comes between the lovers, first in 'The Nationalists', then in *My Mother's House* – and Lily would write death and sacrifice into *Eunice Fleet* two years later, and two years later again, into her third novel, *Tube*.

In *My Mother's House*, Lily presented the predicament of British Jews, particularly Jews whose identity was being diluted by the attraction of partial or full assimilation – which was her own predicament, too. Here she focused on British-Jewish thought, feeling and affiliation, and expanded on many of the themes she had first sketched in her stories in *The Nationalists and Other Goluth Studies*, and grappled with in her adaption of *Daniel Deronda*.

In her sketches, Lily had been simple and polemical about the dangers of assimilation, and had used the parallel compelling attraction of assimilation for Welsh people. The Welsh who dispensed with their Welsh past – their sense of history and tradition, and, above all, language and accent – helped Lily illustrate the threat to Jews, not at the collective level, but at the level of the individual. She wrote assiduously about how assimilation would result in an atrophying of experience, and would create a limited, unsatisfactory emotional and social life. She saw it as a pointless endeavour, for even if Jews cast off everything that identified them as Jews, changing names and accents, and cutting themselves off from their families, they would never be fully accepted as English.

That was her own experience – for now, beginning to move in London literary circles, she encountered the prejudice against Jews that was widespread in the period. This was not an entirely new experience, for although, in common with many Welsh Jews, she recollected no hostility to her as a Jew from Welsh people, in her fiction she attributed such hostility very clearly to those who 'betrayed' their Welsh roots – and to English incomers. Undoubtedly she did indeed experience some prejudice in Wales, and not solely from those who were anglicised or English, though she may well have understood it through that filter, or have chosen to represent it that way for purpose of favourably comparing Welsh and Jewish cultural pride and the national politics that arose from it. For example W. J. Gruffydd, her own fellow tenant in the Rhiwbina cooperative venture – and hardly an anglicised or 'self-hating' Welshman – would some years later publish a profoundly hostile and now notorious diatribe against Jews in the journal *Y Llenor*. Of course whether he had that view when he was Lily and Philip's neighbour, or whether they were ever subjected to it is unknown.[95]

Hostility to Jews, Lily believed, was fundamental and unchanging – and in England was ever-present. In *My Mother's House* she wrote painful scenes of casual daily prejudice which showed that even when Simon and people like him were accepted, it was always a tenuous state, and contingent on not making a 'fuss'. In one London scene at a party, a 'swarthy fellow', a Jewish artist, knocks into the writer Westerley, a new acquaintance of Simon's, and spills coffee on his sleeve, which Westerley mops at with a handkerchief.

'Accident,' said Simon – 'but he might have apologised.'

'What can you expect from a Jew?' said Westerley. 'Ill-mannered, like all his tribe.' There seemed unnecessary venom in the quiet voice. Ted Rendall had strolled up with young Vannick. A look in the latter's eye told Simon he had heard.

Westerley replaced his handkerchief and held out his hand. Simon took it and said,

'Our hostess is Jewish, you know. And so am I.'

'Really?' There was no change in the smooth, cool face. 'Ought I to beg your pardon? You're different, of course. Always pleasant to find the exception.'

Vannick, one of Simon's two friends who has witnessed the exchange, is outraged and he exclaims, '"What about *his* manners, I'd like to know? Thinks he can get away with it by making exceptions – that proves the rule, of course! Oh yes, I know these anti-Semites. You can always spot 'em by the same old tag – 'Bless you, I'm not an anti-Semite – why, my dearest friend's a Jew!' naturally, quite different from the rest of the tribe, and all that."'

The other friend defends Westerley as 'a decent chap' who had a right to feel annoyed, and he tells Simon: '"Now the worst of you chaps is – you're so damned sensitive. It don't seem reasonable to me. Can't you forget you're Jews, sometimes? I don't go about thinking I'm an Englishman all day long.'"

But Simon can't forget – and nor could Lily. For him, as for her, the 'lack of novelty' of that kind of slur made it no less galling: 'A Jew in England, even if he wanted to forget, was not allowed to escape constant reminder.'[96]

It was this kind of small-scale daily reminder of difference that Lily herself experienced, as much as the knowledge of much more serious and threatening forms of hostility, that reinforced her belief that the only true freedom for the Jewish individual could be in a Jewish homeland.

Lily did not yet know Palestine well when she was writing *My Mother's House*, and even though she made it the place of Simon's death, she also presented it in the novel as a haven, a symbol of all that was possible, and a place of regeneration. Zion, for her, was inseparable from any question of Jewish identity or history, and so it is only through an embrace not just of his Jewishness, but his Jewishness restored in Palestine, that Simon's fractured self can eventually be made whole.

By 1931, when *My Mother's House* was published, many of the problems created by the Balfour Declaration were becoming clear. British and Commonwealth forces had begun their conquest of the Ottoman province of Palestine in 1916, and the British government had issued the Balfour Declaration the following year, a declaration full of hope and promise to Jews, and full of dread and threat to Palestinian Arabs. The British Mandate for Palestine, as the civilian colonial administration was known, began in 1921 and continued for twenty-six years. The British Mandate meant that Britain was centrally engaged in international Jewish questions, and British Zionists themselves were in a unique position of influence in the future of world Jewish affairs.

When Lily's book came out, the military conquest of Palestine and the issuing of the Balfour Declaration was a decade and a half in the past, and the British civil administration of Palestine was lurching from crisis to crisis, crises that triggered investigations, Enquiries and White Papers, and hopelessly unworkable solutions. Every aspect of the British Mandatory administration of the region was hotly debated from all sides. Jewish national hopes in Palestine were no vague abstraction to the majority of the British public, but a pressing political and practical matter, with high-ranking supporters and opponents. Its colonial control of the region made the UK responsible for two competing claims to the land, and ushered in decades of insoluble conflict from which, eventually, it would withdraw, turning over responsibility to the UN in 1947. In that political climate, Lily's novel was timely, as it presented in grand, almost epic sweep the full panoply of Jewish and Zionist thought, opinion and experience.

The political landscape of Palestine was in a state of such rapid flux when the UK's military administration changed over to the civil administration of the Mandate years, that it would perhaps have been almost impossible for Lily to situate a novel in the present day. The political subtleties, the realities of administering two opposed national groups, the arguments for and against restricting or allowing immigration of Jews to Palestine, and the growing threat in Germany all combined to create a highly unstable state of affairs. Lily instead situated her novel in the years she herself had known in Wales, giving Simon a childhood that closely matched her own family life, one whose tensions and intricacies of social and political nuance she knew intimately, and which she could accurately recall. That way, she managed to present a compelling personal story of a boy desperate to belong, to be normal, to be part of England – and what this cost him. Instead of the uncertainty of the interwar years that she was living and breathing, she set his life against the backdrop of argument and discussion in the lead-up to the First World War.

Ten years, twelve years after the end of that war, when she was finishing *My Mother's House*, it was still possible for her to write a pacifist hope into her novel, still possible for her to believe in a Jewish homeland achieved through peaceful means, even though she knew the reality of war – or, more accurately, *because* she knew the reality and hopelessness of war. Nevertheless, she was only too aware of what that war had won for Jewish hopes of a homeland, and she wrote her mixed and contradictory feelings about that into the ending of the novel – for it is war that brings Simon finally to Palestine, and to a reconciliation with his Jewish self. When he reveals to Edith his intention to enlist, though his embrace of Zion is something she has wished for, she exclaims in dismay: 'Not that way, surely, oh Lord?' – for both she and Simon's mother 'could only feel appalled at a Judea soaked in blood'.[97]

Though Lily had visited Palestine, she was not yet living there, and her knowledge of it was limited. The reality and complexity of Palestine, with its conflicting claims and violent confrontations, would not appear in her work until her final novel, *The Samaritan*, the sequel to *My Mother's House*, published in 1939.

Many critics praised *My Mother's House*, and Lily read positive review after positive review. The *Eastern Daily Press*, for example, announced it 'a most remarkable achievement … exceptional in its naturalness and vitality'. Not surprisingly, *My Mother's House* had a particularly sympathetic reception in Wales. It was reviewed in English and Welsh, in the leading papers and journals, including the prominent cultural journal the *Welsh Outlook*, and the newspaper for which Lily had herself once worked, the *Western Mail*.

The author of the *Western Mail* review was one 'WHJ', possibly William Hughes Jones, secretary to Ernest Rhys, the editor of *Everyman*. 'Those who insist on the affinity of the Welsh and Jewish peoples would do well to read and ponder this extraordinarily powerful study of a young Jew, born and bred in Wales, whose one ambition was to be a Britisher,' he wrote, under the header 'A Jew of Wales'. But in fact it is not this common Welsh interest that the reviewer focused on, but Lily's Welsh credentials and her skills of observation and expression:

Formerly resident at Ystalyfera, and later at Rhiwbina, the authoress has obviously used to excellent purpose her opportunities to acquire a knowledge of the life and mental outlook of the native folk of Glamorgan. It is also clear that she has been an equally conscientious and industrious student of Jewish mentality and customs. Her sympathy with both races is beyond dispute. In addition, she has an exceptional gift of self-expression. Hence the value and interest of her tale.

His sole mild criticism – 'A glossary would have helped most readers of this striking novel' – was aimed implicitly at certain Yiddish and Hebrew phrases or words, including names of festivals or traditional practices, some of which were not given in translation in the book.[98]

The reviewer in the *Welsh Outlook* was equally impressed by the unusual subject matter, and by the parallels with Welsh assimilation, but less convinced by Lily's skill.

The subject of 'My Mother's House' – the conflicting loyalties of a young Jew – will be new to most readers of the Welsh Outlook; but the fact that much of the action is involved with life in industrial South Wales adds interest to a story which, though sometimes faulty in technique, never fails in vigour and imagination. Miss Tobias's work appeals to readers of Jewish blood – '*Pure Jewish blood – poured out hot in the fires of the Inquisition – poured out cold over the racks in the torture chambers. In defence of the silly old customs that it makes you uncomfortable to keep.*' Yet the problems confronting Simon Black are not really different from those confronting any young Welshman of distinction, tempted by 'glittering prizes' to renounce his birthright.[99]

In strong contrast, a reviewer in the *Jewish Chronicle* managed almost entirely to overlook the Welsh background, context, comparison and cultural portrait in the novel, noting instead its Jewish material. Indeed, although Simon's childhood in 'a South Wales mining village' was acknowledged, and the review credited the novel with forming 'between Wales and Palestine another link than that afforded by the personality of Mr. Lloyd George', the only other mention of Wales was the 'anti-alien riots', which constitutes such a very small footnote to the story that it is surprising the reviewer even noted it – unless, of course, his sole association with Wales was indeed Lloyd George on the one hand and the Tredegar riot of 1911 on the other, as was so often the case.[100] He identified Simon as 'the son of foreign Jewish parents', and summarised his life story in rather different ways to that of the *Western Mail* review:

He is sent to study for the ministry at Jews' College in London, but gradually becomes more and more estranged from his religion and race. Rebelling against what appears to him 'the jargon and jumble of the Yiddish world' he comes to have an unreasoning admiration for 'everything English, good or bad, just because it's English.' Eventually he marries a non-Jewish girl, who is before long untrue to him. Then he finds his soul's redemption through his love for Edith Miller, who may be described as a female counterpart of Daniel Deronda. When the great war comes, he joins the Jewish Regiment and dies fighting in Palestine.

The reviewer betrayed his own anglocentric and metropolitan values, which mirrored those of the *Jewish Chronicle*, and the attitudes of London's Jewish community in the period more generally – a dismissal of Wales as a province of England, and Welsh Jewish experience as a curiosity. Swansea (the novel's 'Dawport') was 'a small provincial community' and its Jewish community 'a provincial congregation'. The reviewer overlooked Lily's unique comparison of Welsh and Jewish struggles with assimilation, and instead read the novel solely as treating 'of the rather hackneyed problems of assimilation and inter-marriage'. Nevertheless, the reviewer acknowledged, the novel 'does so in a decidedly fresh and vivid manner, and discusses certain aspects of Anglo-Jewish life that are new to fiction. Perhaps the most notable feature is that, despite the breadth and variety of the scenes depicted, each separate one is portrayed with a most sure and intimate touch ... The characters may stress the religious, national, or cultural aspects of Judaism; they may speak Welsh, Cockney, Yiddish, or Hebrew – but they are all true to life ... In its scope and comprehensiveness, this is certainly a novel out of the ordinary. The authoress has avoided the danger of generalisation from any one particular type,' he concluded, 'and has shown a remarkable insight into the psychology of all the varied groups that together comprise Anglo-Jewry.' But in *My Mother's House* Lily did not write only about Anglo-Jewry: she was writing at least as much about Welsh Jewry, and about Wales, something which the Welsh reviews recognised.

A review in the *Spectator* was less positive: the critic found the novel 'dignified but forced and to that extent unreal'.[101] Lily was quick to respond to the charge of inaccuracy and lack of realism when it was made privately by Mrs Hyman, a friend and fellow synagogue member in London. Mrs Hyman had read *My Mother's House* and commended the book, but she identified some weak points, including what she saw as being unlikely in Edith's situation – Edith, she felt, would surely have known she was Jewish. Lily responded at some length:

> I want to express my appreciation of the candid note on my novel ... I value your opinions as highly as any press notices I have received – in fact more highly than some!

It is certainly the most gratifying tribute I could receive from friends, that you forgot *me* in the story.

Your view of 'weak points' may well be right. But may I say there is no need to strain belief in the fact of Edith's parentage being unknown? It was not a dead secret (in spite of Lady Hafod's efforts) except to Simon and those who, like him, could not or would not share in the village life. His own parents knew or suspected the truth long before. – As to the long arm of coincidence, I have found that, in Jewish affairs, real life can equal and even surpass anything to be found in novels. I wouldn't dare invent nearly as fantastic and 'incredible' a combination of circumstances as I have actually known and heard of. By the way, I wonder if you are familiar with the romance of a Finchley couple we all know? The husband is of German parentage. He came as a youthful student to England, met a girl in a boarding-house while on holiday at the seaside, fell in love, and wrote home to tell his parents that he was going to marry a Jewish girl. Whereupon they wrote, revealing for the first time that he – and they – were Jews!

My Mother's House was a success, and its subject matter timely. Lily was part of the literary scene in London, enjoying growing friendships both within the Jewish community and far beyond it. Her Labour Party and pacifist connections were wide and strong, both socially and politically, and she took an active role in literary and Zionist circles. It was her next book, however, published two years later, which brought her the widest recognition.

Eight

Between two wars

Lily's second novel, *Eunice Fleet*, was published by Hutchinson in 1933, not long after the Oxford Union Debating Society's notorious 'King and Country' motion, on 9 February, that 'this House will in no circumstances fight for its King and Country'. Lily dedicated the novel to the brothers who had been COs in the First World War, but the publisher placed material on the dust-jacket and included a preface that situated the novel clearly in the present context of an increasing threat of war. 'The young men of the Universities of Oxford and Manchester have given their vote', the preface begins. 'They will, in no circumstances, fight for their King and Country. Their action has been the signal for an outburst of condemnation, but there can be few who do not feel the significance of that now-famous resolution.' It links the resolution to the theme of *Eunice Fleet*, although the connection was tenuous at best:

> *Eunice Fleet* is a novel which has been long awaited and which, appearing now, is particularly opportune. It has, for its theme, the tragedy, the humiliation, the abuse which each one of those young men, if they remain loyal to their faith, may have to suffer in no distant future.

The story, standing as it does for so much, tells how a popular athlete is condemned as a coward and felon, abandoned by his wife to a tragic fate because of his refusal to fight in the last war, and afterward rehabilitated to her memory. While the protagonists are imaginary, the background is one of realism based on experience and observation. From every point of view we have been given pictures showing the horrors of actual battle. Here is a picture of a different battle, but every bit as fierce, every bit as shattering, and every bit as cruel.

Eunice Fleet demands attention. It is a novel which possesses significance for every man and woman; it is beautifully written.

A reviewer for the *Western Mail* responded first to that marketing device, and the wider implications in the present or near future, before examining the book itself: 'Those English and Welsh undergraduates who recently pledged themselves not to fight for their country in certain circumstances would do well to read this story. If, after doing so, they still stick to their decision, there will remain only one more thing to demonstrate their courage – the pacifist's test in war time. Miss Tobias has concentrated all her skill on showing us what that actually means.' But the critic's scepticism about the historical background provoked Lily to respond. 'That she has based her case on historical fact seems incredible. No doubt strange things happened to conscientious objectors during the Great War, but surely the "madness of patriotism" never descended to the depths of cowardly cruelty suggested here. And yet,' he concedes reluctantly, 'there is an atmosphere of realism about this tale.'[102]

This was of course not the first time a reader had raised questions about 'incredible' elements in Lily's writing. She wrote carefully in her own defence, both publicly and privately, and on this occasion, after reading the notice, she immediately sent off a correction to the newspaper's editor. 'Sir, – May I express my appreciation of the "review" of my new novel "Eunice Fleet" in Thursday's Western Mail?' she began her letter, with typical grace. 'Apart from its intrinsic interest, it is a pleasure to me to receive a meed of recognition from South Wales, with which my life and work are so closely bound.' Then she shifted to 'points of accuracy' raised by the reviewer: 'That I have based my case on historical fact, he says, seems incredible. Unfortunately, historical fact not only verifies my tale, but exceeds it. There are chapter and verse for every incident in my book that deals with conscientious objectors. I had personal knowledge of many of the victims, and the descriptions of prison, camp, and barrack cell in "Eunice Fleet" are strictly true. There are citizens of Cardiff who can testify to, and confirm, vital episodes in the book.'[103]

The publisher's marketing strategy also drew the attention of a reviewer in the *Welsh Outlook*, but in this case the review identified a problem with the publisher's characterisation of the book. 'The publishers had a happy inspiration – commercially speaking – when they decked out this novel in a flaring dust-wrapper plastered with reproductions of newspaper paragraphs about the notorious Oxford "King and Country" debate, and describing it as "the story of a man who would not fight!"', he observed. 'But it is not, strictly speaking, that.' *Eunice Fleet*, he pointed out, 'is the story of his wife.'

The review in the *Outlook* was long and thoughtful, but critical, too. Unlike the reviewer in the *Western Mail*, this critic affirmed Lily's accurate rendering of the past, as

> an honest attempt at what is already becoming so terribly difficult – to recall that life of unhealthy excitement, and of equally unhealthy and utterly dismal monotony, experienced by those who stayed at home during the War. The ignorance and brutality of many conscription 'Tribunals'; the beastliness of the 'White Feather' business; the mobbing of a pacifist politician who was to become a 'Nationalist' Prime Minister scarcely a dozen years later; the disillusionment of the soldier on leave … these things are true, and they need saying, not once but many times. Few who saw anything of London and other large towns during the later part of the war are likely to dispute them.

Indeed, he found, 'there is enough evidence of the dirty sordidness of the "Home Front" during those black years to make Miss Tobias's sketches look comparatively mild'. But he was less admiring of the sections set in the present, and of her style: 'the story falls between two stools … The actual writing also is very uneven. In the "Past" section the style is mostly direct, simple, and sincere, but elsewhere, in straining to render the sophisticated present (why does "the present" always think itself the last word in sophistication?), Miss Tobias produces a good deal of rather crude "fine writing." Yet ethically and historically, if not exactly artistically, the book has interest.'

A *Jewish Chronicle* review, in the 'Books and Bookmen' column, was similarly mixed. The reviewer felt that marketing the book in the context of the Oxford Union debate did

the authoress an injustice for it surely did not require this particular piece of topicality to justify an anti-war book by a Jewess. The treatment of conscientious objectors by this country during the War is not a matter on which any decent citizen can look back with any pride, and Mrs. Tobias has told the shameful story with objectivity coupled with a soaring passion. There was never a scrap of paper more cynically torn up than the conscience clause in the Conscription Act, and it is just as well that the national conscience should at long last be cleared by open confession. The authoress wraps up her bitter pill very skilfully in a story dramatically told with some admirable character drawing.

But, as with most of the other reviews, he found her writing lacking in places: 'Here and there she fails to sustain the high level of the central theme, and there is an almost amateurish descent to the penny novelette grade of writing.' However, he conceded that 'this can be forgiven for the work as a whole possesses gripping qualities and no small artistry. Obviously the book could not have been written except by one who had been brought into very close and intimate contact with the experiences described, and this power of verisimilitude carries conviction. Mrs. Tobias is to be congratulated on a notable achievement.'[104]

The criticism in that review and in the *Welsh Outlook*, as with the *Spectator*'s notice of *My Mother's House*, must have stung Lily, but there were plenty of warmly positive comments for the publisher to select and quote from in various advertisements. From *The Western Mail* it selected: 'its power is beyond dispute'; from *Public Opinion*: 'Mrs Tobias is a novelist of exceptional ability'; from Lilian Arnold, in *John O' London*: 'Mrs Tobias is to be congratulated on a very vital piece of work.'[105] The *New Leader* had proclaimed it 'important as one of the few accounts we have had of the conscientious objector in the war'. *Jewish Standard* found it 'A book which no thinking person can afford to ignore'. *Everyman* described it as 'a deeply appealing novel', and the reviewer in the *Manchester Evening News* declared it "well done, moving, sincere', and concluded: 'I liked it.'[106]

Most of the reviews dealt primarily not with the sections of the book set in the present, but with the poignant and moving story of Vincent and his martyrdom, but that was not only because of the publisher's marketing strategy of the book as 'the story of a man who would not fight' – it was also because of the political and social environment in 1933.

The Oxford Union Debating Society's declaration that 'this House will in no circumstances fight for its King and Country' was made in the context of a heightened threat of war. Lily set *Eunice Fleet* during the Asian crisis of 1931, when Japan invaded Manchuria; it looked then as though a more widespread war was inevitable, and though Lily, like so many others, had high hopes about the effectiveness of the League of Nations, they were disappointed. Looking back to the previous war, she found the material for some of her most moving writing, based on the experiences of her brothers and on her own daring and dangerous escapades, but, as the *Outlook* review observed, the novel was in fact about the eponymous character herself rather than Vincent, as she struggled, in the early 1930s, to make sense of her husband's sacrifice, and to find something to believe in in the present.

Eunice Fleet opens in London, where Eunice is managing a lingerie shop called 'Miss Eve', owned by her Jewish friend Hava Casson. Lily used all the first-hand knowledge she'd gained from her aunt's lingerie shop, Madame Foner, in Swansea: the detail makes for some very interesting and useful historical material, should anyone wish to know about women's underclothes, including rubber corsets and silk suspender belts, in the early 1930s. Lily described London evocatively, too: it is all smog and clubs and theatres. Eunice, now in her thirties, has suffered from long years of depression in the decade or so after Vincent's death in prison, and she wrestles with a sense of hopelessness until she meets George Furnall, a former member of the No-Conscription Fellowship who had known Vincent, and whom she herself had briefly met when he'd visited Vincent in prison. Furnall is engaged in political work, and intends to stand as a Westminster candidate, and Eunice hopes that through him, and through what she understands as his work for peace, she might begin to make up for her failure to support Vincent, whose ideals, belatedly, she has come to understand and to share. With this encounter she begins to come alive again, and to go out – to the theatre, to nightclubs, and to meet others involved in the coalition government – it is Ramsay MacDonald's government, though Lily only indicates that obliquely in the novel.

Critics found the wartime sections of *Eunice Fleet* most compelling, for Lily's heart went into the writing of Eunice's memories of war, of the No-Conscription Fellowship, the barracks and military tribunals, and the suffering of conscientious objectors. This was a world Lily did not need to imagine at all: she had observed it with pain and been an intimate part of it in Cardiff between 1916 and 1919. And while the *Welsh Outlook* was critical of the 'sophisticated' present in *Eunice Fleet*, Lily nevertheless evoked the London of the late 1920s and early 1930s with a great deal of accurate detail and closely observed dialogue, which is peppered with the new expressions and idioms of the day. Though she had by then been living there for several years, London was still a new, fresh scene to her as a writer, and she revelled in its vibrancy, particularly the theatre (Eunice, for example, attends the play *Journey's End* by R. C. Sherriff, which opened in December 1928 at the Apollo Theatre and ran for two years in the West End).

Lily lingered on other details of the London scene, too, including the novelty of the new traffic lights, first introduced widely to the city's streets in 1929. That latter detail was not just to establish setting, however, for later on in the novel Eunice deliberately or otherwise ignores the lights, and, distraught, nearly kills herself in traffic. She has been betrayed by her new lover, whose peace position, it emerges – like that of the government more generally – is one of expediency, not commitment. When her lover chooses Eunice's young niece instead of her, Eunice tries to gas herself, but is saved by the postman knocking on the door. Rallying, she decides to follow Jewish friends of hers who have moved to Palestine out of a 'belief in something big, not just in a man'. Towards the close of the novel, that is Eunice's hope, too: that she might find something big to believe in. Nevertheless, as with *My Mother's House*, Lily wrote an ominously suggestive final few lines, for when Eunice's niece comes in, she finds Eunice asleep and 'dead to the world ... Darkness fell, and the door closed quietly.'

Lily had finished revisions to *Eunice Fleet* in September 1932, and soon after it went to Hutchinson, her publishers, she began adapting it for the stage, writing a rough first draft in pencil in a small notebook, which she rapidly filled as the play grew to three Acts. She provisionally called it 'Where Have I Seen You Before?', which is a line taken from the novel, when Eunice sees Furnall for the first time, and is reminded of the past.

Lily wrote the play as a chronological account, unlike the book, giving it an opening in a peaceful and wealthy industrial family home in Cardiff before the outbreak of war, and situating the last Act twenty years later. In the modern section she dealt directly with the Prime Minister and the people around him, rather than obliquely, as she'd done in the novel. In the novel Lily hadn't amended her original admiration for Ramsay MacDonald as a hounded pacifist during the war, but her view of him had changed by the time she started to write the play. In 1931 MacDonald formed a National Government in coalition with the Liberal and Conservative parties, and he was condemned for what many socialists felt was his betrayal not only of the Labour Party, but of the working class, and the party's anti-war past. In the play, though Lily disguises him under the name Bruce Allinson, she condemns him too.

Later on Lily reworked the play, amending names, details and dialogue, and wrote out a new clean copy in ink in February 1933. But in 1933 it was becoming clear that

MacDonald was unwell, and Lily's play languished – first the publication of *Eunice Fleet* itself engaged her, then the distressing news of the predicament of Jews on the continent and in Palestine displaced her interest in it, and her third novel absorbed her. Meanwhile the plans to establish a branch of the family business in Haifa were at last making progress – and Lily's father, Tobias, bought land to build a home for himself where Lily and Philip and other members of the family would join him, for he wanted to live out his final years in Palestine.

In 1934, Lily and Philip travelled by ship again to Palestine. They arrived in Haifa in mid-October, and their presence was announced in the 'Social and Personal' column of the *Palestine Post*, the leading English-language newspaper. The description of Lily shows the new standing that her two novels had conferred on her: 'Mr. P. V. Tobias and Mrs. Tobias, of London, are spending three weeks in this country and are this week at the King David Hotel. Mrs. Lily Tobias is a distinguished novelist, a recent book of hers is "My Mother's House," on a Jewish theme. "Eunice Fleet," published early this year, "the story of a man who would not fight," created a stir. Her husband is a director of Shepherd, Tobias and Co., Ltd., and has interesting plans for a glassworks in Haifa.'[107] It would nevertheless be two more years before Lily and Philip moved to Palestine to live, and in interim the *Post* reported regularly on the progress of the glassworks.

By the time they checked into the King David, the luxury Jerusalem hotel that had opened two years earlier (and which would be bombed twelve years later in one of the worst anti-British acts of Jewish terrorism in Palestine),

Lily's second novel had been widely reviewed, and her third novel, *Tube*, was about to be published.

Tube, like *Eunice Fleet*, was published by Hutchinson, but it proved a much harder sell for the publisher. Even the blurb-writer seemed uncertain what *Tube* was about, and unsure of its value, though certain about the value of Lily's previous book: 'One of the most powerful novels of its season and one which, on account of its uncompromising pacifistic theme, aroused a good deal of comment, was Lily Tobias's novel, *Eunice Fleet*. Now in *Tube* the same author has tackled a problem which, if of less obvious importance, is both original and daring.'

That 'problem' of lesser importance was the 'borderland of the real and the fantastic'. Angela Gane, a twenty-one-year-old countrywoman from 'Canbury' in Norfolk, arrives in London full of eager curiosity. She has a capacity to 'see into' people – a faculty of imagination that the editor of the local weekly paper for whom she worked had tried to curb. Freshly arrived in London, she lets her imagination run free. Angela had worked as a reporter for three years while looking after her grandmother, but her grandmother's death has allowed her to leave the dull, familiar uneventful life of Canbury, 'where it's *too quiet for cats*'. She soon revels in the wild and wonderful delights of metropolitan scenes. 'Was Angela Gane a mystic, gifted with second sight, or was she an ordinary girl whose imagination sometimes helped and sometimes misled her?' the blurb asked. 'Was her schoolfellow the woman in green? Was a child born on the train? Was a Cabinet Minister assassinated in the tunnel? Such are the questions which readers of this extraordinarily interesting experiment will ask.'

Lily certainly did not provide answers in the book. As a piece of experimental writing *Tube* was perhaps not experimental enough in style to overcome the narrative problems of its structure, but its political, national and ethnic themes are nevertheless powerful, and they reveal Lily's abiding concerns – heightened and made urgent by developments in Nazi Germany.

Angela's first trip on the London Underground provides the novel's title: it is both a real journey, in which she observes the people around her with a fantastically-inclined imagination, and also a symbolic journey into the unconscious and the narrative structure of the book.

For the structure of the book, Lily adopted an element of her work for the theatre, dividing it into four parts, which work as four Acts: it opens with Part One, 'Angela enters the tube' and closes with Part Four, 'Angela emerges'. As the blurb suggests, it remains unresolved whether the three sub-stories, which all overlap, are the product of the protagonist's over-active imagination about fellow travellers whom she observes on the train, or of some kind of psychic insight into them, in which she perceives and experiences their whole background. In the end, each also has elements that can be traced to Angela's own reading or memories of childhood stories, so what she experiences could be, simply, Lily's way of writing about the writer's imagination.

The first person whose story Angela 'sees' or imagines is an assimilated Anglo-Jewish woman who is forced to confront her Jewishness by the revelation of her Portuguese *converso* roots. In London, Lily had become friends with Cecil Roth, the outstanding scholar of Spanish and Portuguese Jewish history, and had become familiar with accounts of how converted Jews, forced during the Inquisition to reject Judaism, often only nominally converted, and continued their Jewish practice in secret; some, unwitting, carried on family traditions without even knowing they were Jewish.

The second person Angela 'sees into' is a Welsh Cabinet Minister who is about to betray his working-class roots by marrying into the gentry, and the third is the scarred German émigré fiancée of a Jewish man who has been arrested, tortured and possibly killed by the Nazis. Although Lily wandered farthest, in *Tube*, from her own experience, and ventured into much more unusual and alien fictionalised worlds, she nevertheless wove elements of her own life into the overarching story. Angela's old boss, the editor of the weekly newspaper for which she worked, hired her in much the way the editor of the *South Wales Daily Post* hired Lily. In her characteristic play on names, Lily humorously named this fictional editor Poston, a nod to her real editor, W. H. Stevenson on the *Post*. In other ways, too, she kept close to what she knew, weaving it into the new form: the themes of Jewish persecution, the peril of Jewish and Welsh assimilation, and the immorality of political expediency and betrayal of one's national identity, culture and class. Lily also took those 'incredible' allegations from readers of her previous two novels, and put them to work in the service of fantasy in *Tube*. Here she could not be accused of historical inaccuracy or unbelievable coincidence, because the whole novel, with its three interweaving stories that Angela either clairvoyantly perceives or creates in her fertile imagination, are deliberately incredible, as is the idea of ethnic memory that the whole explores.

Lily was experimenting, but to political purpose, for she still had a message she wanted to convey. As always, she gave her closest attention to Jewish material, and though she was writing something fantastical, her evocation of Inquisition torture is deeply disturbing. Readers might find it, like the tribunal and prison scenes in *Eunice Fleet* somewhat improbable, but in fact she based the scenes on a transcript of the torture of Elvira del Campo, which was published in H. C. Lea's history of the Spanish Inquisition: though the setting is shifted from Spain to Portugal, and the relationships and names are changed, the detail of torture implements, and the methods of torture (including a harrowing description of what is now known as waterboarding) are faithful to that account, and the words of the victim are given almost verbatim.[108] Lily presented the scene, the torture and the victim's words in relentless violent detail – experimenting with fusing fiction and documentary evidence, and extending it far beyond mere fictional effect. Her unacknowledged use of source material is problematic now, of course, in a time sensitive to questions of plagiarism, but that wasn't the concern expressed by reviewers, nor by Cecil Roth, the expert on Spanish Jewry. Some years later, in 1945, when Leo Abse mentioned in a letter to Lily that he had met Cecil Roth, she recalled Roth's response to her novel: 'I knew him in London and visited his flat after his marriage (I had known his wife also before),' she wrote to Leo. 'It was after the publication of my "Tube" and I was flattered by his commendation of my treatment of the "Inquisition" & Spanish history matters – of course he's a recognised authority on medieval Jewish history, especially in Spain and Italy.'[109]

Some reviewers were unconvinced, however. 'An odd puzzling book', reported the *Western Mail*. 'An uncommon book', thought the *Daily Herald*. *The Palestine Post* reviewer was unimpressed: 'The author tends to be somewhat heavy-handed in her imagination and writing. The result is hardly the hazy atmosphere of uncontrolled dreaming, but the sharply-edged effect of a patchwork counterpane.' The following year, in the 'Books and Bookmen' column in the *Jewish Chronicle*, the columnist remembered that Lily had 'perplexed her readers in *The Tube* ... with a strange conglomeration of the Inquisition and the Underground Railway'. Some highly placed pre-publication reviews were cautiously positive, or damned with faint praise: according to the *Times Literary Supplement*, the writing was 'always competent', and according to the *Scotsman*, in *Tube* Lily wrote vividly and kept 'her story charging along at a good pace ... an entertainment of a kind not encountered every day'. *World Jewry* found it 'an interesting and very original experiment'. But the review that gave Lily the accolade of arrival (and which provided a phrase for the marketing blurb) was that in the *Jewish Chronicle*: 'An extraordinarily interesting experiment, and she has succeeded in a way that confirms her position as one of the foremost contemporary Anglo-Jewish novelists.'

Few seemed to notice what Lily was doing by writing in the early 1930s about Jewish persecution, juxtaposing a German-Jewish story and a story of torture and expulsion during the Inquisition. But no one knew at the time what was in store for Europe's Jews, and by the time it emerged, Lily's novel had been largely forgotten and had fallen out of print.

Lily already believed immovably that Jews faced perpetual insecurity without a state of their own, and her belief was underscored by the growing threat of the Nazi Party to German Jews. By 1933, when she was beginning to shape the work that became *Tube*, that threat had become clear to many. A decade earlier, Lily's brother Joseph had gone on holiday to Germany with Max Abse, the brother of Kate's husband (and uncle to Leo and Dannie Abse), and some Jewish friends had taken them to hear Hitler speak in Heidelberg. The experience, he later recalled, told him 'the truth about Germany' and made him 'a profound Zionist'.[110] No doubt his experience informed Lily's fears, too, watching, in 1933, as Hitler was appointed Chancellor, and the Nazi Party began to consolidate and expand its power, and then, early that year, acquire total control. But for Lily, unlike for her younger brother, Hitler's growing power merely reinforced and focused her already unshakeable Zionism.

As conditions for Jews in Germany deteriorated, emigration to Palestine increased, although the government White Paper of 1933 placed limits on immigration, because of heightened Arab-Jewish tensions. Lily and Philip once again travelled on the continent, as did two of Lily's brothers a couple of years later, seeking contracts for their glassworks, and for the planned glassworks in Haifa, but also seeking ways, through the business, to help some Jewish acquaintances and associates whose future looked desperately insecure. Many German Jews believed the threat a temporary setback, however, and did not accept help before it was too late.

Although Lily did not describe Germany in *Tube*, she wrote it as a direct response to the threat that German Jews faced. The novel was, of course, to prove prescient (as was to be the case, horribly for Lily, with her fourth novel, *The Samaritan*), but the experiment – in which she tried a new way of exploring political questions – was not a success: reviewers were more perplexed by the book's structure than attentive to its purpose, and they did not note the warning.

Nevertheless, the publication of *Tube* brought her to the attention of new readers, which had compensations. Between visits to Palestine and to the continent, Lily regularly returned to Wales to see family and friends – her sister in Cardiff, now the mother of four children, and her brother Moss and his family in Swansea. She also retained her social and press connections in Wales, and in the autumn of 1935, the Welsh journal *Y Ford Gron* introduced her in a detailed profile under the heading 'Iddewes sy'n Gymraes' – 'a Jewess who's a Welshwoman', and in the same issue rather belatedly reviewed *My Mother's House*. Not surprisingly the review focused on the novel's parallel Welsh and Jewish message about the need to embrace rather than reject one's ethnic, national and cultural background and identity. The only criticism by the reviewer, 'Y Meudwy', was the misspelling of Welsh words ('iath' instead of 'iaith', 'Saesneg' instead of 'Saeson').[111]

A later issue of the magazine included a translation into Welsh of a section of *My Mother's House* which had been excluded from the published novel for reasons of length. Few if any had observed of the novel the unusually interesting detail of Simon's almost accidental marriage to Jani, a girl from the Welsh colony in Patagonia, although the reviewer in the *Western Mail* had noted Jani's Welsh identity.

But in this Welsh-language context, Jani and her father, 'Lloyd Patagonia', were of particular interest, and it was a more extended portrait of Lloyd Patagonia that was translated and published in *Y Ford Gron*.[112]

Typically of a Welsh-language publication at that time, the profile of Lily established her Welsh credentials by virtue of her fluency in Welsh: 'Bydd yn newydd i lawer ddeall mai Cymraes lân o ran iaith, er mai Iddewes o ran gwaed, yw Mrs Lily Tobias, awdur amryw ramantau poblogaidd' – 'it will be news to many to learn that Mrs Lily Tobias, author of several popular romances, is a pure Welshwoman by language, although she is a Jewess by blood.'

The author provided a brief summary biography about Lily's birth in Swansea, her businessman-father's move to Ystalyfera, her marriage to Philip and their residence in Rhiwbina in Cardiff, and reported that in a letter he received from Lily, she indicated that although she'd been living in London for some years, she still thought of Wales, and retained a connection with people from Ystalyfera. 'Pan ymwelodd côr Ystalyfera amryw weithiau â Llundain, cefais yn eu mysg amryw hen ffrindiau, ac fe ddaethant â bore fy oes yn gryf i'm meddwl,' she wrote – 'When the Ystalyfera choir sometimes visited London, among them I had several old friends, and my early life came strongly to mind.'

But Lily had been quick to reiterate the Welsh and Jewish connections that she had explored in *The Nationalists and Other Goluth Studies* and in *My Mother's House*. 'Ond ar wahân i gysylltiadau personol, y mae ymdrechion cenedlaethol y Cymry lawer ohonynt yn eiddof innau,' she wrote – 'But aside from personal connections, many of the national struggles of the Welsh are my own.'[113]

That political interest out of which she wrote certainly contributed to some limitations in style, but for the most part, though *Tube* had been somewhat risky and experimental, Lily wasn't interested in literary innovation, in the new modernist forms emerging at that time, nor in the reinvention of language. Instead she wanted to bring to the modern romance the heightened drama of political idealism, of dying for a cause – and, conversely, to bring to the didactic or polemical tract the drama of romance, of individual love, representing the ways that political engagement played out in individual rather than collective struggles. Or, as Angela Ingram and Daphne Patai so succinctly put it about a whole generation of women writers in the 1930s whose political focus rendered them quickly unfashionable, the concern 'was not to find new ways to express new forms of consciousness but rather to expose the resilience of old forms of consciousness that prevailed then and that still prevail today'.[114] So Lily brought together in *My Mother's House* and in *Eunice Fleet* the style of the popular modern romance that was typical of the post-war generation of women writers, and the political struggle that typified the proletarian fiction of her contemporary, Lewis Jones, in his didactic novels *Cwmardy* and *We Live*, or of B. L. Coombes in *These Poor Hands*. And like them, she struggled to find a literary voice that could convey the pathos of human experience and the pungency of political statement, struggled to make credible what was somewhat incredible, and to write against the grain of what was popular in that interwar period.

With *Tube*, Lily tried something new, moving away from the overtly political, and creating a fabular and slightly hallucinatory experience of riding on the London Underground, and plunging into what we would now call her characters' back-stories – but what back-stories! A revolutionary stalking a Welsh government minister who has lost his political way and is about to sell out; a red-haired girl descended from a Jewish woman tortured in the Spanish Inquisition; a German-Jewish woman who has been hounded and tortured by the Nazis. Lily was also writing a great deal about her own imagination as a novelist: through her protagonist Angela, who projects herself into other people's lives, imagining characters and experiences, Lily let herself explore what she herself was doing as a writer.

Nine

Palestine at last

In the autumn of 1970, when she was eighty-three years old, Lily looked out over Haifa Bay from the tiled terrace where she took her breakfast – 'an Israeli breakfast, cream cheese with the home-grown peach that follows our spring avocado or, when neither are in season, the perennial olive' – and closed her eyes and recalled Rehov Hatishbi as it had been thirty-six years earlier, when she first saw the plot her father had bought on Mount Carmel. The land had belonged to a monastery on the French Carmel, and had been sold to the Palestine Land Development Company, which purchased land throughout the country and sold it on to the Jewish Agency for Jewish settlement.

Rehov Hatishbi was 'neither street nor road or scarcely a track', at that time in the early 1930s, she recalled. 'Half a gate still hung on its hinges when I entered, turning from the Stella Maris woodland path that led to the monastery on the cliff, to scramble over a wilderness of thornbush and boulder.' There was an expanse of purple sage and nut trees in the fields and wadis, which were peopled only by an occasional shepherd and his goats or cows. She saw again the wildflowers that briefly appear there in spring – red anemones and pale pink cyclamen, and irises – and heard again the sound of jackals in the wadi.

By 1970 it was all gone – the unimpeded view of the Mediterranean, and of 'the mosque silhouetted beside a palm on a distant hill', visible from her balcony, but also less picturesque images, too: 'dark patches from which shadowy knife-handed figures might spring as one walked home late on the lampless roadway.' The wilderness of the mountain slope, once land belonging to the monastery, had been tamed, fenced in, paved over, built up and lit – and, of course, named. The area was now a network of roads, and Villa Merhavia on Rehov Hatishbi had become part of a new neighbourhood built to accommodate the rapidly growing population of Haifa, which had been augmented by the huge influx of new immigrants during and after the Israeli war of independence in 1948.

Lily, writing about these memories in a nostalgic article published in a Cardiff Jewish journal called *CAJEX*, in the winter of 1970, described how her thoughts were interrupted by a drone that became a throbbing overhead: it was a helicopter, bringing wounded soldiers from the border to the hospital. 'I can no longer relax in the peaceful morning,' she wrote. 'There is no peace. I go inside and gaze at the ancestral portraits on my walls. The most recent is that of my father, who realised his life's dream in this "Merhavia"– a family home in the Land of Israel. Further back are the Vallentines, notables of Anglo-Jewry for several generations, among them a founder of the London Jewish Chronicle … the two of them who face me in their Victorian garb were the grandparents of my husband, who came to forge his own link in the historic chain.'[115]

In 1936, Lily and Philip had left their comfortable

London house, 'Havilah', and sailed for Palestine. From then on, Villa Merhavia became Lily's home, which she and Philip initially shared with Lily's elderly father during the final two years of his life (and, for a short time, with Lily's young niece Huldah Abse, who looked after Tobias). It was the family home, presided over by Tobias, the white-bearded patriarch. He, near the end of his long life, had wanted to die in Palestine, where his wife was buried, and Lily and Philip wanted to begin a new form of work for a Jewish homeland, so their interests and needs were of mutual benefit. No doubt the elderly Tobias would not have been able to make such a move on his own, while his support of the business expansion, and his provision of a home for them in the large villa he'd had built suited Lily and Philip's social and domestic needs.

Villa Merhavia was a spacious, elegant pink stucco building with a beautiful view of the sweep of Haifa Bay, and was large enough to accommodate separate living quarters for Lily and Philip, and for one or other of Lily's sisters and brothers-in-law and other members of the family who lived there for periods of time. Lily managed that large home for them, and wrote in her book-lined study, and Philip was director of the new branch of the business. Although there were occasional fallings out – as with Lily's older brothers Moss and Barnett early on – the Shepherds were in many ways a traditionally tight-knit Jewish family, retaining close relationships and working together in the various branches of the family business.

Villa Merhavia would remain Lily's home for the rest of her long life – a home that she would almost lose on several occasions through conflicts with her sister, and through conflicts with the British authorities, but to which she clung doggedly, and to which she kept going back.

Through 1935, the Palestine branch of the family's successful glassworks had been taking off, with funding secured from new investors and the raising of business loans. In November of that year, the *Palestine Post* reported on the investment of £15,000 in Philip's new glass business: it would be known as 'the Palestine Plate Glass and Paint Works (Shepherd, Tobias and Co.) Ltd., Haifa', and was to be built in the industrial zone of Haifa Bay, on land belonging to the Jewish National Fund. Although elsewhere in Palestine there was minimal investment in big infrastructure projects, and those related to security, the harbour in Haifa, completed in 1933, was strategically important, and the growing port city, a truly multicultural part of Palestine where Arabs and Jews lived in close proximity, was the focus of industrial development by the British colonial authorities.[116]

All told, 1935 had been an extremely exciting year for Lily personally and as a writer, even though news at home and abroad was everywhere gloomy and hopeless. It was a difficult time for Jewish hopes in Palestine, for although inter-ethnic violence had abated somewhat, in the aftermath of the riots and massacre in 1929 the British government proposed to restrict Jewish immigration. Not long afterwards, things worsened precipitously for Jews in Germany, leading to large-scale emigration, while at home in Wales, the industrial life of the valleys suffered disaster after disaster in the aftermath of the crash in 1929, and the great Depression that followed through the 1930s created terrible poverty and hardship. Lily still had family in Wales, and was in touch with friends in the Swansea valley, and she wrote about the plight of Welsh miners in her final novel. Unemployed miners from Wales and the north of England were to be seen in London too, and they had made their way into her descriptions of the city in 1935, in *Tube*.

In 1936, however, Lily left all that behind. The cornerstone of the Palestine Plate Glass and Paint Works was laid on a Tuesday afternoon in March 1936. The *Palestine Post* reported on the ceremony, in which a document was placed for perpetuity under the cornerstone, recording the founding of the company. Among its specialities was the manufacture of 'Palmira' mirrors. Lily's brothers Isaac and Joseph were there, along with her father and other directors of the company. At the time, a lot of the demand for glass was met through imports to Palestine, and the directors of the new business, which initially intended to employ some twenty or thirty workers, hoped that the factory would in large part replace that reliance on imports. They also hoped, Philip among them, to be able to produce enough for export too. The family's involvement in the glass industry had travelled a long way from Tobias's first little paint and glass shop in Ystalyfera in the 1890s – but their roots in Wales continued long afterwards. It was no coincidence that Lily's article in a Cardiff journal in 1970, remembering the wilderness on Mount Carmel in the early 1930s, and the changes to Haifa over the years, should appear opposite an advertisement for 'Welsh Glass Works Limited, established 1913'. In 1970, the family business still had factory branches in Swansea, Cardiff and Newport.

Lily missed the laying of the cornerstone, for that spring she was ill, and by early summer had to undergo a routine operation that put her quite out of commission for another month. This was probably appendicitis, although perhaps not diagnosed as such (in later life, Lily had recurring intestinal and digestive trouble, as does her character Edith in her fourth novel *The Samaritan*: Edith has to return to England for treatment for appendicitis, and the descriptions are acute, suggesting Lily's rather close personal experience of the condition). Nevertheless, despite her illness, Lily soon recovered, and she and Philip travelled to Palestine not long afterwards, and together attended the dedication and opening of the factory that autumn.

Though they could not have known it at the time, the year that Lily and Philip moved to Palestine was to be the first in the three long years of the Arab revolt that started in April, just after the laying of the cornerstone of the glassworks. The revolt began with a strike, but soon would become increasingly violent, and would end up shaking British colonial rule in Palestine. At the time, however, despite grim news everywhere, Lily was full with exciting possibilities and change. She and Philip had begun to build a new, challenging shared life – Philip with his aspirations for developing Palestinian industry, and Lily as a writer.

Lily was forty-nine when this new phase of her life began. Now, after all she had committed to in person and in print, she had gone ahead and made the move to Palestine to be part of the Jewish national homeland project – to be something of a Jewish pioneer or colonist, but still within a British imperial framework. For Lily still saw herself at the time fundamentally as British: she was there as a British colonist and a British Jew, not as a Jew seeking an independent state in Palestine – or not yet. Even when her politics did shift, later, to opposition to British colonial rule, and later yet she became a citizen of the new Israeli state, she never abandoned her British citizenship, nor rejected her connections to the UK.

Though she had visited Palestine before 1936, she had not lived there, and the change now was comprehensive. She had grown up with financial insecurity and in straitened circumstances, and had seen poverty around her, but by the time she'd reached adulthood her family was prosperous and secure, and for years she'd lived a safe, settled, relatively easy and comfortable urban life. Now, from the dark smog of London, with its short, gloomy, wet and cold winter days, its coal-smoke and cabbage and cabs, she moved into the intense sunlight and heat of the Middle East, a place of sand and dust and flies, of often unremitting humidity, of a desert wind called the *chamsin* that sent everyone mad, and of cruel, miserable poverty and illness. She had changed climate, food, landscape – and above all, language, for Palestine was a Babel of Middle Eastern and European languages. It was also a place itself convulsed by a rapid rate of change, through immigration of Arabs and Jews, through investment, and through intense, hard labour. Haifa was being transformed – buildings and factories and workshops were going up; new roads replaced tracks; the docks replaced jetties, and industry expanded. There might be poverty, poor sanitation and endemic trachoma, but there were new health clinics, new agricultural practices, and new schools.

Along with the expansion of industry and agriculture, the Jewish settlers began to develop new cultural institutions. Lily had enjoyed London's vibrant theatres, restaurants and concert halls, piano recitals and literary salons and cabarets, and now she began to enjoy and contribute to the development of the cultural life of Jewish Palestine. Soon she began to write reviews of performances for the English-language press in Palestine, and she was a lifelong supporter and patron of the Palestine Symphony (after 1948 renamed the Israel Philharmonic Orchestra) from its beginnings. Lily had always loved the piano, and one of the threads running through *My Mother's House*, which she would take up more fully in its sequel, *The Samaritan*, was the story of Jewish concert pianist Lena, and her ambiguous relationship with Palestine. (Lily herself played, and she owned a Steinway, which she left in her will to the Dounie Weizman Conservatory of Music in Haifa – Gita Dunie Weizman, sister of Chaim Weizmann, was a close friend of hers.)

Palestine was home, either temporarily or permanently, to an extraordinary array of Jewish émigré musicians, artists, writers and thinkers from Europe, and she opened her home to them, holding a salon in Villa Merhavia that attracted many prominent cultural figures in the late 1930s. Lily had to build up her social life by stages, making new connections both within the Jewish community and with the British administrative and military staff and their families. Social life was mostly segregated, however – she and other newly arrived Jews had little exposure to urban Palestinian Arab intellectual or cultural life, which, like its Jewish counterpart, was flourishing. Like many Jews focused on the building up of Jewish 'national' institutions, she was largely unaware of that Arab culture, both because of barriers of language and social convention, but also because of imperial and racial assumptions and prejudices about Arabs as primitive 'natives'. Although through formal British affairs she came into contact with Arab dignitaries and civil servants, the Arab world did not engage her interest: it was Jewish life that Lily focused on, in all its new variety and colour, and the people she socialised with were primarily either familiarly Jewish or British (and American), or both.

Soon, however, the position of British Jews in Palestine became more complicated: the Arab population came under ever greater pressure through land sales, the growing landlessness of the fellaheen, and increasing Jewish immigration, and relations between Arabs and Jews deteriorated. To Zionists, the British response to these problems looked increasingly like intransigence, hypocrisy and double-dealing, and as suspicion and hostility grew, what had been a privileged position for British Jews became, increasingly, a liability – something that Lily would write about in some detail in *The Samaritan*.

Lily had come to Palestine to help in what she and Philip viewed idealistically as the building up of a Jewish national home, but although in her writing she could be unnervingly prescient about some things, she could not see that what was the fulfilment of hope for Jews would be the fulfilment of dread for Palestinian Arabs. Most Zionists and supporters of Zionism saw Jewish settlement in Palestine as a 'return' of Jews to their ancestral homeland. It was, they believed, their inheritance, and theirs by right – both moral right and the legal right conferred by the promise of the Balfour Declaration. It should not be restricted by arbitrary British Mandate edicts, nor by what they saw as the groundless claims of Arab residents or recent arrivals – although some, like Ahad Ha'am, had been more sensitive to the existing

Arab population of Palestine. As conditions for Jews in Germany worsened, Zionists increasingly felt that a Jewish national home in Palestine was not only theirs by right, but by necessity, too.

Lily had grown up with a confident belief in the benign and beneficent values of British society and of the British Empire, and she therefore didn't see anything contradictory about supporting a Jewish national revival in Palestine, and the colonialism that enabled it to happen. In the quite typical imperial worldview of her time, she saw Palestine as a place where British and Jewish 'development' could bring nothing but benefit to a neglected, backward and slothful 'East'.

For Lily, Jewish 'redemption' of the land, the Jewish development of health and welfare services, and the influx of Jewish capital, modern ideas, and methods of agriculture, industry and education, were gifts for all who would welcome them; likewise she saw those who did not welcome them in the typical British colonial understandings of the time as fanatical. That, at least, was how she had seen it before she moved to Palestine – and how she had expressed it in her early idealistic articles about Zionism, and through her protagonist Edith in *My Mother's House*.

Living in Palestine, she found that the reality was more complex, and more challenging, than some of those 'benevolent' British colonial ideas allowed. Almost as soon as she settled in Haifa, in that house with its peaceful vista of sea and wadi, she had to struggle to make sense of the violent conflict of the Arab revolt, which would continue unabated for three bloody years of attack and counter-attack, assaults, bombings, hijackings and murders, leaving the British Mandatory authority overstretched – and the general population, both Arab and Jew, vulnerable, frightened and traumatised. In the early stages of the revolt, however, she was still hopeful, and in her difficult and ambitious fourth novel, *The Samaritan: An Anglo-Palestinian Novel*, she tried to show what the people of the place shared rather than what separated or distinguished them.

Lily had the idea for the novel early in 1936, while she was still in London, and she began to sketch it out before she fell ill in the spring. After her recovery, and her move to Palestine later that year, her progress with the book was held up once again, this time by bereavement, for in the spring of the following year her father died. He was by then elderly, but though he had realised his hope of living and dying in Palestine, his death was a savage loss. Lily had adored and respected her father, and had been close to him all her life: they had shared a Zionist vision and commitment, and had realised part of it together.

Despite her grief, she was able to return to writing, and completed the first half of *The Samaritan* later that year, before she travelled back to the UK to see her family, spending some months there in what would become an annual late summer or autumn visit to England and Wales. After she returned home again to Haifa, she began to work on the second half of the novel in the spring and early summer of 1938, and roughly drafted the final chapter in June.

She had many distractions, though: she was beginning to write reviews and articles for the *Jewish Chronicle* and for the English-language press in Palestine, although, with Philip's successful business, she did not depend on the work for an income to maintain her. Her articles that year included an account of the final sitting of the Peel Commission in Jerusalem, which was set up in response to the disturbances in early 1936, and which resulted in the first recommendation to partition Palestine into Arab and Jewish states. Lily attended the sittings, travelling to Jerusalem regularly for both political and cultural events and happenings. She was distracted by her growing social life in Haifa as well: she attended and held receptions, and supported many educational and charitable institutions and initiatives, fulfilling a conventionally British role for the wife of a successful and prominent businessman, and a member of the establishment. After visiting a school in the old quarter in Haifa, she wrote about the social welfare efforts among the city's poor Jewish children – those of long standing, and more recent arrivals from north Africa and elsewhere in the Middle East.

In May that year, she also held a reception for the Peace Army, an English initiative by pacifists associated with the No-Conscription Fellowship and the Fellowship of Reconciliation, which proposed to intervene in international conflicts with unarmed passive resisters. The connection with Lily derived from her old No-Conscription Fellowship friendships and associations – Maude Royden and Joyce Pollard, the Peace Army's President and Chairman, were visiting Palestine to see what could be done about developing an anti-militarist solution to the growing conflict. The reception included such literary luminaries as the German-Jewish writer Arnold Zweig, and various members of the British establishment.

By 1938, Lily had 'arrived' socially, and her home had become a desirable destination in the genteel British and

American social round in Palestine – but she and Philip were also noted progressive socialists, part of the strongly leftwing atmosphere of Jewish immigrant culture in those years.

It is no surprise that *The Samaritan* was quite long in the making: it was a challenging task to pick up the threads of the narrative and the lives of characters from *My Mother's House*, but still make the work stand on its own. The novel begins more than a decade after Simon's death at the close of *My Mother's House*. Edith, his widow, now thirty-five and the mother of his twins, a boy and a girl, is living in Palestine, still trying to carry on the work that first brought her there as a nurse. The novel opens with a scene of violence – the massacre of Jews by Muslims in Safed, in the Galilee. That massacre, on the 24th of August 1929, was part of several days of violence throughout Palestine that broke out after rumours spread that Jews were taking over the Al Aqsa Mosque in Jerusalem, where tensions had been running high. There were riots in Jerusalem, and Jews were also massacred in Hebron. In the aftermath there was outrage that the British had refused to let Jews be armed in self-defence, or to offer police or military protection or reinforcement.

On that August day in 1929 in Safed, a mob from outside the town rushed into the ancient Jewish Quarter and murdered men, women and children. In the novel, Edith tries and fails to protect a girl from the violence, and after such a traumatic experience suffers a nervous breakdown. She has anyway been assailed by recurrent abdominal trouble, and she is persuaded to return with her children to England for treatment and rest. In the riot, Edith is protected from the violence by a boy called Musa, a Samaritan, and she takes him on as a kind of ward, bringing him with her and her children back to the UK.

Through Edith's sense of some terrible evil at work, in this opening section in Palestine, Lily set up the ominous foreshadowing of what was to come later: the uprising that would begin in 1936. Edith reflects on how things had been relatively quiet in Palestine since the previous outbreak of violence in 1921, but now in 1929 is overwhelmed and full of dread that violence has returned – the tragedy that she feels is "'hatred. The spirit of hatred let loose.'"[117] Though she is persuaded to go back to Britain for treatment, Edith is determined to return to Palestine, and embarks on the sea voyage with reluctance.

Lily describes the journey by ship that she knew so well, where passengers boarded at Haifa and stopped along the way at Alexandria. The scenes on board feature a representative array of passengers – British civil servants and military wives and children, antiquity hunters and archaeologists, Jewish émigrés, and that in-between group of people to which Lily belonged: well-to-do British Jews. Neither quite one thing or the other, British Jews in Palestine were both a privileged part of the colonial establishment, and at the same time not quite one hundred per cent British, but, unlike the immigrants from other countries, were also not entirely free to repudiate or shake off British political positions, understandings and assumptions. In the case of Edith's 'set' this is a gentry group, rather than the new middle class – her grandmother is Lady Hafod, who owns estates in Wales and Devon, and it is among this minor gentry of Lily's imagination that Edith moves socially. As with *My Mother's House*, however, Lily also wove in varied

Jewish and Welsh social scenes, featuring Edith's other grandmother, a pious, gentle continental Jewish immigrant in London, and members of Simon's family who are still in Wales (although they are about to move to America).

As always, Lily compared Wales and Palestine. In the first section, set in Palestine, she attributed to English and Welsh officials and soldiers sharply opposing attitudes to being there: an English soldier, desperate to be home, is caustic about everyone – '"Blasted women! Blasted niggers! Blasted sheenies!"… Bad enough to stew in this filthy hole when all was quiet, the natives behaving themselves, and only an impudent colonist poking his nose in occasionally.'[118] The 'colonist' here is a Jewish colonist, and the 'natives' are Arab, but the whole seething, stinking, sweaty lot of them and 'the reeking cobbles of this arid mountain-side, sucked eternally by the Eastern sun' are all dismissed with disgust. In contrast, Isaac Tudur Watkins, an official in the Mandate administration, is drawn to it all. 'The little brisk figure with the shrewd hatchet-face and the lank dark hair could only be a Welshman,' Edith reflects, 'and the accent of his plaintively-modulated voice could only be that of a particular village of South Wales.' He is, indeed, from Blaemawe, Lily's fictional name for Ystalyfera. As he explains to Edith:

'Next to dear old Wales, I always wanted to be in the Land of the Bible. When I was in Sunday School I could draw a map of the land from Dan to Beersheba, easier than I could draw the mountains of Wales. Indeed, I never troubled much about Snowdon and Cader Idris until I was grown up and went for a holiday to Machynlleth. But when I was ten I could tell our minister where the Valley of Jezreel was ... And the shape of the hills of Gilboa and the Carmel were plain to my eyes as they are now.'[119]

Edith notes 'the warm Welsh kinship, which she welcomes', but wonders: 'full as it was of Biblical bonds, did it strain at the new dispensation?' She asks him, but Isaac is unwilling to talk about his understanding of that week of violence against Jews in 1929, and of the British response to it.

Back in Wales, in the novel's third section, it is Edith's Samaritan ward Musa who notices similarities and differences: 'The change of speech struck his keen ear. He had learned already that another race inhabited the British principality that was once a separate kingdom', and he is intensely curious and wants to know: 'Had the Welsh merged into the English? Did their common tongue supersede the Celtic vernacular? Were their institutions, their system of religion and education, identical? Was there complete political equity?'[120] Edith describes Wales as 'the little country – "no larger" – she quoted inversely the famous parallel – "than the Land of Israel ... There are many Welshmen to whom it *is* the Land of Israel, since they believe they are descended from one of the Lost Tribes."'[121] Musa treats this as an exaggeration until he sees, 'in driving through the valleys, a chain of chapels called Zion, Bethel, Jerusalem, Carmel, and other familiar place-names of Palestine', and he is astonished to see that 'the little dark people are just like Jews'.

Edith is more concerned about the effect of the Depression. 'Everywhere was evidence of a stagnant and derelict life. Docks were idle, pitheads deserted, factories

1. The synagogue, Siemiatycze, Poland, c. 1925. Lily's parents left the town in the late nineteenth century. © Special Collections, College of Charleston Library.

2. The old Ysgol y Wern/Y Wern School, Ystalyfera, which Lily attended as a girl. Courtesy of Gordon Williams and Ystalyfera Electronic Archive Research Group/History and Heritage of Ystalyfera.

3. Portrait of Lily and her husband Philip Vallentine Tobias after their marriage in 1911.

4. Lily with her nephew Leo Abse, Rhiwbina, Cardiff, early 1920s.
© Leo Abse Estate. Supplied by Llyfrgell Genedlaethol Cymru/The National Library of Wales.

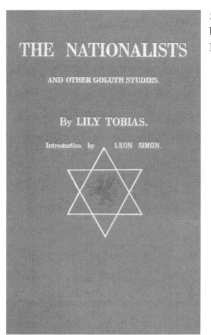

5. The cover of Lily's first book, published by C. W. Daniel in 1921.

6. Anna-Baila Shepherd's grave, Mandate Palestine, c. 1926. Tobias Shepherd (front left) and three other members of Lily's family. The Hebrew inscription reads 'Chana Beila Shepherd of Cardiff, England'.

7. Lily and Philip in London, early 1930s.

(13)

[He nods his head sideways at his colleagues, winking and pursing his lips, as if to invite approval of a crushing phrase.)

Victor (pleasantly) It does, with me. My political and moral views are alike. I think the war is the result of a wrong political conception, which means to me a wrong human outlook, morally and spiritually. I am concerned with the welfare of the masses in every country. I regard war in general as a stupid and inefficient method of settling international disputes. I regard it also as organised murder. And I cannot in any circumstances be a party to murder, or pledge myself to commit it.

Clergyman. Surely you would defend your country if it were invaded?

Victor. Not by military means. I believe there would be no invasion if there were no preparations for military defence.

Lawyer. What nonsense. Do you mean to say if we had no army and no navy, the enemy wouldn't march in?

Victor. Yes. An unarmed population gives no provocation and creates no fear. Without provocation and without fear, there can be no enemy and no invasion.

8. A page from Lily's unpublished play, 'Where Have I Seen You Before?' (1933) based on her novel, *Eunice Fleet*.

9. The grave of Lily's father, Tobias Shepherd. Haifa Old Cemetery, Mandate Palestine, 1936. © Leo Abse Estate. Supplied by Llyfrgell Genedlaethol Cymru/The National Library of Wales.

10. Lily and her sister Freda, in Haifa, Mandate Palestine, 1947. © Leo Abse Estate. Supplied by Llyfrgell Genedlaethol Cymru/The National Library of Wales.

11 and 12. Two portraits of Lily taken during her stay in South Africa in the early 1940s.

13. and 14. Lily reading and in a light-hearted mood.

פ״נ

לילי טוביאס

לבית שפרד

כ״ח ניסן תשמ״ד
LILY TOBIAS
ת נ צ ב ״ה

IN LOVING MEMORY

15. 'Here lies Lily Tobias, of the Shepherd family, 28 Nisan 5744' (30 April 1984). Haifa New Cemetary, Israel.

and workshops closed, furnaces extinguished. Men stood about in queues at labour exchanges, and at gates where any job was offered. Others sauntered hopelessly about the streets, or leaned in apathetic silence against walls. Melancholy towns and still more melancholy villages were full of anxious and disheartened faces.' Visiting a work settlement in the valleys, she deplores 'the wreckage of an active and thriving community'.[122]

In the earlier second part of the novel, 'Journey Back', which takes place on board ship and in Egypt, Lily presented a range of hostile and ambivalent British attitudes to non-intervention in Palestine, and now in the third part, 'England' (notwithstanding that part of it is set in Wales), she explored ideas of the English gentry and English values. Here Edith begins to wonder about her status as an English Jew, though the question had arisen before she'd left Palestine. She had discovered that Saadi, the local Arab policeman, whose wife and son she had treated as a nurse years before, had known in advance of the coming trouble, and had sent his family away. Saadi reassured her, telling her that she and her children and friends were in no danger, but she'd asked, 'am I and my family to be protected as English people? Shall we not be protected as Jews?'[123]

Now, in England, Edith's uncertainty deepens. London moves and distresses her:

The great old buildings and streets, black-fronted, dignified, the later erections with their smooth, light walls, already streaked, already absorbed into the dark old heart of London, stood with an air of immovable, powerful strength. It was a power rooted far and deep, in generations of established life. And so it gave forth this sense of order, of stability, of a profound, rockfast, unimpressionable base. A sense that beat down oddly upon the daughter of Britannia, raw from a pioneer struggle to create and renew ... in it there was not only contrast, but both comfort and dismay. From this mother-source should have come help and sustenance, not thwarting and obstruction. Every step and foster-child was entitled to such aid, in the legitimate effort to find its own feet. 'England promised us,' Esther Hart had cried, that awful day in the hills of the Maccabees. Here at the core of England's mighty heart, throbbing steadily, sending a vital strength through tremendous arteries, one felt the warmth of blood and the bulwark of the parent body.[124]

Edith, seeing this 'Englishness', and feeling acutely its failure to make good on promises, and to support and embrace her, an English Jew in Palestine, is more deeply troubled by its confluence with the revelation of poverty in Wales, but also visible in London, and she begins to wonder for the first time whether that impregnable fastness is built upon deprivation, whether the one is a necessary part of the other, and whether the only solution is, effectively, revolution – to 'cut the threads of human systems'. She worries, though, whether this is possible without 'cutting veins, without bloodshed, without civil and international law'. She wonders, 'Could one cling to such a stronghold, and at the same time wish it destroyed?'[125]

As in *My Mother's House*, Lily set Edith and Jack, a secular socialist Jew, against each other in argument over Palestine. Edith tells him that though things are bad for Jews in Poland, "they are uglier still in Germany." "Oh, Hitler and his crew,"

Jack responds. "Another major blessing of the war, or the peace. But *they* won't amount to much. When things improve economically, the scum will die down." Edith is less sure. "I hope so, but I'm afraid not," she tells him. "A German friend of mine – not a Jew – believes that Jews will soon be hunted out of Germany." Jack is blasé: "Then they can go to Palestine," he says. "That'll make *you* happy, if not them, eh?" But Edith is quick to correct him. "It's not quite so simple, Jack," she explains. "The gates are not open. With the proposed new Commission – oh, these eternal Commissions! – there has been a suspension of immigration. You haven't an idea of what that means to the present waiting list – not to speak of a future one!"[126]

Soon, Jack's views begin to change. He and Edith together attend an Oswald Mosley rally in London, and the scene vividly evokes the atmosphere of Mosley and his fascist Blackshirts' gatherings. In a disturbance at the rally, Jack is seriously injured, and later, in the final fourth part of the novel, 'Palestine', he comes to stay with Edith and recuperate at the nursing home that she's set up near a collective farm in the Jezreel Valley.

Lily's writing of the novel changed course as the unfolding events of the present, in 1936, 1937 and 1938, became more pressing than her original plans: inter-ethnic violence and hatred, which, in the final part of the novel, as in her early stories, she attributed to outsiders and trouble-makers, was beginning to destroy the tentative trust and connection between peoples. Though she was also telling the story of Edith's growing connection with Jack, which provides a romantic tension throughout the book, the urgency of British intransigence intervened, and in the novel Lily tried to explain the predicament of Jews in Palestine, and to appeal for sympathy from British readers. Edith's son David complains that "people in England howl about the expense of British soldiers defending Jews – all the time our hands are tied – they don't know how much we want to be allowed to defend ourselves. But no, we mustn't lift a finger to a trigger, while the bandits get away with every dirty trick." It's enough, he feels, to make one give up, were it not for "what we have at stake. The right of Jews to live in Palestine after dying for it." Edith tells him, "Your father would have agreed with that." But her daughter objects. "I thought he died for England," she says. "It's the same thing," Edith replies, indicating, perhaps, Lily's imperial view at the time of Palestine as legitimately a British colony.

Musa intercedes in the squabble. "Let's leave the British out of it," he says. "This is a matter for Arab and Jew." "The matter being," retorts David, "that Arabs keep on killing Jews." "Arab kills Arab also," Musa tells him. "But it will end when Jew and Arab become comrades." Edith believes that "cooperation is the best way," but Musa proposes that "the two peoples must fuse." When pressed on what he means, he says, "In every way ... They come of the same stock. Their separate ways have created a gulf that is not insuperable. In former eras the two cultures assimilated. With a common economic level and standard of education..." He acknowledges that it would be difficult to make it happen, and suggests that "it may be easier for them to accept a driving force from without – or rather, a force which is outside both peoples and yet partakes of each."

Edith asks where he sees such a force, and he replies: "In the remnant of Israel, that has never left the land – that has guarded the ancient way of Jew and Arab with faith and fidelity – in the mountains of Samaria." Musa means, of course, his own ethnic group, the Samaritans.

When violence breaks out in their own community, Saadi, the Arab policeman, is killed and thrown, like rubbish, on the dung heap. It is Musa the Samaritan – who has spent time both in the Jewish collective farm, with the English and American Jews of Edith's household, and in the neighbouring Arab village – who tries to build bridges, and sets out to bury the murdered policemen, Saadi. He is accosted by a group of young Arab men, who attack him with stones. At the close of the novel, Lily described Musa's almost Christian martyrdom: 'Jews and Arabs were standing together, brothers with heads bowed in a strange truce, the sons of Israel and the sons of Ishmael. The corpse of a murdered policeman lay in the dust at their feet. And between them, hostage or deliverer, was borne the body of the Samaritan.'[127]

Lily invested in Musa what she thought was the best of Christian, Muslim and Jewish belief, and of Arab and Jewish character, and created in that blend a kind of pure and innocent visionary of peaceful coexistence. She had plenty of choices when it came to idealising a cultural or ethnic identity, the way she did Musa's. Muslim, Jew and Christian were only the broadest of terms or distinctions – within each, in Palestine, there were numerous denominations and ethnic groupings. She had closest contact, of course, with Jews and with British Christians, but her contact with Muslims was circumscribed, and in the novel she presented a typical British imperial view of most Arabs as 'natives'.

Nevertheless, in her articles she also indicated unease about 'native' Jews, which is to say members of the longstanding Palestinian Jewish communities, but also Jewish immigrants from other Arab countries, who, with their dark colouring, 'superstitions', and alien ways, including speaking Arabic as a first language, were just as disturbingly different and uncomfortably 'primitive'. Saadi, the policeman in *The Samaritan*, is a noble, troubled and divided figure – but otherwise she described most Arabs in terms of the picturesque indolent squalor of the East, or as loping, slinking, sullen and ominous figures threatening possible violence. Sadly, experience reinforced her circumscribed view of Arabs, both at the time, and later.

In Palestine there was a rich, brightly-coloured patchwork of cultural groups, both major and minor, and among all these Lily chose for her idealised martyr not a member of her own religion and ethnicity, but a member of the ancient Samaritans.

Lily was not the first to idealise Samaritans as a kind of pure, original Jewish community – she had for her source material the work of a Welshman, the Reverend John Mills. His book *Three Months' Residence in Nablus, and an account of the Modern Samaritans* was published in Wales in 1864; for a long time afterwards it remained one of the few accounts in the UK of modern Samaritan culture. By the 1930s, when Lily first encountered living Samaritans, they constituted a very small, tightly-bounded community of a few hundred people in Nablus, where Mount Gerizim was their holy centre.[128] Samaritan beliefs and practices differ from mainstream forms of Judaism, and Jewish religious authorities do not recognise them as Jews. Over the centuries they suffered persecution both by Christian and Jewish rulers for their adherence to their own texts and practices. Lily absorbed Mills's idealised portrayal of Samaritanism and transformed it through Musa. Sadly, however, her hope for the possibilities of peaceful cooperation and coexistence represented in that figure was about to be destroyed.[129]

In June 1938, as she was finishing her draft of the novel, the violence of the revolt came close to home. That month, in an article entitled 'Terror on Carmel', she described what was happening in her own neighbourhood, recounting how she had followed a route where, just an hour earlier, a bus full of passengers had been fired on. 'It was with some uneasiness that I drove along the dark road,' she wrote, 'between clumps of pines and rocky wastes.' She arrived safely at her destination, which was a party held in aid of Haifa schoolchildren. There she met someone who'd been in the bus and who casually and nonchalantly described the incident to her – though fired on, she hadn't even bothered to duck. 'Almost every night afterwards for a week,' Lily wrote, 'the shootings were repeated, at the same time and about the same spot. Police were posted around, armoured cars escorted each bus along the firing-route, and searchlights played on the hills. Sometimes passengers were injured even when they ducked. Always the gunmen got away.'[130]

This was just one site and one incident among many; all around them the unease was high, but Lily focused not on solutions or causes but on the resilience and breezy toughness of Jews getting on with their everyday lives despite the ever-present possibility of ambush or attack. The revolt affected everyone, with curfews and searches, but Jews in particular felt the authorities were not doing enough to curb the threat to them by Arab insurgents. Lily's article was a polemical piece, intended to rally Jewish readers, but also to elicit sympathy.

She sent the article in to the *Palestine Review*, and began work again on the novel – and then, on July 11th, towards the end of that hot summer day, she learned the terrible news that just a few miles away, her husband Philip had himself become one of the victims of the Arab revolt, and had been caught by a group of young Arab men, and stabbed and stoned to death.

How must it have been for Lily, hearing the unexpected ring on her doorbell? In a letter to Leo, she described her delight when, years later, quite without warning, there was a ring at the bell, and she opened it expecting, she said, the postman, only to find Leo's brother Wilfred standing there. He had come to visit unannounced on a sudden day's leave from the army. Though Lily dwelled in her letter on her delight at seeing him, she was not able to disguise what had clearly been a kind of dread. How could a ring at the bell not forever afterwards bring back that unimaginable moment when she learned of her husband's murder?

Later in the day, she went to the morgue to identify Philip's remains. She was never afterwards free of the sight of his mutilated body, and nor was she free of the horror at the way he had died – or the knowledge of who had killed him. Her draft manuscript, which ended with a similar murder, had nevertheless contained the hope of cooperation and reconciliation between Arab and Jew. When, eventually, the following year she was able to return to the novel, to amend it and send it to her publisher, she knew it was flawed, but she could not substantially reshape it. 'Early in July a fresh holocaust of terror broke over Haifa and overwhelmed my life,' she wrote in the Author's Note. 'Almost a year went by before I could take up my pen to fill in a few bare outlines and revise some of the text. For any gaps or redundancies that remain I apologize. But my work must stand by its faithfulness to the spirit and matter of the scene in which it was originally composed.'

The dedication – 'In memory of Philip Vallentine Tobias who fell in Palestine July 11 1938, a sacrifice to the ideals that inspired this book' – was a dedication to her memory of those ideals, too. It was also a dedication to her destroyed hopes. For Lily, her novel *The Samaritan* became a terrible case of life imitating art, and to an extent that was true also of *Eunice Fleet*, *My Mother's House* and in some ways *Tube*. Traumatised by Philip's death, Lily never fully recovered, and afterwards she wrote no further fiction.

Ten

Murder and its aftermath

Lily's article, 'Terror on Carmel', appeared in the *Palestine Review* a few days after Philip's death. A note, appended just before going to press, explained that 'this article by Mrs. Tobias was in type before the news was received of the brutal murder of her husband in Haifa. His car was attacked by a group of thirty Arabs who dragged him out, and stabbed him to death, also injuring his companion, an employee.' The awfulness of the coincidence can have escaped no one who read it – and nor, when *The Samaritan* was published late the following year, could the tragedy of the novel's prescience.

That brief, somewhat inaccurate and dramatic description in the *Palestine Review* of Philip's murder mirrors the reporting in the immediate aftermath of the event. 'Fourteen Casualties in Haifa's Unabated Crime Wave', declared the headline on the front page of the *Palestine Post* the next day, followed by the subheading: 'Shots, Missiles and Knives: Prominent Industrialist Stabbed to Death by Mob.'[131] The paper reported that Philip had been stabbed to death near the Karaman quarry, on the Haifa-Afula road, and identified his foreman, Israel Geller, as 'an employee, Moshe Geller, 30'. The next day, a letter to the editor put the attack somewhere else – in the 'tin hut quarter' at the edge of the industrial zone – and argued that it was an unsafe, unsanitary area that facilitated criminal behaviour and needed to be cleared.[132] Under the headline 'Massacre at Haifa', the *Jewish Chronicle* reported that Philip had not only been stoned and stabbed but also shot.[133]

The *Palestine Post* was full of the news about Philip's murder, but also of the other numerous, escalating murderous attacks on Jews which that week of violence had brought – a particularly notable week in the long spate of bombings, shootings, stabbings and kidnappings that had been going on for two years. In the UK the papers were full of the news, too. Britain was losing control of Palestine, journalists argued. What was needed, one correspondent to the *Jewish Chronicle* suggested, citing an incident in Haifa a few days before Philip's murder, was the imposition of Martial Law.[134] The fact that Philip was British aroused particular indignation, but so too did British inaction. 'What law-abiding citizen can consider his life secure,' asked the Jerusalem correspondent of the *Jewish Chronicle*, 'when, to quote another British eye-witness, the unfortunate and much-lamented death of Mr. P. V. Tobias, of Haifa and Cardiff, at the hands of a berserk Arab mob *occurred within easy striking distance of a British police officer and several armed constables, who did not fire a shot when a defenceless man was being stabbed and battered to death*?'[135]

The *Palestine Post*, calling for a change of British tactics, and reviewing the violence of the previous week, warned that a policy of Jewish non-retaliation should not be misread – and soon enough there was to be retaliation, in a spiralling cycle of armed violence between the two groups in Palestine,

Arab and Jewish, and between both groups and the British authorities.

'With shock succeeding shock, and horror piling up on horror,' the *Palestine Post* writer commented,

> it is impossible not to stop long enough in this melancholy review to express the deepest sympathy with the widow on Mount Carmel and the family and friends in England and in Wales, at the cruellest of fates which has befallen them in the loss of Mr Tobias who, trusting in the British Mandate, exchanged London for Haifa, offering up his energies and his wealth, to be rewarded with the assassin's knife. And as in his life he wrought that others might live, so his death might, and we prayerfully hope it may, make life flower in this unhappiest of countries once more.[136]

The Manufacturers' Association of Palestine published a note in the *Palestine Post* extending their deepest sympathy to Lily and to those involved in Philip's business, the Palestine Plate Glass and Paint Works, known as the 'Palmira' works, after the Palmira mirrors that they manufactured. The *Post* listed the mayor of Haifa among the dignitaries who laid memorial wreaths at Philip's grave.

The day after his murder, a writer in the *Palestine Post* noted that Philip's home on Mount Carmel in Villa Merhavia had 'served as the meeting place of Haifa's workers in all good causes'.[137] On July 15th, in the column 'Notes of the Week', the *Jewish Chronicle* noted that 'English Jews have to mourn the brutal murder of one of their number, Mr. Philip Tobias, who was well-known in Communal circles, and will extend to his talented wife, Mrs.

Lily Tobias, the well-known novelist, their warmest sympathy.'[138]

Lily didn't stay on in Villa Merhavia for long. Two weeks later, in another echo of her novel, she boarded the S.S. *Sphinx* at the new bustling dock in Haifa, and began the arduous ocean voyage back to Britain, following the route taken by her protagonist Edith after Simon's death, and again, after the trauma of witnessing the massacre in Safed.

At first Lily took what solace and refuge she could with her family. In Cardiff, her sister Kate, who all her life remained close to her, and kept a framed photograph of Lily by her bed, looked after her and comforted her. Lily renewed her connection with Kate's daughter, Huldah, who, when she was sixteen, had come to Haifa to look after Lily's father in the last year of his life; and with Kate's three sons Wilfred, Leo and Dannie. It was a renewing of the connection with Leo in particular – he had spent time with Lily and Philip in Rhiwbina as a teenager, and later he would correspond with Lily and stay with her in Haifa while on leave during his military service in Egypt. Lily was also carefully looked after by her dearest brother, Joseph, a doctor with a practice in London; he was by then the father of Annabella, who had been named in memory of Joseph and Lily's beloved gentle and beautiful mother. Two other brothers were in London, too – David, and Isaac, whose daughter Naomi, like Dannie, would become a well-known writer.

Despite her shock and her intense grief, Lily found the wherewithal to pull herself together and somehow carry on. She was not yet able to face going back to Palestine to sort out practical matters arising in the wake of Philip's death, and before long a separate problem would also loom: the question of ownership of her home. The villa in Haifa had legally belonged to her father; it was he who had bought the land on which it was built, and when he had died intestate two years earlier, Lily and her siblings all had a legal share. It was a family property, jointly owned, and Lily and Philip shared the large house some of the time with her sister Fay and Fay's husband Jonas, but soon the absence of a will was to create conflicts over who had a right to live there. That was still to come, and would cause Lily a great deal of distress, but at the time of her return to the UK in the summer of 1938, she had no inkling of how Philip's death and her absence, then and subsequently, would undermine her claim to Merhavia as her home.

Philip's will had named her sole beneficiary of his personal cash assets, and Lily was left sufficiently comfortably provided for financially. The Haifa branch of the family business had borrowed heavily, however, and without Philip there to oversee operations, it soon ran into trouble, and creditors began to make demands. In the interim, her brothers, who, like Lily, were fellow directors and shareholders, were able to keep things going, and to shield her from practical worries while she tried to come to terms with the trauma of Philip's murder.

Lily stayed on in the UK for a year and a half, sustained by her family, but also by her sense of outrage, and her attempt to bring some kind of justice to bear on those who she believed were responsible for Philip's murder. All that she had expressed, through Edith, in *The Samaritan*, had come home to her acutely and violently – Philip had died in the service of an ideal, and to abandon it now would mean being unfaithful to his memory. Lily had been outraged at the British failure to protect Jews from attack in Palestine, an outrage that was now painfully personal, for the police had failed to protect Philip, and she held the government accountable. In September she secured a meeting with the Colonial Secretary, Malcolm MacDonald, and presented to him what she had learned – that Philip's murder could have been prevented if an Arab inspector named Hashem had done his duty and intervened in the angry scene. However, Inspector Hashem was alleged to have done nothing – and, as she understood it from the Jewish constable who'd witnessed events – he had in fact done worse: he had released the man who had been arrested for Philip's murder, and subsequently denied he'd ever had him in his custody.

At the time, the Palestine Police was a complex and unsatisfactory combination of British, Arab and Jewish officers, constables and auxiliaries. Lily's understanding of what had happened derived from the account given by a Jewish constable, Constable Horowitz, who claimed that he himself had apprehended a man he'd seen bent over Philip's body, and had handed him over to his superior officer, the Arab Inspector Hashem, before returning to try and help Philip. Later, when he saw Hashem and asked what had become of the prisoner, the Inspector disclaimed all knowledge of him. Lily presented this evidence to Malcolm MacDonald, the Colonial Secretary, who assured her he would look into it, but on the 8th of November he wrote saying that there was insufficient evidence to bring any action against Inspector Hashem, and that though she had his great sympathy, there was not anything more he could do.

Lily was dismayed, and responded at length some three weeks later, refusing to accept his conclusion. 'I have to thank you for your letter of the 8th,' she wrote to MacDonald. 'I have not acknowledged it until now, because I felt too bitterly the decision conveyed – and did not wish by writing hastily to reflect in any way on your own kind and I am sure sincere efforts in this matter. But I must tell you how impossible I find it to accept such a decision, at least without being more fully informed on what grounds it has been arrived at.' Despite that protestation, she never was given further information, nor the grounds on which the decision was reached. 'As I see it,' she continued, 'the word of Inspector Hashem has been taken against that of Constable Horowitz. That is, the word of an Arab superior officer, who failed in his duty of dispersing a mob near his station, where they were able with impunity to commit a crime some time *after* his arrival on the scene, and in fact while he absented himself at a quiet spot a little way off – against the word of a Jewish subordinate constable who performed his own duty. It is not only a question of the arrest and release of the Arab murderer of my husband. It is also a question of what was done or left undone by the Arab police who were on the scene of disturbance nearly ten minutes *before* my husband drove up.' Lily wondered how much information had been provided and considered: 'Have all these circumstances been placed fully and impartially before the High Commissioner and the Inspector-General of Police?' she asked. 'Were the latter furnished with an explanation by the local Police Superintendent – Mr James – of his refusal to pursue investigations on the spot and at the time?' She was careful to qualify the assertive questioning, by assuring him that she didn't wish to harass him unnecessarily, but, she went on, 'I have learned nothing to shake my conviction that had Inspector Hashem acted properly, my husband would have been saved. With this terrible conviction, I cannot be satisfied to know that such an officer is allowed to remain at his post, free under British administration to connive at further crime.' It was not just these circumstances that convinced her of Inspector Hashem's guilt, however. As she explained: 'I appreciate the fact that numbers of Arab police, known to be disloyal, have been replaced in recent weeks by British and Jewish members of the force. But this only makes it more strange and unacceptable, that the particular Arab officer who I, in common with many other responsible Haifa residents, know to be without honour or veracity, should be retained.' She ended on a rather contradictory note, expressing her intention 'to continue to protest, with all the spirit left to me, against the possibility that others may suffer as I have done', but thanking him for the 'personal courtesy and sympathy' that he had shown.[139]

The courtesy and sympathy expressed in Malcolm MacDonald's letters did little to comfort Lily. Philip's death haunted her, and her pursuit of justice did not provide further understanding or resolution. Nor was she allowed to forget it, either, for his death had received widespread coverage in the press, and she was known for a long period afterwards as the widow of the British Jew who had been so brutally murdered as a consequence of the shortcomings and failures of British Mandatory government policy.

It was a low and difficult time for Lily, but before very long she began again to engage in public affairs, and managed to write and publish a few articles, including, in October 1938, a rather harsh review of *Toward the Jaffa Gate*, by Marina Blount. Lily was an obvious choice to review this English novel set in Palestine, and she found it severely wanting. 'The situation is trite, although much of the setting is not,' she wrote. 'Yet Palestine is used so summarily that, like the map of that scarified country, its wastes are more conspicuous than its fertilities.' Lily went on to damn the writing with faint praise: 'The jog-trot pedestrian style sometimes achieves colour and vividness which is less in the pen than in the material,' she observed, and she found that its lack of engagement with anything beyond the English protagonists' desire for home made 'of the story at least a winter day's diversion.'[140]

Lily's engagement with Palestine and its difficulties was, of course, much more complex, and when the London Conference was held early in 1939, in which the British government sought to negotiate the future of Palestine with Arab and Jewish leaders, Zionists and those opposed to Zionist claims followed its sittings and presentations with close and anxious attention. It was a time of momentous change for the Zionist movement. In 1937, the Peel Commission had recommended for the first time partitioning Palestine into Arab and Jewish states (the latter a very small territory, but nevertheless to Lily a welcome recognition of Jewish claims), but subsequently the government had backed away, and in May 1939, as an outcome of the failure of the London Conference, and to Zionists' outrage and despair, issued a White Paper that retracted the idea of partition, which left Palestinian Jews a minority within a future Arab state. It also imposed severe restrictions on Jewish immigration.

Everything that Lily had attempted when she had been writing her first draft of *The Samaritan* became, again, pressing, for in the novel she had set out what she saw as the great Jewish achievement in the years of settlement since the Balfour Declaration of 1917, as well as arguments in support of Jewish claims, and a reminder of British obligations to honour promises. By the time Robert Hale published the book however, in late 1939, its topicality had already passed, for a few months earlier, the opening manoeuvres of the Second World War had begun, and in the autumn Britain had formally declared itself at war with Germany.

In *Tube*, in 1935, Lily had written obliquely about the threat to Jews by the Nazis, but had not yet grappled with what sort of impact this might have on her dedicated pacifism. Inevitably her experience in Palestine since then had begun to alter her view – not least the view that armed self-defence was necessary in some cases. For pacifists in the Labour Party, particularly those who had taken an anti-war position during the First World War, the situation on the continent in the 1930s – first fascism in Spain, and then Nazism – presented a terrible dilemma. Nevertheless, it was not something Lily was able to write about until later, when, back in Palestine after the end of the war, she encountered camp survivors, and wrestled with the new dilemma of Jewish militarism.

However, at the outbreak of war in 1939, Lily was not engaged with political principles so much as recovery. Part of that recovery had lain in trying to find some kind of resolution to the outstanding questions surrounding Philip's murder. She had continued through the previous autumn to press the Colonial Secretary to investigate the circumstances, but without success: although his words had been kind and sympathetic, he was blandly and diplomatically immovable, restating his position that there was insufficient evidence to warrant further action or enquiry. But Lily had also had the novel to rework, and she'd focused on that to the extent that she could. Despite her conviction that an Arab policeman had colluded first in the murder of her husband and then in the escape from justice of his murderer, she did not amend her work to reflect the newly deepened mistrust she now felt.

When *The Samaritan: An Anglo-Palestinian Novel* appeared, Charles Landstone commented on it positively in a round-up review in the *Jewish Chronicle*, describing it as 'showing a very close study of conditions under the Mandate', and adding that it 'should prove illuminating to those who have little knowledge of the birth pangs of the new National Home'. The novelist Louis Golding found it 'a moving and beautiful work with a story interest that does not falter for a moment', and Frank Swinnerton declared it 'a product of an interesting mind which dwells wisely upon personal as well as national problems'. In a long and detailed review in the *Palestine Post*, 'IHS' wrote that in 'this tale of two lands … it is apparent that the authoress is drawing on a rich background of experience. The result is that this novel is no superficial romance of sensational adventures in the Holy Land … but it is primarily an account of spiritual wrestling, individual and collective.' He acknowledged Philip's murder, and the dedication of the book to him, and observed that 'the sense of sorrow and loss in Lily Tobias's own life pervades, as it could scarcely avoid doing.' But, he went on, 'what gives her work here special value is that it is something more than a record of suffering. Every now and again the dominant minor key is broken by a major chord of triumph.'

The reviewer perhaps read too much of the autobiographical into the description of Edith preparing for the start of a Sabbath with Simon, and Simon not arriving for he had died – because that had already been established in 1931, in *My Mother's House*. But about Musa he was more accurate, for he described him as standing 'within and above the narrative as the embodiment of the ideal running throughout the whole book – the spirit of reconciliation that is to conquer the spirit of hatred'. The reviewer was warmly positive about the book, observing that there was 'hardly an aspect of the Palestine scene which has not been emotionally experienced and faithfully produced. The authoress can make skilful use of even a Royal Commission Report.' He commended the 'acute observation of the English scene; the unemployment and apathy of a Welsh mining district, the turbulence of a Fascist meeting in London (excellently described)'. Although he acknowledged that there were 'jerky passages', he found that the interruptions of the narrative with passages of past reminiscence had 'the merit of allowing a story of psychological tension' to be told 'in a quiet, restrained manner. And there is much sound knowledge of both child and adult psychology.' In conclusion, he endorsed the book fully: 'If I were asked to recommend the book which best conveyed a picture of the significance of events in Palestine during the years 1929-36, I should have no hesitation in recommending this beautifully conceived novel.'[141]

By the time of publication at the turn of the year, Palestine was not the most pressing problem in people's minds in Britain. In 1940 it was the progress of the war, and Lily's fourth and final novel provoked nothing like the response that *Eunice Fleet* or *Tube* had a few years earlier, although it was a more mature and better structured book than either of the preceding two. When it did gain attention, it was often for the connection with Philip's death. Lily's mind was anyway not on reviews by then, but on returning home to Palestine. Her departure was reported in a social column, 'Deborah Says … ', in the *Chronicle*: 'Lily Tobias, whose latest book, "The Samaritan," was recently published, left London last week for Palestine,' the journalist reported. 'With great courage she proposes to resume her life in Palestine, which was so tragically interrupted a year ago last July by the brutal assassination of her husband … The almost prophetic relation of her artistic creation to the terrible facts in real life has been pointed out by many readers of "The Samaritan".'[142]

Because of the war, that return journey was precarious, but Lily set out nonetheless. She was still in considerable distress, recalling later how, in Paris in 1940, she met the *Daily Herald* journalist Jose Shercliff, whom she'd known: 'she cheered me in her flat and saw me off on my way back.'[143]

Lily arrived by troop ship via Beirut in May 1940, shortly before France fell, and before the Mediterranean became a conflict-zone. Nevertheless, the journey was a difficult one. Once back, she was able to help gather relevant information about the glassworks to assist her brothers in putting in a claim of compensation against the government: though there was no hope of criminal proceedings against the inspector who, she believed, had colluded in letting Philip's murderer escape, the civil case for compensation would hold the government accountable in a different way. Her younger brother, David, like Lily before him, managed to secure a meeting with the Colonial Secretary, and the company followed up, according to MacDonald's suggestion, with a formal written memorandum on 5 July 1940.

'Sir,' David wrote, '… at your request we set out hereunder the position relative to the serious losses this Company has incurred in consequence of the political situation prevailing in Palestine and in particular through the murder of our Director Mr P. V. Tobias in Haifa.' The letter detailed the losses incurred and debts owing, stating that 'following the death of Mr. Tobias the situation became acute', and that the business suffered. 'There is no doubt in our minds,' David continued, 'that had Mr. Tobias been afforded, as a British Subject and a Director of a British Enterprise, full protection, his endeavours would have had the result, in view of his business experience, of mitigating our losses, by a re-organisation under his personal supervision … We feel that as a result of the late Mr. Tobias's not receiving that protection which was warranted, this Company has incurred a considerable loss resulting in a severe hardship which is entitled to the most serious consideration of H.M. Government with a view to our being reimbursed to some considerable extent.'[144]

The family's attempt to secure acknowledgement of responsibility was not successful: in its response, MacDonald's office acknowledged that while in a few cases of direct losses compensation had been paid, the kinds of indirect losses detailed in David's letter were excluded from consideration.[145]

Lily's attempt to bring some kind of closure to the case had once again failed, and she was never able to let go of her sense of outrage at the injustice of the whole business. It was bad enough that Philip had been murdered, and so violently; it was worse knowing that it could have been prevented, and being certain that the man who could have prevented it had chosen not to intervene; worse yet was knowing that he had held and released the murderer. That the government would take no responsibility, nor act to remove the inspector from his post, was, on top of all these other factors, an intolerable outrage.

Lily did not remain long in Palestine. The growing Jewish resistance to British colonial rule, like the Arab-Jewish conflicts, was to an extent superseded by the war, and when France was defeated and the Vichy Government installed, the areas that would become Lebanon and Syria, then under French Mandatory rule, became enemy territory on Palestine's northern border. Haifa, as a port city and an industrial centre, became a key target of bombing raids, and some private British citizens who were not part of the colonial administration were evacuated in an emergency manoeuvre, as the armed forces could not guarantee their safety – or, perhaps more accurately, did not want the liability of protecting British civilians. This highlighted one of the differences in status of Jews in British Mandate Palestine: Palestine-born Jews, or those who had immigrated to Palestine from elsewhere (and indeed Palestinians of all ethnicities whose residence dated to the Ottoman period) had a different legal and civic status to Jews like Lily. They were citizens of British Mandate Palestine, not British citizens – but Lily carried full British citizenship, and she, like other British civilians, was also encouraged to leave.

However, by then, with the European war engaged on

land and at sea, returning to the UK would have been impossible, and instead Lily made the much longer journey to the relative safety of South Africa, where Philip's brother and other members of his family lived.

South Africa was far from the active conflict, and it was there that Lily spent the next four years of the war. As she would write to Leo towards the end of her stay, they were shielded from war, at least, but not from racial tensions, nor the tensions raised by the war, for there was strong sympathy with Germany among some parts of the white population in South Africa, and anxieties for Jews were soon augmented by the passage of legislation restricting Jewish immigration. Nevertheless it was a fortuitous move for Lily, for in Johannesburg she encountered a political administration – and a Jewish community – that was strongly supportive of Zionism and of Jewish aspirations in Palestine, and she found a new readership for her work. More importantly, seeking out those members of Philip's family who had remained in South Africa (where Philip himself had grown up), she met a young student called Phillip Vallentine Tobias, who was the nephew of her murdered husband. This young man whom Lily befriended would later become the world-renowned paleoanthropologist Phillip V. Tobias. The two of them developed a very close and lifelong friendship that did not ever subsequently falter. In the young Phillip (whose name was usefully spelled with a double l, distinguishing it from her husband's), Lily was able to find some mitigation of the grief and loneliness she felt as a widow, and after she returned to Palestine in April 1945, they began an extensive correspondence that continued for nearly forty years, almost to the end of Lily's long life.

Lily had arrived in South Africa in 1941, at a time when the country was still a British dominion and had a large and prosperous Jewish community. She wasted no time in making connections and meeting people, and was soon established once again as a writer of note. Here she managed to organise another staging of *Daniel Deronda*, and published several newspaper pieces including reviews and obituaries. Perhaps the achievement that best showed her considerable *chutzpah* was securing a slot for herself on national public radio, which she managed through her typically bold and unabashed use of contacts. These South Africa exploits were remembered later by a journalist called Sadie Levine, who wrote an admiring profile of Lily in 1957.

Levine had known of Lily through *The Samaritan*, which had impressed her and other writers. In the profile she recalled:

> I met her for the first time in South Africa, in the early part of the war. Her visit was at a time when South African Jewry, still precariously balanced between a South Africa allied to Britain and a country in active sympathy with the Nazis, was apprehensive about its future as a community. I remember the mysterious way in which this little, apparently timid, quiet, Welsh-speaking woman, 'got around.' It was not long before she had inspired Mrs. Smuts, over tea, with the wonders of Palestine. She found her way into broadcasting, then practically a 'closed shop.' One afternoon, unheralded and unprecedented, there came over the air the strains of 'Kinneret,' a series of Yemeni songs, some Hebrew lullabies, illustrated in the unmistakeable Welsh accent of Mrs. Tobias.[146]

The two of them met regularly through the 1950s during Lily's annual visits to London, and Levine described Lily admiringly as the Swansea-born 'Israeli novelist, broadcaster and playwright', a designation that would no doubt have pleased Lily enormously. 'Every year,' Levine wrote, 'she leaves her lovely home on Mount Carmel, and pitches her tent, from early summer to late autumn, in a flat in Regent's Park. And every year I take tea with her and put the question: "What are you up to now?"'

Lily told Sadie that she thought of herself as an 'unofficial shelicha' – an emissary – and that 'her mission in life was to carry on the unshakeable faith' of her husband. 'He believed that one could foster goodwill in the face of the most bitter enmity, by peaceful, rational means', Levine reported. 'His faith cost him his life. He died at the hands of the Arabs he was befriending during the "disturbances" in Palestine.'

Given Lily's courage and determination all those years earlier, as a supporter and activist of the No-Conscription Fellowship during the First World War, it was entirely consistent that she should charm her way into having tea with the wife of the South African president, and onto national radio to broadcast a Palestinian-Jewish programme of music.

Lily was bereaved and still caught up in grief, but she was not cowed: wherever she went, she took with her a determination and commitment to her deepest political cause, a commitment not lessened but instead strengthened by Philip's murder.

Phillip V. Tobias later recalled how, in Johannesburg, Lily was able to begin writing again, and became active in the local Zionist circles, and in international Zionist organisations. She lectured in Johannesburg on the subjects closest to her heart, including on the Yemenite Jewish community in Palestine, about which she had made herself something of an expert.[147] She also continued to work as a journalist, publishing several articles on South African Jewish matters in the *Palestine Post* – and she was instrumental in reviving South African PEN, a project with which she would become increasingly involved later in her life.

Lily wasn't happy in South Africa, though; she wanted to go home – home to Villa Merhavia in Haifa, to take up her life again in Palestine. In 1944, as it looked as though the war was coming to an end, she felt increasingly anxious about the situation of the glassworks business in Haifa, and about the state of her home. The business into which Philip had put so much work was in a precarious state, and although she had no personal interest or capacity to be actively involved as a businesswoman, she wanted it saved not only because she had a financial interest in it, but also to honour and continue what Philip had begun. But it was difficult to find the means to travel, and meanwhile her younger sister, Fay, who also had a share in the ownership of Villa Merhavia, had taken over the whole residence with her husband Jonas during Lily's absence. Lily had just organised her journey, in early 1944, when Fay and Jonas informed her that they did not want her back.

'After all my arrangements for departure had been completed,' she wrote to Leo on February 21st, 'I get a letter from my Merhavia "partner" calmly announcing that it's no longer my home, but I can with her gracious permission remain as a guest until I find another roof over my head!'

This was the beginning of Lily's own private war, which dragged on for years, firstly through an unhappy, distressing and anxious correspondence, and then, after her return to Palestine, in miserable daily conflict or hostile silence. But at this early stage she was more outraged than hurt. 'If it were not so lamentable an exhibition of "sense and sensibility!" I'd think it farcical—,' she wrote, acknowledging, however, 'Of course I've been away too long. But I have no intention whatsoever of being anyone's guest while I have – legally as well as morally – a right to my home – a greater right, indeed, even legally alone, than its present occupant – who, instead of being grateful for a share, insists on total possession.'

The prospect of the long and difficult journey had already exhausted Lily, and 'the necessity of complying with innumerable regulations re luggage etc etc' was an extra burden, but her 'nervous forces' were further undermined when she received news of a possible sale of the Haifa glassworks. She thought it was a mistake to sell the business. 'For all I know,' she wrote to Leo, 'it's sold already – to my mind, a stupid step at this juncture. Perhaps, however,' she reflected, touching on a proposal that she had put to him before, 'you still think otherwise – though I still hoped that I might, once on the spot, arrange finances to enable you to join as a partner, if you really cared about it on that basis. I thought at least we might talk it over seriously as soon as opportunity allowed.'[148]

Leo was at the time stationed with the RAF in Cairo. Before the war he had studied law at the London School of Economics, and he was considering his options after demobilisation; the choices he was weighing up were law, business, or writing. He considered the possibility of a role in managing the glassworks seriously enough for Lily to repeatedly discuss the prospects with him for the next two years. But the business was in a perilous state, and in 1942 had gone into liquidation. Notices appeared in the *Palestine Post* in December 1942 and January 1943 declaring that 'the rights of the Palestine Plate Glass and Paintworks (Shepherd, Tobias and Co.) Ltd. ... are offered for sale in satisfaction of a mortgage debt in the sum of LP 2,000, plus interest' (the currency was Palestinian Lira), which was owed to Barclays.[149] Though this process was averted, the 'deal' mentioned by Lily in 1944 did not in the end come off, and subsequently others fell through, giving Lily hope that the business might still be saved and kept within the family.

Lily, in preparation for her return, had to destroy papers, manuscripts and letters, because it was 'impossible to cart so much about'. Overall she was distressed by her circumstances, by the news of British intransigence in Palestine, and by the accounts of Jewish experiences in continental Europe that were beginning to emerge. She felt overwhelmed by a sense of the increasing brutality in human nature, despite having 'all the will in the world to believe otherwise'.[150] Her own deep pacifism, already challenged by the question of how to respond to Nazi Germany, was to be further undermined both by her private war with her sister and by the situation in Palestine.

Although the letter from Fay laying claim – legally and morally – to her home had shocked and upset her, Lily still planned to start her journey back to Palestine, and told Leo he could write to her in Johannesburg up until March 24th.

Afterwards, she instructed him, 'write to the Villa. I hope to be there early in April.' In fact it was another year before Lily managed to leave South Africa and return to Palestine. She was both physically and emotionally vulnerable, suffering from repeated feverish colds, flu, bronchitis and digestive troubles, but also from enervation. Far away in South Africa, oppressed in spirit, pessimistic, lonely, her 'nervous forces' easily depleted, she felt cut off from news of the family, and excluded from discussions and decisions about the business that would affect her – particularly as she felt that, because of Philip, her stake in the business was not just financial but also moral and emotional. Letters often went astray or followed circuitous routes around the globe – the post was unreliable because of the war, but also because people on active service repeatedly moved between postings. At that distance from her family, the lack of response to her letters and long periods of silence made her fear she had been forgotten. When Leo got into trouble in Cairo for helping to organise a parliament for service personnel (and voting in a way that displeased the RAF) Lily didn't learn about it until some time later, and continued to write to him at his RAF base in Cairo long after he'd been returned to England. The extended unexplained silences worried and hurt her by turns, and she was relieved and delighted to get letters when they came. But they often carried brief and unwelcome news about the business, about her home in Haifa, and about family members, and in the late spring of 1944 came the sudden news of the death of her older brother Barnett – she had had no idea that he'd been ill, and worried again that she was being left out of family affairs. Frustrated by the space limitations of the 'airgraph', Lily welcomed the prospect of being able once again to write letters when a new airmail service to the UK was established that summer.

Though she knew that she had been away too long, and that she needed to return, both the difficulties of travel during the war and her own exhaustion and depression made organising and effecting the journey too much. Four months after the 'definite' March departure date she'd given to Leo, she once again confided in him about her distress at the prospect of travelling, but she was also uncertain of her reception in Haifa. 'I've had no reply to my letters saying I'm arranging to go home,' she wrote to him in July. 'As you know, I've wished to do so for a long time … But I'm much bothered by the travelling formalities etc & hope to be able to go by air, though there are no facilities for me at present. All friends who have recently gone by sea complain bitterly of "ghastly voyages" … and I don't feel equal to that sort of thing, especially in my present state (a second bout of flu' within a couple of months has left me feeling pretty low!).'[151] When she met an old friend, Bernard Joseph, in Durban, his greeting, 'What! Are you still here? Time you came back!' filled her with delight: 'The first words of invitation to "come home" that I've heard,' she wrote to Leo.[152]

Lily wanted to go home, but home also held terrible memories of grief and loss. The conflict and confusion over the house and the business only deepened her emotional turmoil, and although she felt keenly that she was being ignored and forgotten, and that she needed to be in Haifa to put things right, she deferred making decisions, unable to cope with the burden of it, and perhaps the burden of memory that return to Palestine would provoke.

Over that distance, Lily relied on Leo as an ally and confidant, and he in turn confided in her about his doubts and aspirations, particularly his increasing uncertainty about what to do after demobilisation. He was then twenty-eight, and although very politically minded and involved, had not yet considered embarking on the political career for which he would become well known and, on occasion, notorious. Lily understood that work in business might not prove fully satisfying to him, but still urged him to consider taking on the management of the glassworks in Haifa. She wanted desperately to retain the business in the family, not only to ensure her own greater financial security but also to keep Philip's work going: it had been his enterprise and vision, but also an integral part of their shared life together and of their plans for the future, and to let it go would be a form of treachery to his memory. But behind her appeals to Leo lay another hope, too: to have Leo in the business would also mean she'd have, in Haifa, an ally and a support, at a time when the family was deeply divided and in conflict both over the business and over her father's legacy. She was also very fearful of the hostile reception that was waiting for her on her return.

She wrote to Leo persuasively, therefore, urging him to consider the business possibilities, pointing out the plans of the entrepreneur Solel Boneh to develop vast post-war building and housing schemes in Palestine which, she believed, would hugely increase the demand for glass within the country and put the glassworks on a sounder footing.[153] Over that year, Lily felt her distance from things more and more acutely. When her brother Isaac wrote, suggesting that the best way of 'clearing up this mess' (the mess of the bankrupt business with its several business creditors and investors demanding payment) was to let the bank sort things out, and to give Fay legal authority, she objected categorically. Her own interests were being repeatedly overlooked. She learned from Isaac that Fay had bought out the financial interest of an associate named Ben, who had invested a sum of money at its start. Although, as she wrote to Leo, nothing could relieve her more, 'so far as minor matters are concerned, than to know that this man has no further claim on the business,' she exclaimed: 'but everyone seems to have forgotten to consult me first especially as to *my* claim on *him*.' Ben had behaved appallingly after Philip had been killed, she told Leo. 'Phil lent him (out of our joint private account) £720 (for the business) which was to be returned to us,' she explained, 'and actually part of it he returned to Phil in two cheques, which were to be banked on the fatal day. —Well, the wretched man robbed the dead, filching the cheques for himself – It's not a thing I care to recall, but it ought to be remembered. The £720, by the way,' she added, 'was part of the proceeds of sale of our London home. So I think I have a just claim from every point of view.' The memory upset her, and dwelling on it seemed to her hopeless: 'I don't suppose anything will ever come of it, and remembrances only agitate me in vain,' she concluded.

To Lily's dismay, her efforts, at this distance, to secure Leo in a position that would, she felt, benefit them both, backfired badly. Leo did not tell her directly that he didn't wish to take on the job, but she learned of it through her brother Isaac, who detailed to her his own efforts to keep the business going, and his decision in the end to sell.

Carefully, and without attaching blame, she wrote to Leo that 'it seemed from [Isaac's] references to your declining to take on the job that this was, in the end, a deciding factor. At the same time I received a letter from your mother resenting the unsatisfactory nature of the proposal made to you – she felt it offered no secure prospect and might prove a repetition of old trouble.' Lily had rushed to try to repair the damage. 'I cabled Isaac to offer you partnership with shares, if not too late (that is, if the factory were not already sold). I also wrote him by airgraph detailing my reasons. And I wrote to your mother similarly, telling her that as far as I could personally secure your future I would do so, but that your "coming in" was entirely subject to your own inclination. – But I also received a letter from Fay fulminating against "the boys" for deciding too late to sell – the offer of purchase in question having been withdrawn two days before the acceptance from London arrived. So now I don't know where exactly we all stand in the matter.' Lily's hopelessness and pessimism took over. 'Whatever happens,' she wrote, miserably, 'I suppose I shall be blamed. But to that sort of blame I'm indifferent. I wanted and still want – if feasible – to preserve the business in the family & am prepared to do my utmost to secure it.'[154]

Months later, she was still trying, but no longer held much hope that the business could be saved. Her sister Freda had the same views, but she doubted that the two of them could do anything about it. 'Unless there is a man to carry on, it's impossible,' she wrote helplessly to Leo in October. For someone who had fought for the right of women to vote, who had argued for the recognition of women's contribution and leadership, particularly within Jewish culture and within the Zionist movement, and who had portrayed successful and competent women in her fiction, this suggestion of needing to rely on a man sounds surprising, but perhaps it is not the contradiction that it might at first appear to be: Lily herself was not a businesswoman, and nor were her sisters – and nor was she interested in or capable of becoming one in her fifties. It was her brothers who knew the business, and in their absence she had hoped that Leo, who was also interested, and had worked at one point in the Cardiff branch, might take up the same role.

In the end, her efforts came to nothing: Leo did not go into business in Haifa, but instead on demobilisation he took up law and established a legal practice that would become the largest in the Welsh capital, before he entered politics and became an MP, first for Pontypool and subsequently for Torfaen. How different the course of his life, and Lily's, and that of their home country might have been if she had succeeded in persuading him to go into the business in Palestine: though Leo sponsored many progressive measures, it was he, as a backbench Labour MP, who shaped the Referendum on Devolution in 1979, and helped foster harsh and long-lasting divisions and hostilities in Wales, hostilities that continue into the present.

At last Lily made the difficult journey home from Johannesburg to Haifa early the following year, flying at the end of February to Belgian Congo, and waiting there for a seat on an aeroplane onwards to Egypt and from Egypt to Palestine. Because of misinformation and mix-ups, she was stranded for several weeks in Stanleyville (now Kinsangani, in the Democratic Republic of Congo), something she would later remember in an article published in the Cardiff journal *CAJEX* in 1961. Lily was travelling with two other Jewish women, and they stopped for a couple of nights in Elizabethville (now Lubumbashi), only to find their hotel reservation was non-existent, and hotel rooms unavailable. Abandoned in a cafe, they sat 'at a flyblown table, spread with dubious refreshments, stared out at the sandpitted street shimmering in the noon day heat, and debated what to do'. It was agreed that they 'must find some Jews' – and so they looked in a French telephone directory for a Jewish name, and were rescued and hosted by a young Jewish family. A few days later they travelled on to Stanleyville, making a nightmare journey in an ancient transport plane – 'dirty, cramped, and airless – apparently even toiletless, since mailbags were piled against an inaccessible door', and that 'wretched flight of 800 miles in stifling heat' turned them out, 'green and reeling with fatigue', into an airport from which there was only a weekly service from Lagos to Khartoum, a service that was booked up for the next three months. The resthouse in which they had expected to spend one night became their insect-infested home for several weeks. On the first night, they were put in touch with another Jewish family: by coincidence it turned out that it was the beginning of Passover, and though the others were exhausted, Lily accepted the invitation to a Passover seder, and 'was soon being driven along the dark forest roadway into the town. A snake skidded across from the impenetrable density of foliage on one side to that of the other.' Lily recalled that she seemed 'to be veritably in the jungle where Stanley greeted the lost explorer with his famous understatement – "Dr. Livingstone, I presume?" Fantasy, if not terror, was in the air.'

Eventually, after fruitless cables and appeals, and the intervention of a new arrival from South Africa, similarly stranded but with better connections, Lily found that they could bribe their way onto a flight, but only by paying in Belgian francs, which none of them had. In despair they returned to the Jewish shopkeeper who had hosted Lily for Passover. He listened to the story. 'Then, without a word, took keys from his pocket, opened his safe, drew out thick bundles of Belgian franc notes, and handed them' to the three women and the newcomer. 'Strangers, who could give him only our words – and I.O.U's which might never have been honoured. But we – some of us – were Jews. Stranded – bound for the Land of Israel. And he was a fellow-Jew.'[155]

All told, it took Lily a month and a half to get home. She arrived in Haifa in April 1945, in time for the sight of anemones flowering wild on Carmel. The war in Europe was over, but for Lily a new conflict, both within and beyond her home, had just begun.

Lily truly had been away too long. Trees had grown up in her absence and blocked the view of the sea from the villa; the political situation in Palestine had shifted, and her home, for which she had longed, was no longer her home. Fay and Jonas had claimed it, and were resolutely opposed either to sharing it or giving it up.

Initially Lily did not have to fight with them openly about her legal right to live in Villa Merhavia, which they had repudiated in letters – letters that were not subsequently referred to. When she first got back, the atmosphere was one of apparent frosty 'polite acceptance' – a relief for her, particularly as on her arrival she fell ill with a severe case of dysentery.

Leo, distressed by her accounts in letters to him, and by letters from his mother Kate about the nastiness of the situation, suggested that Lily might come back and make her home with them in Cardiff. 'Your suggestion touches me deeply as proof of real concern, both on your mother's part and on your own,' she wrote back on May 20th. 'I know very well I should not lack for affection in staying with her, and I hope it will be possible for a time later on.' But she was too recently returned, and at too great a cost to her wellbeing, to leave again, and nor was she willing to give up the fight for the right to her home. She also felt she needed to be 'in the place which fulfils most deeply other needs' – her spiritual needs, and her political needs.

Lily was exhausted after 'the long strain of living away and the vicissitudes of the journey home'. She couldn't face thinking of the future, though she acknowledged to Leo that the difficulties she found herself in had come from her 'having "drifted" and failed to make or rather to effect certain decisions in the last few years – much has been lost or forfeited because of my absence – but I'm really too tired to make much effort now, in any direction.'

The factory was at last to be sold, and any thought or discussion of it agitated and depressed her, and she regretted the missed opportunity with Leo. 'I should have been back at least a year ago,' she wrote. 'We could then have met and talked about much, and perhaps I could have done something really helpful and mutually satisfactory.' As much as regretting the practicalities she regretted not having his company and support – at home once again in a frosty, unwelcoming atmosphere, she wished for his presence. 'How I wish you could walk over the Carmel with me!' she exclaimed to him, melancholy. Her possessions, shipped from South Africa, had not yet arrived, and wouldn't arrive for several months, and she missed her typewriter in particular.

Lily had put a great deal of her writing energy into letters during those war years – adrift and often ill and, in the latter years, depressed, she had not been able to engage in anything substantial, although she'd had the idea for another novel in hand, and did produce a few articles. Now that she was home, she hoped she would be able to focus again on writing, and by July she was feeling better and in higher spirits: 'I'm resuming all sorts of work here and hope to carry on!' she wrote to Leo. Sadly, that optimism didn't last, for the 'polite acceptance' of her presence by her sister and her sister's husband came to an end, and soon it turned into a vicious open conflict.

The conflict was one of the chief subjects in correspondence and conversation throughout the family: Leo's older brother Wilfred, who was then stationed in India; Leo himself; their mother Kate, and Lily's other siblings. Lily was miserable about it, and her pitiful letters to Kate distressed Kate greatly. Lily enjoyed a respite in August when Fay and Jonas were away on holiday, and she felt well enough to go down to the sea to swim for the first time since coming home, but the respite was brief. Another of Lily's nephews, Ezra, the son of her brother Moss, lived not far to the south in Karkur, the garden village settlement venture in which Lily and Philip had invested some money. Ezra observed his two aunts' growing discord with dismay and distaste. He thought Fay was in the wrong over it all, but declined to say anything or get involved, and Lily was without support, except long distance. According to Ezra, Fay's claim on precedence lay in her assertion that it was she who had retrieved the house from the neglect it had fallen into after Lily had left, that she had put immense time and effort into it and that it was her home, but Lily, he told Leo, stuck to her guns, though she said little. Things deteriorated between Fay and Lily so badly that they ceased to talk to one another, and Ezra found their behaviour – what he described to Leo as their snubs, pettiness and cattishness – utterly childish: he thought they ought both to be spanked.[156]

All the family hoped that their sister Freda, who planned to visit from the US, would be able to effect a truce, and Isaac too intended to visit, but their trips kept being put off, and then Palestinian visas for British subjects became difficult to secure. Lily kept hoping they would come, and that they could help mediate and resolve the dispute. Despite her misery, she was able to be humorous at her own expense. 'I'm advised "to keep a stout heart" until then. "Stoutness" is all,' she wrote to Leo in October. By November, she could no longer keep her own counsel about what was going on, and she told Leo: 'Though no actual physical violence has been applied, every other form has been used to drive me away – now I can no longer endure in silence. Having been consistently insulted and humiliated, abused in the vilest terms, I too must bestir myself to defend my rights.' Leo had asked her to pass on his regards to Fay and Jonas, but, she explained, 'I no longer speak to those who have called me by every foul epithet & ordered me to "clear out" – so please don't ask me to convey your greetings to them.'[157]

Lily confided in Leo, but she kept the detail of what was

going on from Phillip when she wrote to him back in South Africa. Phillip was then an undergraduate, and Lily enjoyed a different relationship with him, one which maintained her connection to South Africa, but also provided a family link with her husband. She felt protective towards Phillip, and wrote to him encouragingly about his university studies and interests, but did not burden him with the detail of her difficulties, mentioning only that she hoped they would soon be resolved. They weren't, and in January Lily couldn't cope anymore. Feeling persecuted, ill with flu, and without the means to look after herself, and no one to look after her, she left Villa Merhavia for the nearby Carmel Sanatorium – 'for rest and recuperation after flu' etc', as she put it to Phillip delicately; everything she had detailed to Leo about the abuse she only hinted at in that 'etc' to Phillip.

A clearer picture of Jonas's behaviour in particular emerged after Leo's older brother Wilfred visited unexpectedly a little later, in February. By then Lily had somewhat recovered, and had moved back into Villa Merhavia. That visit by Wilfred 'was truly the most thrilling thing that had happened to me for quite a while!' Lily told Leo. 'I went to the door at the ring of the bell, thinking it was the postman, and there stood Wilf!'

Wilfred had arrived in Palestine on his way back to England from military service in India, and had twenty-four hours of leave to visit family in Haifa while his plane was serviced in Lydda. As Lily and Fay were still not on speaking terms, he saw them separately, and his revelations about Fay's husband Jonas shook Lily badly. 'Wilf was horrified at the domestic "situation",' she told Leo. 'His impression of J. as a "man without pity – ruthless – and bent on remaining sole master" (of the Shepherd-Tobias family property!) proves a very strong illumination of much that had been dim and not too easily perceived – or believed in – before. Easier, however, to perceive after the behaviours which led to my being forced to go to the Sanatorium.'[158]

Lily was desperate for kindness, describing her sister and brother-in-law in extreme terms as 'two Nazis who have done disgraceful things in their determination to hound me out of my home'. Although the meaning of that epithet has of course changed with time, this was nevertheless an indication both of Lily's feeling of being helpless and persecuted, and of her loss of perspective and sense of proportion. Wilfred's sympathy comforted her hugely: 'I simply cannot express how I loved seeing him,' she wrote to Leo.

By the autumn of 1946, the prospect looked better, and a solution to sharing or dividing the property seemed to be in hand, helped by the intervention of lawyers and by other members of the family. Lily was more optimistic, though she had managed to do little work, as the situation in the house was so disabling. 'I must pray for a better year to come for my personal life,' she wrote to Phillip in September, at the Jewish New Year. Sadly, however, it was not to be. Just as her domestic situation seemed about to be resolved, the political situation in Palestine intervened, for the end of the war in Europe had not brought peace to the Middle East. On the contrary, it had merely shifted the focus of the simmering conflict, which was about to spill over into armed revolt.

Eleven

From Palestine to Israel

Lily's domestic difficulties were not everything or even the main thing that preoccupied her on her return home to Haifa. She was by then nearly sixty years old, and desperate, after years away, to get settled and re-established. Harassed by her sister at home, and struggling to find a solution, at the same time she was enraged and appalled by the predicament of Jews – both refugees in Palestine and survivors and refugees seeking entry. The British, wishing not to inflame Arab public opinion nor change conditions, kept in place the provisions of the White Paper of 1939, which had restricted Jewish immigration and the sale of land to Jews, and had cracked down on illegal Jewish immigration. Now boatloads of survivors were sailing for Palestine, and the British navy enforced a maritime blockade, turning back refugees, sometimes returning them to the countries from which they'd fled, or incarcerating them in new concentration camps in Cyprus and elsewhere, where conditions were terrible. During the 1936-1939 Revolt, Jewish groups such as the Irgun had mounted attacks against Arabs, often in retaliation for Arab attacks on Jews, but now, after the war, they shifted the focus of paramilitary or terrorist activities to the British, in repudiation of the White Paper policies.

Lily's outrage at conditions turned at times into despair. Though she welcomed the end of the war in Europe, and anticipated the imminent fall of Japan, she didn't feel it held much hope for Palestine. 'Many little clouds looming over the horizon may develop into great storms,' she wrote to Leo in May 1945. Still not fully recovered from dysentery, she had not yet got back her strength. 'I haven't been about much but from all I've seen and heard, victory for democracy won't help to solve our problems – if dirty intriguers get their way.'[159]

Three months on, and the future political solution to tensions and conflicting demands in Palestine was no clearer, though the growing knowledge of the scale of the Holocaust, and the moral outrage on behalf of survivors and other Jewish refugees from the continent, was beginning to play its part in shaping things. 'Nobody knows what's going to happen to Palestine, but meanwhile life is easier here, though costly,' Lily wrote in July. 'Flotsam and jetsam from the horror camps are arriving – though far too many seem to be left behind. Though free from torture & murder, they don't seem to be the Allies' pets, and our desire to welcome and care for them here inspires little response.'[160]

Lily was sure that the tension between Arab and Jew in the spring of 1945 was an exaggerated 'hocus pocus' – Palestinian Arabs, she felt, were not so keen to be stirred up, but she doubted that things would be left alone. The pressing circumstances of refugees from Europe guaranteed that it would be impossible for Britain to maintain the status quo. Jewish groups broke the British naval blockade and smuggled refugees in. Some made it through the blockade, and others were intercepted and detained in British camps within Palestine. Lily was dismayed by the circumstances of

Holocaust survivors who were being denied entry into Palestine, and also those who made it through the blockade. She wrote to Leo on the 28th of November, 'If you – "No Zionist", you say – can observe of the Bevin statement, that "this outrageous piece of procrastination which affects the miserable remnant of our people I've seen here leaves me furious" – how should I feel, living among those who alone in the world wish to welcome and care for the "miserable remnant" and are mown down for exercising their right to do so?'[161]

But it was not just the situation of survivors, or the restriction on immigration to keep from inflaming tensions between Arabs and Jews: it was the future of Jewish national aspirations in Palestine that was at stake. The Jewish paramilitary groups that had largely cooperated and supported Britain through most of the war years now banded together to cooperate in a coordinated armed revolt against the British. The revolt began in November 1945 and was not called off until the following July. In November the massed tanks, guns, and closed roads that Lily saw everywhere, and what she described as the 'new war against the Jews in their homes', infuriated her: 'The dead bodies of our men, shot down while crossing a field, unarmed, are already buried, and the nearest hospitals unable to accommodate all the injured children,' she told Leo.

Britain responded to the armed revolt with a harsh military crackdown, and the experience hardened Lily's feelings and destroyed what was left of her anti-militarist position, already challenged by the war and its aftermath. 'You note,' she wrote in response to a letter from Leo, '"more and more I feel Judaism our religious tradition, is what we stand and fall with"

– well, I'm like the woman who wouldn't agree to cut the living child in two. Such a separation of religion and national tradition seems to me now more of a fallacy than ever – all the more specious, too, because Bevin has trotted it out to bolster up his evasions in the form of "Zionists and other Jews" – at best, the term "Zionist" is for the Diaspora, with its need of propaganda to show up the sham Jewish life there.' Lily was referring to Ernest Bevin, Foreign Minister in the new Labour Government, whose strictures against immigration were severe – to him, Jews were not a nation, but a religious group. Back in 1938, Lily had begun to question her own Britishness and the meaning and role of being a British Jew in Palestine; the British response to the Arab Revolt, and the failure of the Mandatory authority to investigate Philip's murder had contributed to her growing mistrust, but by the end of 1945 she felt no ambivalence about it, and she was caustically dismissive and unambiguous. She sympathised strongly with Jewish opposition to British rule: 'Here nobody thinks of "Zionists." All are just Jews, living as Jews in the Jewish national home. Dying as such too. Lighting the first candle tomorrow night in memory of the Maccabeans will be no empty ceremony in Palestinian homes. Certainly now, as in their days, Jews have to defend their lives on their own soil,' she wrote, and added '– alas, the modern Romans are the British.'

The situation of British Jews in Palestine was now even more precarious, and their possible allegiances suspect. 'It is we British Jews who have most to deplore and grieve over,' she observed. 'No wonder those who are officers here are being hastily posted out of the country. One of them has just phoned me to say goodbye. He is heartbroken about being sent off to Egypt tomorrow – obliged for no reason apparently except that he's a British Jew to leave his important and valuable work in a military hospital here.' She interrupted her letter to run errands down in the town, and on her return described an unusual and, to her, a moving sight: 'a number of cars parked in a street bearing printed slips which quote Churchill "We shall fight them on the beaches" – Palestinian Jews have wit as well as courage,' she wrote, proudly. 'We shall see whether it will prevail.'

Lily felt both the larger conflict and the conflict within her home had clear non-negotiable moral imperatives. In despair she exclaimed to Leo, 'Pacifism and appeasement are a dead failure!! – a belated discovery, you'll think. But one clings to the illusions of a lifetime, somehow.' The loss of those 'illusions' took her political affiliations and understandings in a new direction, one in which Palestinian Jewish needs were now the absolute priority. Nevertheless, she was far removed both socially and politically from the militant ideologues behind the violent revolt: though increasingly critical of the British position, she still identified strongly with the UK, something that she did not share with Palestinian Jews and Jewish immigrants from the continent. But though her Zionism did not shift so far over from its early pacifist vision as to become an ideology of 'by any means necessary', as it was for the underground militant groups who organised and implemented the violent revolt, it did nevertheless begin to create unbridgeable differences between her and Leo. Leo was then and subsequently deeply suspicious of Zionism and nationalism in all forms, and though he had been her confidant and a source of support and succour in the difficult early 1940s, she found his politics increasingly unpalatable, and she turned more and more to her other nephew, and husband's namesake, Phillip.

The Jewish revolt was officially suspended the following year, in July 1946, but that did not result in the end of hostilities and attacks. 'Troubles here have increased, though they are not necessarily continuous and sensational,' she wrote to Phillip in September 1946. 'It is the political outlook which has grown more gloomy – and a corresponding military domination which in its turn exasperates the civil population and evokes sporadic outbursts. You are right to pray that "people of whatever persuasion or party may be filled with a more rational and a more humane spirit" – Such a spirit, however, seems to be lacking chiefly in the hearts of the authorities who have the power to grant justice but persist in withholding it. There are, in consequence, many vain and tragic sacrifices. – We must hope that the New Year will bring better things.'

The Jewish New Year that autumn did not bring better things, either personally or politically, and Lily bemoaned the British policy of military control. 'We all hope that the mishandling of the "Palestine problem" will give way to wiser methods, before too much hostility is engendered,' she wrote to Phillip in October. Again, as had happened towards the end of her time in South Africa, she was too distressed to concentrate or write, and was still waiting for the intervention of her brothers and sister Freda in her struggle with Fay. It was, she told Phillip, her personal situation that preoccupied her still, for the political conflict was not yet affecting her directly. 'The majority of our people here are, as always, peaceful and averse from violence,' she told him, 'but the desperation of the minority is due to despair of justice, and indeed of common humanity in the treatment of the wretched D.P.'s – It is a vicious circle which cannot go on.'[162] But the revolt was not only a despairing response to the predicament of Displaced Persons that she was referring to – a despair, and a response to that despair with which she could sympathise. It was also a violent uprising against British colonial rule, which would have a marked impact on the decision taken by the UK government just two years later to wash its hands of the problem of Palestine. At the time, however, Lily could not see that clearly, nor the direction that things were going.

Shortly afterwards, the political situation affected her much more directly: the area of Haifa where she lived, up on the strategic heights of Mount Carmel, was declared a closed military zone, and in February 1947 her home and the homes of her neighbours were requisitioned by the British army. 'I know I ought to have written,' she apologised to Phillip months later, in July, from Lev HaCarmel Hotel, 'but I've gone through so much during these last months that it hasn't been possible to be a good correspondent. You will see from this notepaper that I'm living in a hotel. I was obliged to move here in February, when the Villa was requisitioned.'

It was a sad irony that the loss of Lily's home came at the very moment when her siblings had finally arrived at a viable solution to her domestic conflict, and a further irony that the domestic conflict and its solution mirrored the conflict beyond her home, too: she and her sister could not live together, but neither would give an inch of what they believed they each had a right to. Just as separation through partition was the proposed solution for Palestine – partition into separate Arab and Jewish states – so separation (and later partition) would prove to be the only solution for Villa Merhavia.

The requisitioning of Lily's home and the imposition of martial law in parts of the country meant that her brothers could not visit from England, but her sister Freda had arrived in January for a visit from America, and with her sympathetic company Lily felt a new sense of support. She sent a snapshot of the two of them to Leo, taken outside the WIZO Children's Home on the day of its opening ceremony on February 25th. It was an amusing shot, the two of them carefree, but their heights distorted. 'When I collected the snap from the photographer I thought there was some mistake,' she told him. 'I didn't recognise Freda. In fact she didn't recognise herself!! Even though I'm sitting & she's standing, she isn't so tall.'[163]

Lily was without a home for more than a year. 'I can't tell you here of all the difficulties, hardships and vexations involved,' she wrote to Phillip, although she acknowledged that her suffering was small compared to the thousands who were 'harried from pillar to post, deprived of homes and businesses, and even of personal liberties, by the "authorities" who aren't concerned that any number of innocent persons and indeed whole communities should be so shamefully penalised for the offences of a few.' Parts of Haifa were under curfew, and 'all sorts of unpleasant things are done and threatened,' she told him in July. But in the neighbourhood of Lev HaCarmel Hotel where she was staying, things were a little easier: 'So far this part of Mount Carmel is free of restriction on movement although we are kept awake at nights by explosions & firing, and cannot of course get from the spot,' she wrote. 'But explosions & firing don't affect us as much as the inhumanity and treachery of politicians and their tools.'[164]

At the time that Lily's home was requisitioned, in February 1947, the British government resolved to hand over to the UN the responsibility for solving the conflict in Palestine, and the UN proceeded to develop a plan to partition Palestine into Arab and Jewish states. That conflict – between Palestinian Arabs and Palestinian Jews, and between both groups and the British – was focused and intensified by the majority UN Resolution vote, on November 29th, in favour of partition. This constituted for the first time an absolute commitment to the establishment of a Jewish state, something that Jews in Palestine had been fighting for through diplomacy and violence – and something that Palestinian Arabs had been resisting, through diplomacy and violence – for three long decades. The UN vote was for Lily, as for most Zionists, a moment of heady euphoria. Thousands listened to the live radio broadcast from the UN of the achingly slow progression of countries announcing their vote in favour, or against, or their abstention. The UN Resolution required a two-thirds majority to pass, and it got such a majority, thus making the creation of a Jewish state an international commitment. Palestinians and Arab states rejected the resolution, not least repudiating from the outset the UN's right to decide partition, which violated the right to self-determination.

After the UN vote, the armed conflict intensified, ushering in the long violent months of the so-called 'unofficial' war that lasted from the 29th of November until the following spring, when, on May 14, 1948, Britain officially ended the Mandate, and at midnight David Ben-Gurion declared the independence of the new Israeli state.

The UN vote for partition, the increased conflict, and the anticipation of an independent Jewish state filled Lily with a fierce and resolute patriotism. Although she was still living in the Carmel hotel, she was focused and energised, and became a feverish correspondent with friends and family, despite the irregular and unreliable postal service which was often suspended. She didn't know if her letters ever reached her correspondents, and was certain that most letters sent to her never arrived. 'Our mail services have almost ceased to function,' she wrote to Phillip in January 1948, after having received two letters at once from him. 'I haven't received anything from London for over a month & I have no idea if my letters have even gone out of the country – in fact I've been told that none go out.' Nevertheless she was still receiving occasional post and magazines from South Africa: she kept up with *Trek*, to which she'd subscribed while living there, a magazine in which Phillip was beginning to get published.

Phillip was politically active as a student, and later that year he would be elected President of the National Union of Students, a body that was at the forefront of campaigning against apartheid, something with which he was centrally involved. Lily admired his capacity to deal with contested issues in a balanced way. But she was much more interested in his future plans, and her hopes about him began to replace the hopes she had invested in Leo two years earlier – not the hope that he would take up a role in the family business, but at least that he would come to Palestine as a lecturer, perhaps at the Medical School in Jerusalem – 'For there will be a Medical School on Scopus,' she wrote to him emphatically, giddy with euphoric resolve, and underlining the words heavily. It would be a medical school to serve the Jewish State! We wade to our objectives through blood and tears – and God alone knows how many of us will survive to see them realised. The flower of our youth is being sacrificed daily – our truly heroic youth – boys and girls of surpassing bravery and endurance. I cannot now tell you their tale. But I want you to know that there was never a time in Jewish history, when so much was done by so few.

By then, in January 1948, the British administration had begun its withdrawal and departure from Palestine, and barely intervened in the skirmishes between Arabs and Jews that were really the opening movements of the official war that would break out in May. The British military had relinquished her house, although, despite now being empty, it was still off-limits to her. 'I went to see it (by special permission to pass the military barriers of the zone) last week, and am in touch with the authorities who have promised me a decision soon,' she wrote hopefully. 'On the day I went there, there was heavy firing and bomb explosions in the town below and I was warned against flying bullets & shrapnel. Yet on the spot itself, all was peace and beauty – a tragic contradiction.'[165]

Fired with renewed political will, and full of hope that she could soon return to her home without the distress of sibling conflict to mar it, Lily was able to begin writing again. When, eleven days after her letter to Phillip, there came the news that Mahatma Gandhi had been assassinated, she was very quick to respond – for she had met Gandhi in London in 1931, and he had made the deepest impression on her.

Gandhi was assassinated on the 30th of January, and immediately on hearing the news Lily drafted an article entitled 'A Memory of Gandhi', intending it to go to the

Palestine Post. However, just as she was about to send it to Jerusalem, she heard the news of 'the vile attack' on the *Palestine Post* building – it had been bombed. 'It was a mercy more lives weren't lost or more people injured,' she wrote to Phillip on February 4th. 'The whole building was wrecked, machinery ruined, and all files etc destroyed. In spite of the appalling destruction and loss, the P.P. bravely came out with a single sheet (printed at another place) on the same day.'

She was afraid that it would take the *Palestine Post* a while to get back on track, and the moment for her article would be lost, so she asked Phillip if he might help her place it in a South African publication. She had sent it to *Trek*, being unable to think of anywhere else, but asked them to send the manuscript on to Phillip in the event that they could not use it. As it happened, she had been too pessimistic about the capacity of the *Palestine Post* to recover: the paper published her article the following week, on February 13th. 'It's the first time I've ever written about Uncle Phil—' she wrote to Phillip, although this wasn't strictly true, for in 1940 the *Palestine Post* had published a poem of hers entitled 'In Memoriam'. Still, that poem hadn't named Philip, but referred only to 'our dead who lie so still'.[166]

In her *Palestine Post* article, Lily recalled the time she had met Gandhi in 1931 in England. 'The Mahatma's visit to London was marked by political conversations with high dignitaries, by interviews, by platform speeches at crowded meetings in the great hall of Friends' House in Euston, and lionizing by the most brilliant English society,' she wrote. But despite this high-level attention, he stayed in the East End in the community organised by social campaigner Muriel Lester, who had founded Kingsley Hall. Lily knew Muriel Lester through pacifist connections, and she and Philip would very likely have been among those who attended the opening of Kingsley Hall. The building had been officially instituted in July 1927, with a ceremonial symbolic laying of foundation stones by many of the prominent figures of the pacifist movement. These included people from Lily's No-Conscription Fellowship days and from Rhiwbina, such as the prominent Welsh pacifist George M. Ll. Davies, who had been involved in the company that set up the Rhiwbina tenants' cooperative (he might well have been the model for one of the pacifist socialist figures who appeared in both *My Mother's House* and in *The Samaritan*). The event also included people Lily had met subsequently in London, such as Sybil Thorndike and John Galsworthy from the theatre world. This group intersected with the group of people who set up PEN International, of which Lily was a founding member. But though she knew Muriel Lester through these connections, she met Gandhi through her husband Philip, as she explained in the article:

Muriel Lester gave a reception at which a limited number of Quaker friends and fellow-workers were presented to the guest of honour in the simple building. The coveted invitation we received was due to the fact that my husband had in his boyhood known Gandhi in South Africa, and had ardently championed his cause. Few white people – the officially-styled 'European' section of the population – sympathized with the Indians or supported Gandhi in his self-punitory crusade. Among the few was the modest youth who, to the scandal of his order, 'hob-nobbed with the coloureds', openly professed his admiration for their leader, and espoused his cause in the British press.

Lily recalled how completely overwhelmed she had felt when she was introduced to Gandhi.

> I was so awed and confused that I hardly knew what was being said; but the beaming smile on the almost fleshless face and the friendliness of the unexpectedly rich tones reassured me. I felt my hand taken in a firm grip, and heard the words I have never forgotten – 'I am glad to meet you, Mrs. Tobias. I knew your husband when he was a little boy – but he was not married then – ha! ha! ha!' The hearty laugh astonished me. I was still too confused to realize that the Mahatma had made a joke. It seemed that Gandhi, himself married when he was a 'little boy', teased me humorously with my husband's bachelordom at that early age. There was a very simple, human side the great personality of the Mahatma.

Gandhi's death sobered Lily, reminding her of her own once deeply held pacifist convictions, and those of her husband. 'We mourn the dead who die so wastefully,' her article concluded. 'But let us believe in the resurrection of that power of righteousness which the individual generates for the sake of humanity, even while the assassin strikes again and again at those great and small, who challenged evil at the price of their lives.'[167]

Although Lily had renewed her writing, she found it difficult to concentrate in the midst of conflict. This was not the only barrier to publication, however: she found the unreliable post and the long silence from publishers disheartening and discouraging. The *Zionist Record* in South Africa held onto manuscripts of hers for months without a response – 'in one case for 6 months, in another for over 18 months!?' she told Phillip. 'I'm disgusted with them, as you may imagine!'

Despite these setbacks, she did manage to place an article in *Palestine and Middle East*, an annual publication that functioned as a Jewish Yearbook of Palestine – and here she was in truly august company: her name and article, 'Village Festival in the Emek' (an account of a dance performance in a Jezreel Valley kibbutz) was listed in the 'principal contents' along with articles by David Ben-Gurion, Chaim Weizmann and Moshe Shertok (later Moshe Sharett), the leaders of the Jewish government-in-waiting.[168]

In this article, Lily compared her visit to the kibbutz in the autumn of 1947, when the sight of a British soldier struck fear, with her first visit, in 1941, when she had 'sat with Britons talking of "home", and singing songs of nostalgic amity in Saxon and Celtic – for the score of boys were from England, Scotland, and my native Wales.' It was an irony, she thought, that the first time she had visited she had accompanied a group of British soldiers who were 'welcomed in friendliness by the settlers', whereas this time, in 1947, she came to attend a festival which, during earlier rehearsals, had been interrupted by the arrival of British troops, who had surrounded the place 'with a cordon of armed vehicles, forbidding ingress or egress while a search was made … presumably for terrorists and arms'. But the fear of the British army had by now become her fear too: 'now, the Palestinian crowd of fifteen hundred visitors and settlers assembled at the fringe of the trees to watch a holiday spectacle, were relieved to be free of the sight of British uniforms, to look apprehensively at an approaching officer, relaxing only as we recognised a local guard and heard his Hebrew accents.'[169]

In the spring of 1948, Lily's dislocation finally came to an end and she was at last able to move back into her home. However, the peace that this gave her was short-lived, for on the 15th of May, the day after the establishment of the State of Israel, and its declaration of independence, full-scale war erupted, when the newly-declared state was invaded by the armies of Egypt, Transjordan, Syria, Lebanon and Iraq.

The nature of that war, and of the 'unofficial war' leading up to it, remains the object of intense scrutiny and conflicting interpretation, not least because of the large-scale and devastating displacement of the Palestinian Arab population. Lily, living through it, and reading and listening to the Jewish media accounts of unfolding events, was not troubled by ambiguity in her understanding. Passionately patriotic, she reported on the progress of the war with zeal, pride, and intense excited hope for the future dream not only of survival but of success.

Lily celebrated the departure of the British in the months leading up to independence – in an article in the *Palestine Post*, she reported how those who were able to return to live within the military zone on Carmel, 'could share once more with the lizard its isolation and solitude, and become oblivious of the barbed wire and checkposts of alien authority.' There were difficulties of passes and permits and soldiers living in the military zone, but she was relieved to be home despite the challenge. Then, at last, it was the end of the Mandate:

There came the day, after countless rumours, that the British were leaving … when the highest civil authority, having abandoned officialdom in Jerusalem, arrived at Haifa to embark on the ship of departure. I watched the last symbols

out at sea from the Carmel check-post, past which cars came
and went with dignitaries busy with farewells. R.A.F. planes
circled the port and dipped in salutation, while a salvo of guns
echoed through the hills. A Welsh guard, whose homely accent
established a bond between us, gave me illuminating details
of personnel and movement … Only the most recent
importations, coming hidebound into new roles, showed the
outmoded British 'superiority to the native', supported by one
old die-hard who said, while the cocktails flowed, 'We must
keep these Jews down.' … The military authority hung on. But
a few weeks more, and the last remnant of the army, too,
departed. This time there was no flourish of pennons and
salutations, and scant ceremony at leavetakings. A departure
without dignity or finesse. Almost as silently as the legendary
– and contemporary – Arabs, who 'fold their tents and steal
away,' the last British military chiefs and guards abandoned
their Carmel posts. One day I saw my neighbour the G.O.C.
driving past as usually, escorted by his Scots bodyguard, to
and from his beflagged commandeered residence; next day
the general, his escort, and his flag had vanished. And one
morning, soon after, unwept, unsung, and unseen, the last few
British guards disappeared from the checkposts at either end
of the Carmel zone.[170]

The British were gone, but the military zone remained
nevertheless: overnight the personnel changed to Jewish
soldiers, and the language to Hebrew, but Lily was willing to
accept the restrictions, understanding that there were security
issues. She was ambiguous about some aspects of the new
order, however. 'We were stirred and intrigued by other
changes. Arab families still in residence were suddenly

evacuated from our midst and removed with their belongings by Jewish police to Wadi Nisnas. Jewish children from outpost settlements were brought in and lodged in empty houses, to which, after they were vacated by the British, the former Jewish residents had been ready to return.' That was Lily's sole reference to the forcible Arab depopulation of the area, and to the catastrophe that the Israeli war of independence was for Palestinian Arabs. Like so many others, she remained silent then and since about the cost of Israeli independence, which, even if it was not clear to her at the time, was clear to all after hostilities ended, for everywhere throughout the new state there were ruined and empty Arab villages, and towns with Arab neighbourhoods empty of Arabs. But Lily, in war, was focused on Jewish national survival. 'Today the news has burst upon us,' she concluded her article, 'the zone is no longer a zone! The barriers are down, guards are gone, and buses are running through! It is a great day for the Carmel. We are free. We are free in the State of Israel.'

It was not the end of the war, of course, either for her, or for the new state: over the next nine months there were periodic ceasefires, and lulls in the intense fighting, but the conflict did not finally end until January of the following year. During one of those ceasefires, in September, Lily sent New Year's greetings to Phillip and his father Joe, but asked rather sharply why they had not been in touch for many months, particularly after the re-establishment of direct post. 'We are living here in a time of historic events,' she told them. 'Great troubles, great progress. At present Haifa is quiet and we move about freely.' But that wasn't to last, for the ceasefire came to an end in October, and the renewed hostilities continued until January 1949. No matter how frightening and dangerous it was, Lily was determined to be courageous in her letters, and to praise repeatedly what she saw as the extraordinary endeavour of the new state. She sent everyone sets of the first postage stamps printed by the new state of Israel, and exhorted Phillip to keep and cherish his – 'they will be a collector's pride!' she predicted.

In November she at last received a New Year's greeting from them both, and wrote back passionately about Israel: 'You've probably heard something of events here — the great fight of Israel against tremendous odds, still continuing but with an amazing record of victory in a brief time — and remarkable feats of organisation in the new state —. Haifa came triumphantly through a fearful ordeal. Our black-out has been lifted but we are still not free of visits from enemy planes, though nothing much has happened —'

In the quieter situation during that autumn hiatus in the war, Lily was able to enjoy her surroundings again. 'Our long summer has only just broken, and it's now cool and rainy,' she wrote, 'but today I picked some lovely little purple crocuses on the field behind the house.'

When at last she did hear properly from Phillip, a letter rather than a greeting card, he had the momentous news of his election as President of the National Union of Students – and the terrible news of the progress of oppression under apartheid, and resistance to apartheid. 'While it gives me much pleasure to hear of your progress and prospects in the academic world,' Lily wrote back, 'I am much saddened by your account of things developing in S.A. – I had heard & read of these trends, but did not know they were so actual and so drastic in practice and intention. It is indeed depressing.' But that seemed far away compared to the immediacy of war in Israel – and Lily at war felt emphatically patriotic, shifting from the personal to the collective, and identifying herself utterly and unquestioningly with the just cause of the survival of the new Jewish state: 'Here with all our troubles we have rid ourselves of the atmosphere of persecution and the burden of being bestraddled (old-man-of-the-sea-like!) by alien rulers. Our youth are free and independent, unhampered by inferiority complexes and in fact completely unconscious of anti-semitic prejudice & hatred – Fighting on our own land for our own national safety and independence is quite another matter than fighting under masters who may at any moment kick, eject, or enslave the fighters.'

Once again she found the heroism of the present in the celebration of the winter festival that marked Jewish resistance in the past: 'Now in this time of Chanukah celebration we see again after the centuries our present-day Maccabees in armour around us.'

In November 1948, in the midst of war, Lily had moved a very long way away from the pacifist idealism of her youth and young adulthood. In 1916, when she was twenty-eight, she had written to the editor of the *Jewish Chronicle* about the moral necessity of objection to war, and about her conviction that 'such views must necessarily become embodied in "practical politics" if there is to be real civil and international peace. That Jews should, in common with fellow-citizens of other faiths, hold war in abhorrence as an irreligious as well as stupid method of settling national disputes, ought not to cause surprise.' Further, she had added, 'the pacifist does not propose to abolish war by sentiment only. It is necessary to call in reason and construct machinery, revise policies, and create understanding of such a nature as to reduce international friction to a minimum, and in the event of its occurring to proceed to a settlement on lines other than those entailing the barbarity and wastage of war.'[171] But now, in 1948, scarred by the murder of her husband, disillusioned by what she felt was the failure of pacifism, and the impossibility of peaceful accommodation and cooperation, and caught up in a collective fight for survival, she not only justified but celebrated a war-like ethos: 'Normally it is a grievous thing to be at war, and we do not want to see our youth devoting their energies only to warfare – but if it has to be done, then the spirit prevailing here can only be termed the finest form of patriotism.' She did still feel the need to qualify that sentiment, however, concluding, 'May it soon be diverted into the service of peace.'[172]

Soon afterwards another ceasefire was negotiated, and this time, at least for Lily in Haifa, and for those in many parts of the state, the war was largely over. By April, evacuee children from the kibbutzim near the frontlines who had overrun her neighbourhood were returned to their homes, which were once again relatively safe. Lily described their non-existent notion of private property and personal possessions, including her own property and possessions, in a humorous article in the *Palestine Post* that spring, which celebrated their departure less for the quiet it would bring than for the peace and security it represented.[173]

A little later, in the summer, she praised the resolute, battered new state in a poem entitled 'A Liberty with a sonnet to Liberty' which appeared on page 4 of the *Palestine Post*.[174] It marked the arrival and interment in Israel of Theodor Herzl's remains two days earlier, on August 17th. Her first publication in the *Jewish Chronicle*, when she was a girl of sixteen, had been about Herzl – 'Sir,' she had written to the editor, about Herzl and the Uganda plan, 'Within his own pure heart the vision of Zion alone sat enthroned, and not for a single instant did he swerve from the idea he had proclaimed of reaching the original goal – Palestine! … Our aim, like his, should be the Palestinian goal – and the Palestinian goal alone!'[175] Now, in 1948, at the age of sixty-one, it had come full circle: 'Herzl! Thou should'st be living at this hour; Israel hath need of thee', the sonnet began, and it appealed to Herzl's ghost to 'Give us manners, virtue, freedom, power' – qualities that Israel would certainly need.

Lily had lived to see the state established which she'd dreamed of, longed for, and worked towards through some forty years of her life. Over the next few years she would see the young state gain many of those qualities she wished for it, would see it threatened, see it prevail, would celebrate its successes and praise its achievements. She never wrote or in any way acknowledged doubt, or qualified her patriotic embrace of the Jewish state – and fortunately for her, she did not live to see the shift in world opinion, which came to view Israel's exercise of power, that last in the list of desirable qualities, taking precedence over all others.

Twelve

Family and frailty

Early in 1949, Lily voted in Israel's first general election, and the three men beside whom she had been published the previous year in the *Palestine and Middle East Review* were appointed as the leading figures in the first government: David Ben-Gurion as Prime Minister, Moshe Sharett as Foreign Minister, and Chaim Weizmann as President. After the ceasefire in January 1949, Lily's hopes and anticipations about the new state were high. On February 28th, just four days after Israel signed its first armistice agreement with Egypt, she wrote optimistically to Phillip: 'Now that the world is recognising us – Britain too! – we can expect to make progress in many ways. Peace and the establishment of good international relations will have a magic effect on this extraordinary little country.'

Sadly, if predictably, peace and the establishment of good international relations failed to materialise. Lily had lived through two world wars, had experienced at close hand the long conflict of the Arab-Israeli war of 1947–49, and she would live to experience the numerous Middle East wars that followed the establishment of the Israeli state: the Suez-Sinai War of 1956; the Six Day War of 1967, the Yom Kippur War of 1973 and the first Lebanon War in 1982 – as well as the increasing attacks during the 1970s and early 1980s by the Palestine Liberation Organisation, the Popular Front for the Liberation of Palestine and other groups.

Nevertheless, after the end of the 1947–49 war, Lily enjoyed something of a respite from troubles at last. She led an active, engaged life in the next two decades, and travelled widely – to the UK, to Ireland, on the European continent and in the US. She spent several months each year in the UK and on a couple of occasions for most of a year, though she was always relieved and happy to return home to Haifa.

The various siblings who had a part ownership in Villa Merhavia had at last between them resolved the dispute over residence, and Fay and Jonas did not return from their new house after the requisition by the army was lifted. Instead Lily lived alone in the place she had made her home with Philip some ten years earlier – and at last it became once again a genuine home, and a peaceful place.

In the autumn of 1949, Lily was host for the High Holy Days to members of her family: her brother Joseph from London, and two of her sisters – Kate from Cardiff and Freda from New York. When Freda had made her welcome visit in 1947, which had been a comfort to Lily, she had ended up staying in Palestine for nine months. She and her husband felt a strong bond with the place and wanted to spend more time in Haifa, and it was they, instead of Fay and Jonas, who came to share Villa Merhavia with Lily. Unlike Fay, who had laid exclusive claim to the house, and had treated Lily with such hostility, Freda and her husband made no such claim. The villa was too large a house for Lily to keep alone, both practically and financially, and although sharing the villa meant dividing it into two apartments with separate entryways, this relieved some of the burden she felt. The prospect of altering the building made her unhappy, but she accepted that it offered a sensible solution to the difficulties she was having, particularly with recurrent health problems, in managing such a large home on her own.

While Villa Merhavia was full of builders Lily stayed in London, remaining for several months, as she would now do most years, at 'The White House' in Richmond. Long since prone to intestinal and respiratory illness, her health began to deteriorate, and so did her eyesight. She became quite ill, and had to undergo surgery. She was slow to recover fully, but nevertheless she returned to Palestine to live in her newly appointed flat, and began again to entertain, holding musical evenings and dinner parties, though with less energy than before. As had been the case in the 1930s, with Philip, and in South Africa, she managed to orchestrate meeting and often playing host to many prominent people who were passing through, including politicians, academics and eminent cultural figures. When she heard that one of the world's most celebrated anthropologists, Raymond Dart, was to visit Israel, she wrote to her nephew Phillip, who knew him: 'When is Professor Dart due in Israel?' she asked him. 'Will he be in Haifa? – And if so, would he have time – or inclination – to contact me?'[176]

The disruption of building work had unsettled Lily, and she was often unwell in the 1950s and easily exhausted by travelling, but she recovered her sense of well-being, and throughout the 1960s was busy, positive and engaged. She still travelled for her summer's visit to the UK each year, preferring to travel by sea than by air, and she took an active part in the social and cultural life of Haifa, reporting to Phillip on all comings and goings of dignitaries, celebrities and her family.

After the four years she'd spent in South Africa she was always interested in what was happening there, and she followed the news of apartheid oppression with dismay. 'I have read a good deal in the local and world press that comes my way of the deplorable situation in S. A.,' she wrote to Phillip, who reported to her his own responses and his political activities. 'I can indeed well understand the repercussions on academic and professional life and truly on all liberal thought – and that effect on you and your colleagues [of] the impending legislation. The planned protests no doubt involve terrific strain, yet the compulsion to carry on, even in the face of defeat, must seem undeniable. I feel with you deeply in this effort – both because of my sympathies with the principle at stake, and because of the personal problems raised.'[177]

Increasingly, however, Lily was most interested in the lives of members of her family, and those of her four high-achieving nephews in particular: Leo, with his increasing political prominence; Wilfred, a highly regarded psychiatrist; Dannie, with his growing literary reputation – and her husband's nephew Phillip, whose high-profile scholarly achievements and political engagements filled her with pride. Some years earlier, in 1944, when both Wilfred and Leo had mentioned Dannie's poetry, she'd exclaimed to Leo: 'It's curious that you both wrote me about Dan's "poetic effusions" as if I had seen them – whereas until your letters I had no idea that Dan had ever written a line of verse!'[178] Now she praised all three of Kate's sons to Phillip, and vice versa. Wilfred she described as 'truly brilliant in his sphere.'[179] Leo, then a solicitor, had 'narrowly escaped being elected as a municipal councillor' and was a 'potential M.P.!!' All three, she wrote, 'are brilliant young men in different ways.' She praised Phillip to them, too: 'Dannie had tea with me and we talked of you,' she reported to him when she was staying in London. 'He said he would be very pleased to correspond with you … He is going to get me a copy of his poems to send you. It would please me very much if you and he could form a friendship. I must tell you that he and his brothers were very interested in your previous letter, which I imparted to them (as you know it was of particular interest re S.A.) and their comment was "Why, he sounds like one of *us*!" So now you'll know that I have talked as much to them of you as I have talked to you of them.'[180]

She followed her nephews' lives with close attention, and after her niece Naomi Shepherd moved to Jerusalem, she included her growing reputation as a writer in her interests too. The development of relatives' careers filled her with pride and delight. 'I wonder how many audiences seeing Professor Tobias for the first time reconcile his charming dapper appearance with the image they have formed of a shaggy-bearded recondite figure,' she wrote, 'possibly mumbling like the dear old Cardiff University Professor I knew, who always lectured to himself (in undertones) rather than to his students, hopelessly (or joyously) fingering their blank notebooks! Though I myself haven't heard you lecture, I'm pretty sure you don't mumble, or, I hope, swallow your words in a rapid inarticulate flow like that of our Professor Isaiah Berlin, whose Weizmann Memorial Lecture I sat through without understanding a single sentence of the truly brilliant speech until I read it afterwards in print!'[181]

She was eager for the two sides of her family to meet. Initially, when her nieces were still young and single, she positioned herself (not always with huge subtlety) as something of a matchmaker; she described them in enthusiastic terms to Phillip, and was proud of their academic promise (Naomi, Isaac's daughter, was at Oxford, and Joseph's daughter, Annabella, was at Cambridge). They were, she wrote 'both very attractive and intelligent girls, each entirely different, but both charming and could tell you all about university life in England etc etc – Naomi has entered into all sorts of activities in Oxford and is on the staff of Isis – writes stories and articles, I believe! These girls could entertain you very much with their chatter!'[182]

That was true too of any and all intelligent, lively, single Jewish women she met who had connections to Israel or South Africa. Nothing ever came of her matchmaking, however, and Phillip never married. Gradually Lily let the role of matchmaker go and she became instead something of a *shelicha*, an emissary, between the two families related through her marriage to Philip. Even in this context she never stopped being an emissary or propagandist for Israel, either (as she described herself when interviewed for the profile in 1957 in the *Jewish Chronicle*), for when Phillip finally managed to travel from South Africa to Israel, she was very moved by his report of feeling that, rather than visiting for the first time, he had come back. 'It was what I would have wanted you to feel if I had been able to define even to myself what I anticipated of you,' she told him after his return home to South Africa. 'Nothing so certain was in my mind, only the longing that for you as for no other visitor there would be the consciousness of being "at home" – Your being here was to me indeed not just a visit. It was almost like a dream fulfilled … I shall not now, any more than I have ever done, make claims or demands or try to outline a future – but your own expressed emotions arouse in me, I must admit, a conviction that what George Eliot's prophetic creation called "the leaven" really works.'[183]

After many years of anticipating, imagining and trying to orchestrate a meeting of the two sides of her family, her hopes were realised when Phillip visited the UK, although on that occasion she wasn't able to join them. But it filled her with joy when all the family met up at last in 1955, when Phillip was at Cambridge for a year, and she was able to attend High Holy Days services with him at the Great Portland Street Synagogue in London. That year Lily spent many months in the UK, and the two of them travelled to Wales together to see her sister Kate and other members of the family.

Lily's intense interest in the family's doings wasn't always appreciated and wasn't always reciprocated; some members resented or brushed off her attentions, feeling the pressure of her high expectations of their behaviour, particularly in the matter of staying in touch, visiting relatives and passing on messages. She often relied on Phillip to act on her behalf in practical matters, such as contacting friends for her in South Africa, and she was surprised and put out when he was slow to follow up on contacts and connections that she tried to set up for him. When two of her nephews married non-Jews, she was hugely upset by what she felt was a betrayal of their Jewishness, and she amended her will to reflect her unhappiness with them (later, however, she

amended it again, making Dannie her literary executor, and
bequeathing to him all copyrights and royalties in her work).
At the same time she valued and relied on their interest in
her, and was warm and effusive in her appreciation of any
kindness to her.

One of the interests that became a strong commitment,
after things had settled down in 1949, was PEN
International, the writers' organisation set up to defend
freedom of expression and to advocate for writers suffering
under political oppression. Lily had been a founder-member
when she'd lived in London, and it was she who had been
instrumental in reviving PEN in South Africa during the
time she lived there. In the 1950s, she attended the PEN
Congresses every year, and reported on them in the Jewish
press – and advocated for the congress to be held in Israel.

Throughout the 1950s, 1960s and the early 1970s, Lily
continued to publish articles – reviews of cultural events,
and responses to current affairs – in the *Jerusalem Post* (what
had been from 1932 to 1950 the *Palestine Post*), the *Jewish
Chronicle*, and elsewhere. Later, in the 1960s and 1970s, her
articles appeared in *CAJEX*, the magazine of the Cardiff
branch of the Association of Jewish Ex-Service Men and
Women. These included a description of her neighbourhood
on the Carmel in Haifa, an account of her journey home
from South Africa when she was stranded in Belgian Congo,
and, in 1967, some 'Notes on the Arab-Israeli War'.[184] She
thus returned, towards the end of her life, to publishing
where she had begun: in Wales.

Perhaps the highest literary moment arrived for Lily in
1974, when her adaptation of George Eliot's novel *Daniel
Deronda* was performed again in London in the lead-up to

the centenary of the book's publication. The *Jewish Quarterly* in London published a substantial excerpt from her newly revised play, and a reading of the play was also given at Hebrew University in Jerusalem in April 1976, part of a series of public lectures marking the centenary. It was staged again in Haifa two years later as a fundraiser for WIZO, the Women's International Zionist Organisation, and in tribute to Lily. This was a moment of recognition for one of Lily's works which, though she knew was flawed, was nevertheless of the deepest importance to her, particularly now that she felt George Eliot's early Zionist vision had been fulfilled.

Her most tangible and lasting contribution in the post-war decades, however, was not a literary one, nor something to which her name was publicly attached. In the aftermath of the Six Day War in 1967, she endowed a research post at the Haifa Technion in memory of her husband. The Philip Vallentine Tobias Chair in Glass and High Temperature Technology was directly related to her husband's work, and to his vision of developing industry as a way to develop the capacity of the country. The idea and the planning for the endowment had begun much earlier, and its reach was wide: at the time there was no department at the Technion that directly related to this research, and as a consequence of her endowment, an institute was set up in close cooperation with an existing department in glass technology at Sheffield University in England. As she wrote to Phillip in 1964, after the anniversary of his father Joe's death, there was a need 'not only to fulfil the duties of remembrance, but what is rarer and harder, the duties of memorial, in a form to endure – This is now one my problems.'[185] In this she succeeded.

Years earlier, she had intended to leave a bequest to the

Technion, but was advised that this might get eaten up in death duties, owing in part to her dual citizenship – for, despite her total commitment to Israel, and self-identification as an Israeli, she had never relinquished her UK citizenship: England and Wales were the countries where most of her family still lived, and where she spent a considerable time each year.

In place of the bequest, she was advised that she could make a living legacy – and see it effected in her lifetime. It took many years to realise, but the result was indeed a permanent and effective memorial to Philip. Marking the fiftieth anniversary of the Balfour Declaration, in October 1967, the Technion held a dinner to honour Lily's endowment. Arthur Blok, who had been the first director of the Technion when it opened in 1924, described Lily as 'a lady of many gifts: she is shy, modest, gentle, with a maximum of goodness in the minimum of physical proportions.' Lily's own explanation of the endowment was that it should 'complete the purpose of my husband's life – the strengthening of industry in Israel.' Years later, in 1980, near the end of her life, she wrote to Phillip about visiting the Technion on the anniversary of his uncle Philip's murder. She'd been invited to attend 'for the usual annual gatherings and functions of the Technion Board of Governors', but the date was still the saddest in the year for her, more than forty years on – the day she would light her annual kaddish candle for Philip. 'I don't know if you realise how appropriate it was for me to be on the ground of the special memorial I had been able to establish there,' she wrote, 'and to meet there (after a long absence) the Technion executives who had helped me to establish it and receive from them and many old friends very warm greetings. It more than relieved the tension of my day.'[186] Back in 1967, at the event marking the establishment of the Chair, the Technion had presented Lily with a glass candelabra created in the university's glass workshop in recognition of her contribution. An American journalist reported that this would be 'a symbolic link with her husband's pioneering work as she lights her Sabbath candles and recalls what her father, Tobias Shepherd, and her husband, Philip Tobias, read on the Sabbath from the Pirkei Avot: "It is not thy duty to complete the work, but neither art thou free to desist from it".'[187]

That was the principle by which Lily lived. She certainly never felt free to desist from the work – the work at all levels: spiritual, political, literary, and personal – but also that most basic work, to 'go on', as she put it, when she felt at her lowest, when it felt pointless. 'I am now so tired mentally and spiritually,' she had written at a particularly bad point in 1952, three days after the anniversary of Philip's death, 'that I don't feel I can ever "go on" again.'[188] But she did – then, and subsequently. At no time in the forty years after her husband's murder was she ever free of her deep sense of loss, augmented and complicated as it also was by her grievance over the injustice that had been done in its aftermath. However her sadness, and her sense of human tragedy, of the tenuousness of happiness, and the vulnerability of the individual, had long preceded even that particular grief, and suffused her writing. After her own death in 1984, Phillip wrote a detailed tribute to her memory in the *South African Jewish Times*. It was full of praise for her achievements, particularly for her writing, but also poignantly described her life's deep and abiding grief:

'Through all her writing,' he noted, 'there shone an intense spirituality, a Jewish and Zionist fervour, profound feeling, a sad and brooding (though not humourless) contemplation of life, often overlaid with pathos and tragedy.'[189]

Some fourteen years earlier, when he himself had written to her in his twenties about his uncertainties and unhappiness, she had responded sympathetically. He'd expressed a belief that happiness did not exist in the present, 'but more in recollection of the past', and this she had rejected: 'That cannot be true, at least not for a young man of twenty-eight. I am more than twice your age, and life has forced me to discard or to ignore the past and concentrate *only* on the present – not that I find happiness in it, for there is no longer any joy in my life. You see I no longer look to the future – and this is where the great difference lies between the earlier and the later years of one's life.' She apologised for philosophising or generalising – 'I know that every individual existence is determined by special features,' she wrote. 'Even those of us in intimate contact with each other seldom know or even guess at such factors – as you truly say, even one's friends are nine parts strangers to one's soul.' Though she realised that she could not understand all that troubled him, she assured him: 'But I do know – and feel some of the causes, and only wish I knew how to help you to overcome them. At the moment I can only add that I love and believe in you – in that inner self which is not content with material honours and successes, however well-deserved.'[190]

Lily had lived through immense grief, and a time of great upheaval and conflict, but she had seen her way through danger and violence with courage and resolve, determined to 'go on' despite obstacles, with a kind of dogged spiritual will even when she was most alone, most grief-stricken and in despair. Well into her eighties she continued to entertain artists, writers and prominent figures in her home. As a long-time patron of the Israel Philharmonic Orchestra from its earliest days as the Palestine Symphony, she held regular receptions for musicians and conductors, including one for Yehudi Menuhin. But she was suffering from an ever-growing catalogue of ailments – severe arthritis that made it hard for her to write, rheumatism, worsening intestinal problems, back and neck pain that for a while necessitated wearing a brace, and cataracts. Her poor health made travel difficult and then impossible, and she became isolated from her family, and for the first time had to mark the High Holy Days alone.

In 1980, when she was ninety-three years old, the city of Haifa formally recognised the significant contribution Lily had made to its cultural and educational life. She was amused and honoured at the same time, and self-deprecating when she reported the news to Phillip: 'you may care to know that I – your humble aunt – am receiving an award on the 28th of July from the Haifa municipality – that of Honorary Citizenship!'[191] Such recognition was the culmination of forty-five years of commitment to the development of the city, both as a generous patron of the arts and of education, and as a host to artists, writers, dancers, musicians and dignitaries. She had 'entertained' extensively at Villa Merhavia in the 1930s, opening her home for receptions, such as the one she'd held for representatives of the Peace Army in 1938, and for the literary salon she held for writers such as Arnold Zweig; and later, before she left for South Africa, and before her feelings about the

British administration had soured, welcoming Welsh soldiers who were far from home.

In her last years, increasingly frail, suffering badly from arthritis and poor eyesight, she withdrew from public life entirely. With ever-increasing frequency her contemporaries died – acquaintances, close friends, and family. Kate's husband passed away, and then Phillip's father, whom she'd known in South Africa, and Philip's brother Walter, and then an old friend of hers from Wales, Sarah Griffiths, who had been part of her social circle in London (Sarah Griffiths had been the organising secretary of the National Union of Teachers). When Lily's sister-in-law Celia had died in 1966, Lily had written a warm 'In Memorium' to her in the *Jerusalem Post*. Celia, married to Lily's brother Isaac, had been centrally involved in the Zionist movement in England, and had been first secretary of the Women's Zionist Federation.

Then one by one Lily's siblings themselves died – Sol and Isaac, and finally her favourite brother Joseph in 1980, when she herself was ninety-three. After Philip's murder had injured her so irretrievably in 1938, what had enabled her to manage had been the support of her family, and in particular the support of her brother Joseph.

Joseph had been everyone's favourite: he was loved, admired and respected by all the family. He was a warm and intelligent man, who had worked all his life as a London doctor, and had no time for family schisms and feuds. He had cherished and admired Lily. When he was interviewed in 1976 for the Museum of Welsh Life at Sain Ffagan, in Cardiff, he had spoken warmly about her, encouraging his interviewer, David Jacobs, to contact her in Israel. 'She's a woman of eighty-eight,' he said. 'She writes brilliantly. She's written novels in the past. She dramatised *Daniel Deronda*. She's a widow [and] a remarkably clear speaker. And most interesting: her mind at eighty-eight is lucid.'[192]

When Joseph died in 1980 Lily was lost. His death was to her a final and unbearable blow. 'I do not know when you will get this letter,' she wrote to Phillip, who was on holiday at the time. 'Grievous news should not be hurried,' she added, and then, referring to news in the plural, perhaps a result of Hebrew influence, 'neither should they be long delayed'. A cable had come to her and Freda, and Freda's husband, stating that their beloved brother had passed away that Friday night in hospital. 'Of course I knew only too well of his sufferings,' she wrote, 'but I knew too from his frequent letters to me that he still hoped for recovered health – I *did not* anticipate this sudden end. I cannot – dare not – tell you how it has affected me. But it seems as if the light that lightened the darkness of my own life for over forty years – that light has gone out – and I am groping for what is left [that is] good and desirable to sustain my depleted resources for a little longer. I don't wish to harass you – I know you will also feel Joe's loss deeply, not only for my sake – he was my wonderful brother from early youth – we were and continued to be even when separated in perfect sympathy and mutual understanding. I cannot – cannot – see my life without him – without his letters – without the hope however faint that we should meet again – Dearest Philly, you are much to me ... Can one's heart be broken twice? – the pieces, if not healed, again be irretrievably shattered – '[193]

She did somehow recover, though – did manage, despite her 'depleted resources', and despite the grief over the death of her sister Kate the year after, to keep going, and she was well enough to receive Phillip when he travelled to Israel the following autumn. Afterwards she sent him a New Year and birthday card telling him: 'all who met you on the last night of your stay enjoyed it – including your hapless aunt!' But in fact she'd been anxious about her limitations, and about her ability to offer him the hospitality she would have liked. 'Awaiting your news – I hope of a good journey without mishap … and having had no disappointment in Haifa!'[194] When he did reply, after a delay, with a warm thank-you, she was relieved, for she had sensed a disappointment: 'It seemed as if it was something that I did and didn't do, that I should or "oughter to have done" – or simply *was*! –Yet how could it have been otherwise with my deplorable condition? My delight in seeing you at all here should have been enough for me, if not for you. So where was the disappointment I sensed?'[195] It was not disappointment, as his thank-you letter to her revealed, but ill health and emotional strain, and his account of difficulties saddened her. So too, though she was grateful for the thought, did his wishes to her for a happy Hanukkah.

'It wasn't and couldn't be, lonely and isolated as I am from all celebrations and activities,' she wrote sadly. 'Yes, I still have friends – thank God – who sometimes visit me – and even recall happier times together.' She didn't dwell on her sadness, however. Looking through old documents and papers she'd brought back with her from South Africa, she'd recently discovered a poem of hers that she'd forgotten about till then. 'Yes, writers who are not poets sometimes are guilty of breaking into verse!' she told Phillip. 'It had been set to music – no less! – by a woman I met in Johannesburg

… Will this absurdity amuse you?' she asked with typical self-deprecating humour in the midst of her sadness. 'Tell me something more of the emotional strain you've suffered,' she went on – 'I wish I could soothe it,' and she signed this, the last letter she would write to him, 'with all the love that's left in my bereaved heart.'

Postscript

A cover-up

When Lily died in 1984 at the age of ninety-six, only her family and close associates publicly remembered her. Along with the family's formal announcement in the *Jerusalem Post*, the Technion published a notice in the paper with a misspelling of Philip's name that would have irritated Lily exceedingly: 'The Technion mourns the death of Lily Tobias, and extends condolences to her family on their sad loss. Both Mrs. Tobias and her husband, Phillip Valentine Tobias, will long be remembered for their close and generous association with the Technion and the Faculty of Chemical Engineering.'

For the nearly forty-six years that Lily lived as a widow, she was always associated publicly with Philip, but most often because of the terrible circumstances of his murder. In a note to the *Jewish Chronicle*, Dannie mentioned her novels, but stated rather baldly that, after she and Philip emigrated to Palestine, 'alas, her husband was soon stabbed to death by an Arab and Lily subsequently never wrote another book.'[196] His belief that it was because of the trauma of Philip's death that Lily stopped writing fiction was shared by his brother Leo. Their cousin Naomi also identified Lily with the murder of Philip. 'My earliest memories of Lil are

– 267 –

of a little old lady (she seemed to me old, but I was a tiny girl), dressed entirely in black, with a very drawn, sad face,' Naomi recalled – this was in London, shortly after Lily was widowed. In her memoir Naomi described Philip as 'a mild man with muttonchop whiskers', who 'had been dragged from his car and knifed to death in the Arab town during the revolt of 1936. His widow, who wrote novels, kept his study untouched in that villa, I was told, like Queen Victoria after Albert died.'[197]

The memory of Philip and of their shared life sustained Lily, but she was never free of her grief over his loss, the trauma of the manner of his death, or her certainty that it could have been prevented. Nor, despite kind sympathies and assurances she received from the Colonial Secretary, was she ever free of the conviction that, behind the scenes, there was a cover-up of the circumstances surrounding the arrest and release of Philip's murderer.

Lily never knew it, but there were good grounds for that conviction. In the papers of the Colonial Office held at the National Archives in Kew, there are two folders of documents dealing with Philip's death.[198] In addition to the evidence that she herself handed over to Malcolm MacDonald, the Colonial Secretary (the statement by Constable Shimon Horowitz, and statements by Israel Geller and Lothair Kach, two of the passengers in Philip's car), there is an extensive correspondence about Philip's murder and the allegations against the Arab inspector, Inspector Hashem, between Colonial Office civil servants, the Colonial Secretary himself, the office of the High Commissioner in Jerusalem, and various members of the Palestine Police Force.

MacDonald, on receiving Lily's evidence, approached the High Commissioner, asking him to enquire into the circumstances, and the High Commissioner, Sir Harold MacMichael, in turn appealed for information from Saunders, the Inspector-General of the Palestine Police. Down the chain the enquiry went, from police headquarters to Barker, the District Superintendent of Police, to the Acting Assistant Superintendent, to British and Palestinian officers and constables. There was little doubt, the District Superintendent reported back to police headquarters in Jerusalem, that Constable Shimon Horowitz had indeed arrested a man – but there was no evidence, he went on, that he had handed him over to anyone, and there was therefore no evidence with which a case could be brought against Inspector Hashem. Flanagan, the Acting Assistant Superintendent, had questioned Hashem and several British police constables, two of whom had spoken to Hashem before, during and after the riot, and had not seen a prisoner in his custody.

The evidence against Hashem, an Arab inspector, derived from Horowitz, a Jewish constable. Barker, the D.S.P., deemed it likely that Horowitz, in the excitement and chaos, had lost hold of his prisoner, and was trying to pass on the blame. It was highly unlikely, he thought, that a Jewish constable would have handed over a prisoner to an Arab inspector when there were British constables present, and Saunders, the Inspector-General, agreed. This was reported to the High Commissioner, who in turn reported accordingly to the Colonial Secretary at Westminster.

The letters show clearly that assumptions and inferences were the basis for concluding that there was no evidence of wrongdoing, but political sensitivity coloured those assumptions: there was considerable interest in not aggravating political unrest and mistrust of the police by giving weight to a Jewish subordinate against an Arab superior.

In his own account, Horowitz stressed that Hashem was his superior officer, and he made clear that it was entirely in keeping with their relative positions that he should do as he claimed to have done. But there was also considerable personal animus in his account, not least in his allegation that Hashem had approached him from an area near the Arab cafe where no unrest at all was taking place; Hashem, it could be inferred, had not intervened at all, and this was the basis for Lily's belief that, had he done his duty, Philip's life could have been saved.

Horowitz's detailed six-page statement shows that when, later on the night of Philip's murder, Acting Assistant Superintendent Flanagan questioned him, Hashem, and a British constable who had accompanied Horowitz, there were considerable barriers of language. Horowitz did not speak good Arabic, and Hashem evidently did not understand Hebrew or English very well. The questioning immediately after events was haphazard, inconsistent and slapdash: Horowitz was questioned by both Flanagan and Hashem, but it wasn't until five days later that Flanagan questioned Hashem – an interview at which Horowitz was not present.[199]

Whether Horowitz lost hold of his prisoner or handed him to his superior who let him go, it is clear he was in an invidious position, for it was he who had failed to protect Philip. Though armed with a rifle, he had not used it, and he had turned away from the car and left Philip to fend for himself. Other eyewitness accounts reported in the press described Philip being pulled from his car, whereas Horowitz stated that Philip must have ignored his injunction, and got out of the car to try to escape. The fact that Philip's body was found between the car and the crowd suggests that the former was true: had he got out of the car to flee, he would have run from the crowd, like Geller and his other two passengers, in the direction from which they had driven. Geller's account also complicates that given by Horowitz: Geller had no recollection of any police constable instructing Philip or himself to remain in the car; indeed he had no recollection of seeing 'any police at all'. Geller's statement also indicates the barriers of language: he said he did not speak Hebrew well, and gave his account in German.[200]

Lily evidently trusted Horowitz's version of events. Given the extraordinary distress she was in, and the fact that her husband had apparently been targeted as a Jew by a group of Arabs, and given her pre-existing suspicions about Hashem, and about Arab members of the police more widely, it is perhaps understandable that her reading of things would have been coloured by ethnic assumptions and prejudices. Finding sympathy from a Jewish constable, it is not surprising that she would have overlooked the inconsistencies between reports and focused on the strong possibility of corruption by an Arab policeman.

Whether Horowitz or Hashem lost or let go of one of Philip's murderers, and whether or not the Arab, British or Jewish police did enough or indeed did anything to intervene is impossible, now, to say. However, the way the Mandatory authority was managing the Arab uprising was already under intense scrutiny, and, resisting calls for the imposition of martial law in place of the civil police force, all parties would have wished to avoid any public enquiry into these circumstances.

In his letter to Lily later that year, in November 1938, MacDonald, the Colonial Secretary, assured her that the High Commissioner and the Inspector-General of Police had 'given the matter their personal attention, and,' he went on, 'in the light of their investigations, I can only accept the conclusion that sufficient evidence is not obtainable on which a charge could be framed against the Moslem Inspector concerned.' He sympathised with her desire for clarity, but concluded: 'I am satisfied that further investigation would lead to no useful result', and pointed out to her that, as indicated in his answers to questions in parliament, 'we have been relying less and less on Arab members of the police force in Palestine during recent weeks, and employing greatly increased numbers of British and Jewish policemen.'[201]

In the private correspondence, the High Commissioner, writing to the Inspector-General, specified that he did not want an official investigation, but asked him to 'look into the matter personally' when he was next in Haifa, and to find out from the D. S. P. or Flanagan if there were grounds to the accusation by Horowitz, without revealing Horowitz's name. Privately there was acknowledgement among the civil servants that the outcome was 'not altogether satisfactory', but that there was not really sufficient evidence to take any action.

Subsequently, when Lily at last replied to MacDonald's letter later that November, there was a great deal of back and forth in the Colonial Office about whether he needed to answer her, and whether the High Commissioner in Jerusalem should be informed. They agreed that he could not add much to what Lily had already been told unless there was a formal enquiry, 'which would be open to objection because of the publicity involved'. The Colonial Secretary might write with a little more detail to that effect, one civil servant proposed, but another objected that though 'one must sympathise very deeply with Mrs. Tobias in her bereavement … it seems to me that she should be given no further encouragement to elaborate her allegations regarding the conduct of the Arab police, and of Inspector Hashem in particular.' Further, he pointed out, 'It must be remembered that the bomb explosion in question was an outrage on a scale almost unparalleled even in Palestine's history of terrorist activity, and the immediate control executed by the police and military forces was a remarkable achievement.' A response by another notes: 'I question whether it is really necessary or desirable to say anything more. It is clear that nothing that we may say will satisfy her; and I can see no object in continuing a painful & fruitless correspondence. No. 9 [MacDonald's November 8 letter to Lily] did not promise a further communication, & I doubt whether he expects to hear from her again.'

In the end, MacDonald wrote Lily a bland letter assuring her that the matter had been carefully investigated, and that it did not rely solely on the word of a Moslem inspector against that of a Jewish constable. He pointed out that the testimony of two British constables would weigh heavily in Hashem's favour in court, and that in such circumstances there was no further action he could usefully take.

Lily, of course, did not see any of that correspondence, but she knew full well that it was not lack of evidence but lack of political will that drove the decision not to launch a formal investigation. How infuriated and devastated she would have been had she known how little evidence was gathered, and on what tenuous grounds the Inspector-General, the High Commissioner and the Colonial Secretary had reached their conclusions.

Philip's murder alone could not have shifted Lily's anti-militarism and humanism, but his murder, combined with British intransigence and injustice, and her profound sense of being let down by the government all contributed to her decisive shift towards a Jewish militarism that was utterly at odds with the political beliefs in which she had grown up and by which she had lived. Perhaps more than anything else, that shift was the most grievous outcome of Philip's death, for Lily's humanism and her anti-militarism were what had brought the two of them together and what they had worked for together in their shared life as political organisers and, in her case, with his support, as a writer.

Afterword

An uncovering

By the time Lily died, her work had been forgotten, and her books, published in the 1930s and out of print for decades, had long since disappeared from view. Indicative of her eclipse even within Jewish circles, the *Jewish Chronicle*, the paper to which she had contributed so frequently, published only the brief notice that her nephew Dannie had sent in, without even affording it the respect of turning his report into a formal obituary: 'Mrs Lily Tobias (née Shepherd), the doyen of the Jewish-Welsh novelists, who died in Haifa recently, was born in the little village of Ystalyfera in the Swansea Valley in 1887, writes Danny Abse' [sic], it reported. Dannie noted the name of Lily's first book, and claimed, mistakenly, that subsequently 'Hutchinson published several of her novels which were well received, as was her adaptation of George Eliot's "Daniel Deronda," performed at the Q Theatre in London' (Hutchinson only published *Eunice Fleet* and *Tube*; *My Mother's House* was published by Allen & Unwin, and *The Samaritan* by Robert Hale).[202]

Lily's loss of literary reputation was typical of the fate of so many woman writers. Neither modernist nor radical in style, nor, after her move to Palestine, any longer part of the literary world of England or of Wales, she was not valued, and went out of print, and was then forgotten – and, being forgotten, disappeared. In her case, that pattern was further strengthened by her move to Palestine at precisely the moment of her literary arrival; in Palestine, Hebrew, which she was not able to master as a writer, became the dominant language, and here too she was eclipsed and forgotten.

How ironic it was that in Israel the success of the Hebrew revival should in part become such an insurmountable obstacle for Lily when she had embraced and celebrated it, and worked towards its achievement. She had expressed that overtly, but also more indirectly – through her embrace and support for a Welsh-language revival. That support was clearest in a brief piece that was published, in 1933, in the short-lived magazine *Kith and Kin*, a publication of Cardiff University's Jewish student union. This was another excerpt that had been omitted from *My Mother's House*, allegedly for reasons of space. However, its subject matter, as with the excerpt published two years later in Welsh, in *Y Ford Gron*, suggests that the reason for its exclusion from the novel might not have been space, but politics. Here Lloyd Patagonia, who is passionately supportive of Jews both individual and collective, expounds to his wife and to Simon on the Welsh, on the predicament of the language, on the persecution of Welsh speakers, and on the hopes for Welsh independence and what it would offer – all of which is a direct equivalent to the Jewish and Hebrew arguments that Lily made elsewhere in the novel. At the opening of the scene, Lloyd Patagonia's wife complains to Simon about her husband's behaviour, which has just got him in trouble: "'It is his own fault, whatever, for not leaving them alone. Preaching at everybody, always telling they are wrong about something or other, at them about the Seventh Day, or learning Welsh in the schools and having Welshmen instead of Englishmen in this and that about the place. A lot of the ministers and schoolmasters are against us, and the boys do hear them talk, and then they mock at us in the road."' But when Lloyd objects, she exclaims to him:

'I don't wonder at them being mad with you, when you do insult them for not talking right—'

'Insult them!' Meurig Lloyd was a little indignant now. 'It is they who insult their own tongue by the way they use it – or abuse it, rather. Why should I not tell them of their mistakes? It is the duty of any Welsh man who understands his language… You know well they are not taught Welsh in school … Please God, that will come soon. There is teaching already in some parts. Things are better than they used to be – why, when I was a boy –' he turned to Simon – staring moodily at the floor – 'I was whipped by the master for speaking Welsh to my friend.'

'Rather extreme, wasn't it,' muttered Simon.

'Extreme? Aye, everything was extreme in those days. There was no chance for the Welsh at all. Neither for their land, their language, nor their religion. It was more than extreme. It was persecution.' He raised his voice slightly and wagged a finger into Simon's discomfited face. '*We were treated as if we were Jews*. Do you know those words, my boy? They are not mine. No, indeed! The first man to use them was Prince Llewellyn … '

'But that was centuries ago,' objected Simon. 'There hasn't been anything like that in recent times. I know there was some trouble in the sixties about tithes and tolls and such things,' he added, anticipating the interruption that began to bubble from the old man's lips. 'But it isn't fair to call that persecution. Of course, Jews are always being persecuted – in other countries – not here. I mean there's a lot of prejudice and so on. But in Britain Jews have their political and religious freedom. And so have Welshmen, naturally ... Do you mean to say that they didn't – even fifty years ago?'

'I'm telling you, my boy, they didn't. There was so little freedom in religion, and politics, and education, that scores of us emigrated to America – some to the United States, some to Brazil, some to Chile and some to Patagonia. In Wales our nationality was being crushed out of us ... we were not free to worship as we wanted, we were not allowed to own the soil that belonged to us, we were not able to elect men of sympathy to represent us, and we were even punished for talking in the language of our fathers.'

Lily wrote into the end of Lloyd's passionate speech an optimistic view of a new homeland: '"Inspired we were with the vision of an independent community, the creation of a new Wales. Our government would be carried on in Welsh, all the offices of state, as well as the religious services, the schools, the courts, and trade ... At last our own language, our own dear language".'[203]

It is ironic, given how she represented passionate support of Welsh-language culture and of the Hebrew-medium revival of national Jewish culture, that she should be excluded from being able to publish work in either one, because the medium of education and writing was, for her, English: like her protagonist Simon, it was through English that she sought to make a mark, and 'get on'.

However, it was to be in Wales, and as a Welsh writer, that she would be recognised. It is unlikely that Lily ever read a profile that had been written about her in 1958, which was published in Keidrich Rhys's journal *Wales*, and in which the author, Mimi Josephson, placed Lily at the forefront of Welsh Jewish writing.[204] Had she seen it, she would no doubt have commented on it, delighted but self-deprecating, to her nephew Phillip. That article shows her status even then, some twenty years after her final novel was published. However, Lily's work remained forgotten and hidden until 1989, when the first *Blackwell Companion to Jewish Culture* was published. Here she had a well-informed and detailed entry written by Vera Coleman, who acknowledged that Lily's 'was the only Welsh voice among the Anglo-Jewish novelists of inter-War years'. Coleman describes *My Mother's House* as presenting 'as well as the spiritual pilgrimage of the protagonist, a panorama of contemporary Anglo-Jewry, portraying with penetrating psychological insight its various political, religious, and cultural milieux'.[205] Even with this record, however, unless one already knew about Lily and was looking her up, one would only have come across her by accident.

By the 1990s, Lily's disappearance from view was about to change. Critics in the fields of Anglo-Jewish literature and of Welsh literature in English were beginning to reassess and redefine the respective canons, not least in their consideration, often for the first time, of excluded women writers. Jane Aaron, collecting material for an anthology of Welsh women's short stories in 1996, almost included one of Lily's pieces of fiction from *The Nationalists and Other Goluth Studies*, but had to omit it because of space constraints. The time was ripe, however, for Lily's recovery: the field of Welsh writing in English as an academic subject was beginning to blossom, and, with devolution, Wales was beginning to reinvent itself.

In 2000, at the beginning of research for a PhD, and following up on two passing references by Leo Abse in his published work, I searched for Lily in the catalogue in the National Library of Wales in Aberystwyth, and found her books. I won't ever forget the cold shiver of excitement I felt when *The Nationalists* was placed in front of me, and I saw on its cover the embossed emblem of a Welsh dragon and Jewish Star of David. The book did not have a dust jacket, and it wasn't until thirteen years later that I saw it as it had originally appeared, with bold, large text on the cover, describing it as 'A collection of eight stories about Jewish and Welsh life and character. The author's remarkable gift for presenting pathos and humour gives these stories a general human interest. Jews, and Welshmen who love "Land of their Fathers," will find interesting and instructive matter.'

That discovery of Lily led to the republication in 2004 of her second novel, *Eunice Fleet*, in the Honno Classics series, which assured her a place not only in the canon of Welsh writing in English, but also that of British Jewish literature. Her Welsh Jewish work was unlike any other, and for that alone she deserved attention.

In 1933, in *Kith and Kin*, she had appeared alongside none other than David Lloyd George, the Welsh Prime Minister under whose government Britain issued the Balfour Declaration, and who was thus the architect of the hope and disaster that would be Palestine from 1917 onwards. 'The people of Wales – musical and literary, and at heart profoundly religious – have in these characteristics many points of contact and sympathy with the Hebrew race,' Lloyd George wrote in his Foreword celebrating the new magazine. 'No one can ignore the benefactions which mankind has reaped in past history from the genius of the Jewish nation, and I am glad to think that this fine tradition is being maintained un-impaired today.' That Welsh and Jewish comparison must have delighted Lily, but so, too, would the august association with Lloyd George – just as, five years later, her appearance in print alongside David Ben-Gurion, Chaim Weizmann and Moshe Sharett would have filled her with pride.

Lily died just three years before the beginning of the Intifada, the Palestinian uprising that would definitively change world opinion about Israel and about Zionism, a change that makes her politics now look woefully naive and limited. Yet her work, and her politics, was of its time in the best way, too, for it offers a unique view of political affiliations, hopes, understandings and perceptions – as well as cultural links and connections – that would be otherwise difficult to imagine, including that remarkable intersection between Welshness and Jewishness, and between pacifism and nationalism, which coloured and shaped her long life. Whatever the particular cultural interests of her fiction and journalism, her life itself was extraordinary, as was her resilience, her courage, her strength – and her self-deprecating modesty. Lily's story shows the fortitude and achievement of a woman who had little formal education, who experienced numerous obstacles and terrible losses, and who was driven by a political will to produce, against powerful odds, an unusual body of work, and to lead a full, rich, and challenging life, despite her deep sorrow and, ultimately, her abiding loneliness. Repeatedly she wrote to her nephew Phillip that one must just 'go on' – and that is precisely what she did. In the old Hebrew tradition: may her memory be a blessing.

Notes

PROLOGUE

[1] Private Statement made by Pal. Police Constable Shimon Horowitz, 1938, Colonial Office Papers, National Archives, London, CO 733/372/6 1938 (discussed in greater detail in Chapter 10).

[2] 'Zionism and Militarism: some other considerations', *Zionist Review* 4.5 (September 1920), p. 90.

CHAPTER ONE

[3] The following portrait of Ystalyfera draws heavily from Bernant Hughes's two self-published books on the town's history, *Ystalyfera Memories* (1996) and *Stepping Stones in the History of Ystalyfera* (1990), and from the pages of *Llais Llafur*.

[4] A mezuzah is a small box containing a Biblical text that Jews affix to their doorposts according to Jewish law.

[5] Joseph was interviewed by David Jacobs as part of the Oral History Archive at the Museum of Welsh Life at Sain Ffagan on 8 November 1976 (6010-6011).

[6] Bernant Hughes, *Stepping Stones in the History of Ystalyfera*, (Ystalfera: Bernant Hughes, 1990), p. 136.

[7] *My Mother's House* (London: George Allen and Unwin, 1931), pp. 29–30.

[8] Israel Zangwill is perhaps best known for his 1892 novel *Children of the Ghetto*, about London's Jewish East End, which Lily would have read. He was a hugely popular novelist, commentator and playwright (his 1914 play *The Melting Pot* is often given as the original source of the term 'melting pot' to describe multiculturalism.

[9] John Minkes, 'Shepherds in the Valleys', *The Magazine of Cardiff New Synagogue* 10 (April 1997), p. 4.

[10] Hughes, *Stepping Stones in the History of Ystalyfera*, p. 136.

11 No doubt, however, Lily would have objected to an editorial which, in condemning the Conservative Government, referred to 'their gang of Jewish capitalists' (*Llais Llafur*, 9 December 1905).

12 This was Leo Abse's recollection, though he misremembered the paper's name as the *Red Dragon* (letter to the author, 27 November 2000). A profile of Lily in the Cardiff Jewish journal *CAJEX* also mentions her having published her first story in *Llais Llafur* at the age of 12 (Henry E. Samuel, 'A Welsh Emissary in Israel', *CAJEX* 8.2 (1958), p. 51.

13 *The Samaritan. An Anglo-Palestinian Novel* (London: Robert Hale, 1939), p. 98.

CHAPTER TWO

14 Leo Abse, interview with the author, London, 2002.

15 Naomi Shepherd, *Alarms and Excursions: Thirty Years in Israel* (London: Collins, 1990), p. 2.

16 Dannie Abse, *There Was a Young Man from Cardiff* (Hutchinson, 1991), p. 5. Dannie would hardly remember Anna-Baila, except through family stories, as she died in 1926, when he was three.

17 Dannie Abse, *Ash on a Young Man's Sleeve* (1954; Cardigan: Parthian Library of Wales, 2006), p. 21.

18 Leo Abse, letter to the author, 22 December 2000.

19 Leo Abse, interview, 2002.

20 *My Mother's House*, p. 245.

21 *My Mother's House*, p. 49.

22 *My Mother's House*, p. 256.

23 Interview, 2002.

CHAPTER THREE

24 In addition to material in the *Jewish Chronicle*, much of the material on Kishinev and its reception and on the Aliens Act relies on chapters by Lara Trubowitz, Nicholas J. Evans and Ben Gidley in Eitan Bar-Yosef and Nadia Valman (eds), *The Jew In Late-Victorian and Edwardian Culture: Between the East End and East Africa* (Palgrave, 2009). My own chapter in the same volume contains material on Lily Tobias, some of which

this biography corrects.

[25] Quoted and discussed in fascinating detail by Lara Trubowitz in 'Acting like an Alien: 'Civil' Antisemitism, the Rhetoricized Jew, and Early Twentieth-Century Jewish Immigration Law', in Bar-Yosef and Valman, *The Jew in Late-Victorian and Edwardian Culture*, p. 73.

[26] 'Czar's offer to Poland: autonomy to oppressed peoples. Local Polish resident's views', *Llais Llafur*, 22 August 1914.

[27] See *South Wales Jewish Review* (April 1904), p. 49 for an account of Goldsmid's presence at the opening of the Cardiff synagogue in 1897.

[28] Trubowitz, 'Acting like an Alien', pp. 72–73.

[29] *South Wales Jewish Review* (May 1904), p. 65.

[30] *Jewish Chronicle*, 18 September 1903.

[31] *South Wales Jewish Review* (February 1904), p. 30.

[32] Leo Abse, interview, 2002.

[33] Lily Tobias, *The Nationalists and Other Goluth Studies* (C.W. Daniel: London, 1921), pp. 13–19.

[34] Mark Levene points out the misnaming of the Uganda proposal in 'Herzl, the Scramble, and a Meeting that Never Happened: Revisiting the Notion of an African Zion', in *The Jew In Late-Victorian and Edwardian Culture*, p. 202.

[35] For a discussion of the Uganda proposal and British Jewish attitudes in the Zionist movement see Joseph H. Udelson's *Dreamer of the Ghetto: The Life and Works of Israel Zangwill* (Tuscaloosa, Alabama: University of Alabama Press, 1990). See also Mark Levene's different reading in 'Herzl, the Scramble, and a Meeting that Never Happened'.

[36] *Jewish Chronicle*, 12 August 1904, p. 16.

[37] Letter to the editor, *Jewish Chronicle*, 19 August 1904, p. 19. Theodor Herzl had died on 3 July 1904.

[38] For information on Kathleen Manning, see Sybil Oldfield's biography in the *Oxford Dictionary of National Biography* (2004), *www.oxforddnb.com/index/66/101066994*. In a later letter to the *Jewish Chronicle* in 1920, Manning, by then Lady Simon, wrote that she had once been known as 'the little Philosemite' for her work in Zionism in its early days (9 July 1920, p. 42).

CHAPTER FOUR

[39] *Jewish Chronicle*, 1 December 1905. pp. 4-5.

[40] There is a moving first-person account, 'Memoirs of Revolutionary Years' by Shmuel Pyeker, included in the *Kehilat Semiatycze* (the community of Semyatitch), edited by E. Tash (Tel Aviv: Association of Former Residents of Semiatich in Israel and the Diaspora, 1989). The chapter is published in translation at www.jewishgen.org/yizkor/siemiatycze1/siemiatycze1.html. See also Dov Rabin, 'Siemiatycze', published by jewishvirtuallibrary.org.

[41] *Jewish Chronicle*, 22 September 1905, p. 28.

[42] *Cambrian*, 22 September 1905, p. 3

[43] *Cambrian*, 26 February 1904, n.p.; also *Cardiff Times*, 27 February 1904, p. 8.

[44] *Cambrian*, 26 August 1904, p. 2.

[45] See Paul O'Leary, *Claiming the Streets: Processions and Urban Culture in South Wales, c. 1830-1880* (Cardiff: University of Wales Press, 2012).

[46] Dannie Abse, *There Was a Young Man from Cardiff*, p. 5.

[47] 13 January 1911, p. 16.

[48] Leo Abse, letter to the author, 22 December 2000.

[49] Leo Abse, ibid.

[50] *The Nationalists and Other Goluth Studies* (London: C.W. Daniel, 1921), p. 21.

[51] Colin Holmes, 'The Tredegar Riots of 1911: Anti-Jewish disturbances in South Wales', *Welsh History Review* 2.2 (December 1982), pp. 220–221.

[52] Leo Abse, 'A tale of collaboration not conflict with "the people f the book"', *New Welsh Review* 6.2 (1993), p. 18.

[53] Leo Abse, 'A tale of collaboration', p. 18. For a discussion of the historians' debate on the Tredegar riots, see Ch 1 in Donahaye, Jewish Writing in Wales (PhD thesis, Swansea University, 2004).

[54] 'Well-known novel dramatised: playwright's life in south Wales', *Western Mail*, 22 January 1927, p. 7.

[55] Leo Abse, letter to the author, 22 December 2000.

CHAPTER FIVE

56 Iorwerth Peate, *Rhwng Dau Fyd* (Dinbych: Gwasg Gee, 1976), pp. 84–99. See also K.O. Morgan, *Rebirth of a Nation* 1880-1980 (Oxford: Oxford University Press, 1982), p.127.

57 *Llais Llafur*, 2 October 1915, p. 2.

58 It is not clear who the letter was intended for, as it is not addressed to a named individual: it is likely that it was to be used as the basis for letters to several people to whom the family might appeal for help. The letter is in the possession of a family member.

59 Military Service Bill debate, Hansard, HC Deb, vol 77, cols 949–1074 (5 January 1916).
http://hansard.millbanksystems.com/commons/1916/jan/05/military-service-no-2-bill

60 K. O. Morgan, 'Peace movements in Wales 1899-1945', *Welsh History Review* 10.3 (June 1981), p. 412.

61 Leo Abse, letter to the author, 22 December 2000.

62 Leo Abse, letter to the author, 27 November 2000.

63 *Llais Llafur*, 1 July 1916, p. 2.

64 I am very grateful to Aled Eirug for bringing this to my attention – the letter is dated 29 August 1917 (Catherine Marshall papers, Cumbria Record Office DMAR 4/55).

65 Lily Tobias, *Eunice Fleet* (London: Hutchinson, 1933), p. 101 [Honno, p.95]. The novel was republished by Honno Press in their Classics series in 2004: page references are to the original, followed by the 2004 edition in brackets.

66 *Eunice Fleet*, p. 145 [pp.139–140].

67 For an account of the events at Cory Hall, see Brock Millman, 'The Battle for Cory Hall, November 1916: Patriots Meet Dissenters in Wartime Cardiff', *Canadian Journal of History*, 35.1 (April 2000), pp. 58–83; the text also appears in Millman's book *Managing Domestic Dissent in First World War Britain* (2000; Abingdon: Routledge, 2013).

68 *Eunice Fleet* p. 145 [p. 139].

69 Letter to the editor, *Jewish Chronicle*, 28 January 1916, p. 11.

70 *Merthyr Pioneer*, 10 June 1916, p. 1.

71 *Merthyr Pioneer*,1 July 1916, p. 2.

72 Lily Tobias to NCF, Catherine Marshall papers, Cumbria Record Office DMAR 4/55.

CHAPTER SIX

[73] *Jewish Chronicle*, 25 July 1919, p. 30.

[74] Paul Goodman, *Zionism in England, 1899-1949* (London: Zionist Federation of Great Britain and Ireland, 1949). This is the update of an earlier edition published by the English Zionist Federation in 1929.

[75] It was also published a few months later in the *Canadian Jewish Chronicle* on 16 July 1920, pp. 14–15. Other pieces in the *Zionist Review* include 'Mine Own Vineyard', 2.9 (January 1919), pp. 161–163; 'The Purim Ball' [Junior Zionist Supplement] (April 1919), pp. 9–11; 'The Onus' (September 1919), pp. 82–83; and 'Daughters of Zion' (February 1920).

[76] 'Daughters of Zion', *The Nationalists*, pp. 88–96.

[77] Lily Tobias, 'Zionism and Militarism: some other considerations', *The Zionist Review* 4.5 (September 1920), pp. 89–90.

[78] Paul Goodman, 'Jewish and Welsh Nationalism', *The Zionist Review* 5.10 (February 1922), p. 161.

[79] Letter to Leo Abse, 11 October 1945, Leo Abse Papers, National Library of Wales, G/a/246.

[80] It was either typhoid, dysentery or cholera that killed her; the recollections of family members are contradictory.

[81] Lily Tobias, Author's Note, 'Daniel Deronda, A Play', *Jewish Quarterly* 23.3 (autumn 1975), p. 8. Lily also recalled later productions, with revisions to the text, one of them in 1945 in Johannesburg, and another in 1974 in London. It was excerpts from the latter work that the *Jewish Quarterly* published in 1975.

[82] For a portrait of the theatre, and some background to the staging of *Daniel Deronda*, see Kenneth Barrow, *On Q: Jack & Beatie de Leon and the Q Theatre* (London: The deLeon Memorial Fund, 1992).

[83] Jack de Leon's letter of 7 January 1927 in the *Jewish Chronicle* (p. 44) drew readers' attention to the forthcoming production.

[84] *Morning Post*, 16 February 1927. The *Palestine Post* published a rather inaccurate notice about the play 'adapted by Lily Tobias (author of The Nationalists and other tales of Jewish life)'. *Palestine Post*, 6 February 1927, p. 1.

[85] *Jewish Chronicle*, 18 February 1927, p. 82.

[86] *Jewish Chronicle*, 25 February 1927, p. 19.

[87] *Jewish Chronicle*, 19 April 1929, p. 50.

[88] Tobias, 'Daniel Deronda, A Play', p. 8.

[89] Lily Tobias, 'Links with George Eliot', *Jewish Chronicle*,16 March 1951, p. 9.

[90] 'Well-Known Novel Dramatised – Playwright's Life in South Wales', *Western Mail*, 22 January 1927, p.7.

[91] *Jewish Chronicle*, 17 January 1969, p. 9.

[92] Minnie Temkin, letter to the editor, *Jewish Chronicle*, 24 January 1969, p. 8.

CHAPTER SEVEN

[93] WHJ, 'A Jew of Wales', *Western Mail*, 21 May 1931, p. 13.

[94] Tobias, 'The Onus', *The Nationalists and Other Goluth Studies*, pp. 51–54.

[95] W. J. Gruffydd , 'Nodiadau'r Golygydd', *Y Llenor* (spring 1941), pp. 1–4.

[96] *My Mother's House*, pp. 490–491.

[97] *My Mother's House*, p. 516.

[98] WHJ, 'A Jew of Wales', *Western Mail*, 21 May 1931, p. 13.

[99] GWR, 'My Mother's House', *The Welsh Outlook* (April 1932), p.12.

[100] See Neil Prior, 'History debate over anti-Semitism in 1911 Tredegar riot' for the continued disagreement over interpretation of the riots – 19 August 2011. www.bbc.co.uk/news/uk-wales-14582378.

[101] *Spectator*, 16 May 1931, p. 36.

CHAPTER EIGHT

[102] 'The "C.O."', *Western Mail*, 4 May 1933, p. 13.

[103] *Western Mail*, 8 May 1933, p. 9.

[104] 'Books and Bookmen', *Jewish Chronicle*, 12 May 1933, pp. 21–22.

[105] Advertisement, *Western Mail* 18 May 1933, p. 18.

[106] Advertisement, *Western Mail*, 6 July 1933, p. 6.

[107] *Palestine Post*, 17 October 1934, p. 5. In fact *Eunice Fleet* had been published in the spring of the preceding year. 'The story

of a man who would not fight' was the strapline of the publisher's advertisement, and of the book's dustjacket.

108 H. C. Lea, *A History of the Inquisition in Spain* (1906). An excerpt is reproduced in Howard M. Sachar's *Farewell Espana: the World of the Sephardim Remembered* (Vintage, 1995).

109 Letter to Leo Abse, 11 October 1945, Leo Abse Papers, National Library of Wales, G/a/246.

110 Joseph Shepherd, Oral History Archive, Sain Ffagan.

111 Y Meudwy, 'Buchedd Arloeswr, Hanes Canu a Nofel am Fywyd Iddewig', *Y Ford Gron*, 5.9 (Gorffennaf 1935), p. 211.

112 Lily Tobias, 'Llwyd Patagonia', *Y Ford Gron*, 5.12 (Hydref 1935), pp. 275, 279 (translated by 'M.T.').

113 'Ymysg Pobl', *Y Ford Gron*, 5.9 (Gorffennaf 1935), p. 204.

114 Angela Ingram and Daphne Patai (eds), *Rediscovering Forgotten Radicals: British Women Writers 1889-1939* (Chapel Hill: University of North Carolina Press, 1993), p. 9.

CHAPTER NINE

115 Lily Tobias, 'The Street of the Tishbite', *CAJEX* (December 1970), pp. 31–33. *CAJEX*, the publication of the Cardiff Association of Jewish Ex-Servicemen and Women, was later renamed *Bimah*, and continues to publish matter of interest to the south Wales Jewish community.

116 See Naomi Shepherd, *Ploughing Sand: British Rule in Palestine 1917-1948* (London: John Murray, 1999), p. 15.

117 *The Samaritan*, p. 24.

118 *The Samaritan*, p.14.

119 *The Samaritan*, p. 39.

120 *The Samaritan*, p. 178.

121 Perhaps this 'famous parallel' refers to Balfour's maiden speech delivered on 21 June 1922, in which he observed: 'Here you have a small race, originally inhabiting a small country, I think about the size of Wales or Belgium.' Quoted in Christopher Sykes, *Cross Roads to Israel* (London: Collins, 1965), p. 18.

122 *The Samaritan*, p. 179.

123 *The Samaritan*, p. 27.

[124] *The Samaritan*, p. 202.

[125] *The Samaritan*, pp. 203–204.

[126] *The Samaritan*, p. 175.

[127] *The Samaritan*, p. 320.

[128] A decade on, their community would be divided by the 1948 war, which left half the population within the borders of the new Israeli state, and half in the Jordan-occupied West Bank. Reunited after the 1967 war, they became divided again in the wake of the second Intifada, and the building by Israel of the separation wall and fence.

[129] Mills himself had been a missionary to the Jews of London, but had made himself rather unpopular with his denomination for his failure to achieve converts, and for his overly warm sympathy with Judaism, explored in his survey *The British Jews*, which was published in English in 1852. Losing support for the mission, he travelled to Palestine, where he stayed for three months in Nablus with another Welsh missionary, the Reverend John Bowen of Pembrokeshire, and made a close study of the area and of Samaritan culture.

[130] 'Terror on Carmel', *Palestine Review* (July 1938), p. 200.

CHAPTER TEN

[131] *Palestine Post*, 12 July 1938, p. 1.

[132] A.B., 'Haifa's Tin Hut Quarter', *Palestine Post*, 15 July 1938, p. 8.

[133] 'Massacre at Haifa' [Subheading 'Haifa Bomb throwing'], *Jewish Chronicle*, 15 July 1938, p. 22.

[134] 'Massacre at Haifa', p. 22.

[135] 'Has government lost its head?' *Jewish Chronicle*, 22 July 1938, p. 25.

[136] 'Change of Tactics?' *Palestine Post*, 12 July 1938, p. 6.

[137] 'Prominent Industrialist Stabbed to Death by Mob', *Palestine Post*, 12 July 1938, p. 1.

[138] 'Notes of the Week', *Jewish Chronicle*, 15 July 1938, p. 8.

[139] Lily Tobias to Malcolm MacDonald, 23 November 1938, Colonial Office Papers, National Archives, London, CO 733/372/6 1938.

[140] Tobias, *Jewish Chronicle*, 28 October 1938, p. 12.

[141] IHS, *Palestine Post*, 17 March 1940, p. 7.

[142] 'Deborah Says … ' *Jewish Chronicle*, 24 May 1940, p. 19.

[143] Letter to Leo Abse, 25 February 1946, Leo Abse Papers, National Library of Wales, Aberystwyth, G/a/313. All correspondence between Lily and Leo referred to in the following is held in this archive.

[144] David Shepherd to Malcolm MacDonald, 5 July 1940, Colonial Office Papers, National Archives, London, CO 733/452/5 1940.

[145] Letter to David Shepherd, 25 July 1940, Colonial Office Papers, CO 733/452/5 1940.

[146] Sadie Levine, 'An Unofficial Emissary', *Jewish Chronicle*, 27 September 1957, p. 22.

[147] Phillip V. Tobias, 'A tribute to Lily Tobias – Author, playwright and Zionist', *South African Jewish Times* (September 1984), pp. 81–82.

[148] Letter to Leo Abse, 21 February 1944, G/a/3.

[149] *Palestine Post*, 6 December 1942, p. 2, and 28 January 1943, p. 3.

[150] Letter to Leo Abse, 21 February 1944, G/a/3.

[151] Letter to Leo Abse, 20 July 1944, G/a/36.

[152] Letter to Leo Abse, 28 August 1944, G/a/39.

[153] Letter to Leo Abse, 10 May 1944, G/a/14.

[154] Letter to Leo Abse, 28 August 1944, G/a/39.

[155] Lily Tobias, 'Jews in the Congo: a personal reminiscence', *CAJEX* (December 1961), pp. 55–59.

[156] Ezra Shepherd to Leo Abse, 20 October 1945, G/a/249.

[157] Letter to Leo Abse, 28 November 1945, G/a/262.

[158] Letter to Leo Abse, 25 February 1946, G/a/313.

CHAPTER ELEVEN

[159] Letter to Leo Abse, 20 May 1945, G/a/198.

[160] Letter to Leo Abse, 23 July 1945, G/a/224.

[161] Letter to Leo Abse, 28 November 1945, G/a/262. Ernest Bevin was then Foreign Minister.

[162] DPs were Displaced Persons (refugees) from continental Europe. Letter to Phillip, 27 October 1946. Professor Phillip

Tobias Papers, Historical Papers Research Archive, The Library, University of Witwatersrand. All the following quoted correspondence between Lily Tobias and Phillip V. Tobias is held in this archive. I am grateful to the estate for permission to quote.

163 Leo Abse Papers, Llyfr Ffoto 4922, 49226017839/91.

164 Letter to Phillip, 28 July 1947.

165 Letter to Phillip, 19 January 1948.

166 'In Memoriam', *Palestine Post*, 18 July 1940, p. 6.

167 'A Memory of Gandhi', *Palestine Post*, 13 February 1948, p. 4.

168 David Ben-Gurion, Chaim Weizmann and Moshe Shertok were, respectively, the future Prime Minister, President and Foreign Minister of the first government of Israel. Other contributors included E. M. Epstein on film, and pieces by Israel Beer, Henry Wallace, and S. Prai.

169 'Village Festival in the Emek', *Palestine and Middle East* 10–11(1948), p. 219.

170 'End of a Chapter on Carmel', *Palestine Post*, 4 August 1948, p. 4.

171 Letter to the editor, *Jewish Chronicle*, 28 January 1916, p. 11.

172 Letter to Phillip, 27 December 1948.

173 'Mount Carmel loses its young invaders', *Palestine Post*, 27 April 1949, p. 4.

174 'A Liberty with a sonnet to Liberty', *Palestine Post*, 19 August 1949, p. 4.

175 *Jewish Chronicle*, 19 August 1904, p. 19.

CHAPTER TWELVE

176 Letter to Phillip, 31 December 1961.

177 Letter to Phillip, January 1957.

178 Letter to Leo Abse, 28 August 1944, G/a/39.

179 Letter to Phillip, 17 October 1952.

180 Letter to Phillip, 14 January 1951.

181 Letter to Phillip, 15 October 1959.

182 Letter to Phillip, 17 October 1952.

183 Letter to Phillip, 30 November 1961.

184 'The Street of the Tishbite, *CAJEX* 20.4 (December 1970), pp. 31–33; 'Jews in the Congo', *CAJEX* 11.4 (December

1961), pp. 55–59; 'Some Notes on the Arab-Israeli War', *CAJEX* 17.3 (September 1967), pp. 20–22.

[185] Letter to Phillip, 10 February 1964.

[186] Letter to Phillip, 5 July 1980.

[187] 'Chair in Glass Technology, *Technion Journal* 3.5 (January 1968) p. 25.

[188] Letter to Phillip, 15 July 1952.

[189] Phillip V. Tobias, 'A Tribute to Lily Tobias', p. 82.

[190] Letter to Phillip, 1 November 1953.

[191] Letter to Phillip, 5 July 1980.

[192] Joseph Shepherd, interviewed by David Jacobs, 8 November 1976. Audiotape. Oral History Archive, Museum of Welsh Life, 6010-6011.

[193] Letter to Phillip, 3 December 1980.

[194] Letter to Phillip, October 1981.

POSTSCRIPT

[195] Letter to Phillip, 12 January 1982.

[196] *Jewish Chronicle*, 8 June 1984, p. 22.

[197] Naomi Shepherd, *Alarms and Excursions*, pp. 2–3. During the years that she was away, and during the years that Villa Merhavia was under army requisitioning, Philip's study certainly would not have remained untouched, and it is likely that Fay, taking over the villa in Lily's absence between 1941 and 1945, made changes to that room that would have deeply upset Lily. Fay and Jonas married in November of 1938, just four months after Philip's murder, while Lily was still in deep mourning, perhaps an indication of an early lack of sympathy and understanding between the sisters. (In her will, drawn up in 1977, Lily left to Annabella, daughter of Joseph, and namesake of Lily's mother, 'my diamond earrings (now in the custody of my sister Mrs. Fay Israeli) which belonged to my mother.' It would seem the feud between the two remained till the end of Lily's life.)

[198] The correspondence is in CO 733/452/5 1940 and CO 733/372/6 1938, Colonial Office Papers, National Archives, London. The evidence discussed here is in the latter folder.

199 Private Statement made by Pal. Police Constable Shimon Horowitz, 1938, CO 733/372/6 1938.

200 Private Statement of Israel Geller, 1938, CO 733/372/6 1938.

201 Malcolm MacDonald to Lily Tobias, 8 November 1938, CO 733/372/6 1938.

AFTERWORD

202 *Jewish Chronicle*, 8 June 1984, p. 22.

203 'Kin, if not Kith', *Kith and Kin* 1.1 (March 1933), pp. 21–23.

204 Mimi Josephson, 'Dual Loyalties', *Wales* 4 (December 1958), p. 17.

205 Vera Coleman, 'Lily Tobias', in Glenda Abramson (ed.), *The Blackwell Companion to Jewish Culture from the Eighteenth Century to the Present* (Oxford: Blackwell Reference, 1989).

Selected works
by Lily Tobias

BOOKS

The Nationalists and Other Goluth Studies (C. W. Daniel: London, 1921).

My Mother's House (London: George Allen and Unwin, 1931).

Eunice Fleet (London: Hutchinson,1933). Republished by Honno Classics, 2004.

Tube (London: Hutchinson, 1935).

The Samaritan. An Anglo-Palestinian Novel (London: Robert Hale, 1939).

PRINCIPAL ARTICLES AND OTHER WRITING

'Jewish Women and Palestine', *Socialist Review* 88 (January-March, 1919).

'Zionism and Militarism: some other considerations', *The Zionist Review* 4.5 (September 1920).

'Grace Aguilar as Jewish Protagonist', *Jewish Chronicle Supplement*, 29 August 1924.

'Kin, if not Kith', *Kith and Kin* 1.1 (March 1933).

Where Have I Seen You Before? Ms. Unpublished play.

'Llwyd Patagonia', *Y Ford Gron*, 5.12 (Hydref 1935).

'The Land of Israel: the Last Sitting of the Commission', *Jewish Chronicle*, 2 April 1937.

'Terror on Carmel', *Palestine Review* (July 1938).

Review of *Toward the Jaffa Gate*, *Jewish Chronicle*, 28 October 1938.

'In Memoriam', *Palestine Post*, 18 July 1940.

'A Memory of Gandhi', *Palestine Post*, 13 February 1948.

'Village Festival in the Emek', *Palestine and Middle East* 10–11 (1948).

'End of a Chapter on Carmel', *Palestine Post*, 4 August 1948.

'Mount Carmel loses its young invaders', *Palestine Post*, 27 April 1949.

'A Liberty with a sonnet to Liberty', *Palestine Post*, 19 August 1949.

'Links with George Eliot', *Jewish Chronicle*, 16 March 1951.

'Jews in the Congo: a personal reminiscence', *CAJEX* (December 1961).

'Some Notes on the Arab-Israeli War', *CAJEX* 17.3 (September 1967).

'The Street of the Tishbite', *CAJEX* (December 1970).

'Daniel Deronda, A Play', *Jewish Quarterly* 23.3 (autumn 1975).

Acknowledgements

It is my great regret that this book was not ready in time for Dannie Abse to read it: as Lily Tobias's literary executor, he provided generous permissions, and personal encouragement. The late Phillip V. Tobias shared invaluable memories, sources, and photographs, and I am grateful for permissions and access to his correspondence in the Phillip V. Tobias Papers in the Historical Papers Research Archive at The Library, University of Witwatersrand. The late Leo Abse was also a wealth of information, and I am grateful to him too for his permission to access and reproduce correspondence, and to Ania Abse for permission to reproduce photographs from the Leo Abse Papers at the National Library of Wales. Many other members of the family have offered information, documents and photographs. My thanks in particular to John Minkes for detailed family history, and to Naomi Shepherd and Annabella Shepherd, who have both been so helpful and supportive.

Librarians and archivists are the unsung heroes of the researcher. My particular thanks to the exceptional staff at the National Library of Wales, to archivist Alison Harvey at Cardiff University, and to the librarian demi-gods at Swansea University. Thanks also to the staff at the Zionist Archives in Jerusalem, and at the Historical Papers Research Archive at the University of Witwatersrand. My warmest gratitude to Thandisizwe Myataza, without whom I would not have been able to consult the correspondence between Lily Tobias and Phillip V. Tobias.

Alyce Von Rothkirch very kindly passed on to me several *Western Mail* references, and Aled Eirug shared information about correspondence in Catherine Marshall's papers. I am very grateful to him also for comments on the chapter dealing with conscientious objectors, and to James Vaughan at Aberystwyth University for his reading of some of the Middle East material. The mistakes that remain are, of course, my own.

There are always too many people to thank individually for their help and support, but I am very grateful to friends and family members who have taken an interest, asked provocative questions, listened to worries, and tolerated my obsessive behaviour. My thanks, too, to those friends who helped with translations from Welsh. This book would not have been possible without a commissioning grant from the Welsh Books Council, and I am grateful for that support. Finally, my huge appreciation to Caroline Oakley – a forthright editor combining just the right proportions of critical challenge and warm encouragement.

Index of names

Abse, Dannie 18, 26, 27, 70,
127, 164, 197, 253, 254, 257,
267, 275, 284, 286, 299
Abse, Leo 18, 24, 25, 27, 38,
39, 51, 74, 79, 80, 82, 92,
118, 119, 123, 125, 127,
162, 164, 192, 197, 209,
212–220, 223–227, 229,
230, 232, 235, 237, 253,
254, 267, 280, 284, 299
Abse, Wilfred 26, 192, 197,
224, 226, 227, 253, 254
Aguilar, Grace 23, 119, 120,
130, 297
Balfour, Arthur 85, 290
Balfour Declaration 85, 107,
108, 141, 142, 177, 203,
259, 280
Bassett, Tom 83
Belgian Congo 220, 257
Ben-Gurion 236, 242, 250,
281, 293
Berlin, Isaiah 254
Bevin, Ernest 230, 231, 292
Blok, Arthur 259
British Mandate 1, 121, 141,
142, 177, 178, 183, 196,
201, 204, 208, 231, 236,
243, 271
Brockway, Fenner 91, 92, 93,
94, 99
Brockway, Lilla 91

CAJEX 170, 221, 257, 284,
290, 292, 293, 294, 298
Chappell, Edgar L. 81
Churchill, Winston 232
Colonial Secretary 55, 199,
203, 207, 268, 269, 272,
273, 274
Daniel Deronda vii, 44, 48,
107, 108, 120, 122–128,
129, 130, 131, 137, 138,
146, 210, 257, 264, 275,
288, 298
Dart, Raymond 252
Davies, George M. Ll. 240
de Leon, Jack 123, 288
Eliot, George 23, 44, 48, 55,
108, 122, 123, 124, 125,
126, 131, 137, 138, 256,
257, 258, 275, 289, 298
Evans, Caradoc 123
Federation of Women Zionists
125, 263
Fellowship of Reconciliation
103, 180
Ford Gron, Y 165, 166, 276,
290, 297
Fox, Cyril 83
Fyne, Simon 62, 64, 74
Galsworthy, John 125, 240
Gandhi, Mahatma 238–241,
293, 297
Goodman, Paul 111, 119, 288

ABOUT HONNO

Honno Welsh Women's Press was set up in 1986 by a group of women who felt strongly that women in Wales needed wider opportunities to see their writing in print and to become involved in the publishing process. Our aim is to develop the writing talents of women in Wales, give them new and exciting opportunities to see their work published and often to give them their first 'break' as a writer.

Honno is registered as a community co-operative. Any profit that Honno makes is invested in the publishing programme.

Women from Wales and around the world have expressed their support for Honno. Each supporter has a vote at the Annual General Meeting.

For more information and to buy our publications, please write to Honno at the address below, or visit our website:
www.honno.co.uk

Honno
Unit 14, Creative Units
Aberystwyth Arts Centre
Aberystwyth
Ceredigion
SY23 3GL

Honno Friends
We are very grateful for the support of the Honno Friends:
Gwyneth Tyson Roberts, Jenny Sabine, Beryl Thomas.

For more information on how you can become a Honno Friend, see: http://www.honno.co.uk/friends.php